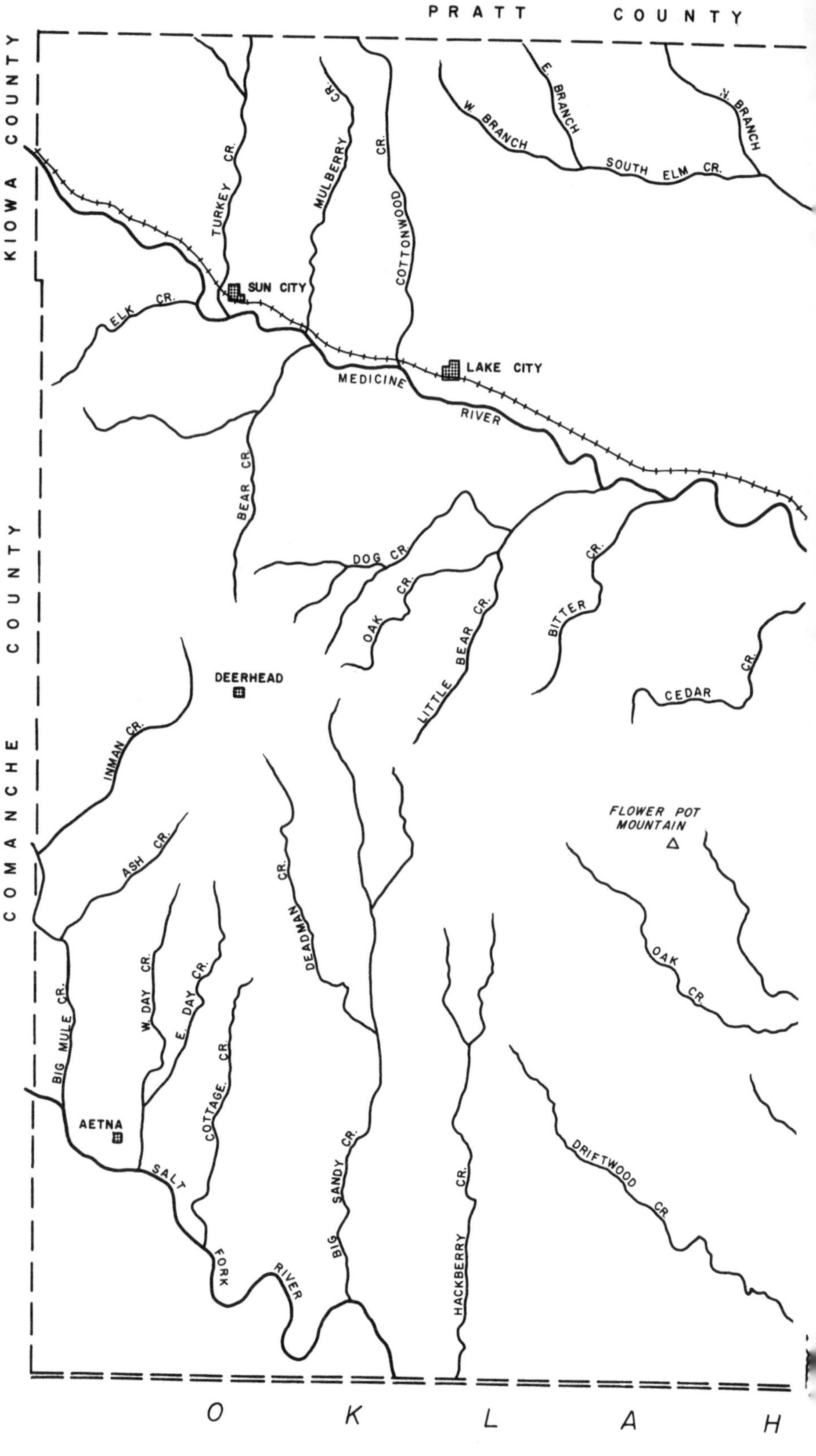
PRATT COUNTY
KIOWA COUNTY
COMANCHE COUNTY
OKLAH
TURKEY CR.
MULBERRY CR.
COTTONWOOD CR.
W. BRANCH
E. BRANCH
N. BRANCH
SOUTH ELM CR.
SUN CITY
ELK CR.
LAKE CITY
MEDICINE RIVER
BEAR CR.
DOG CR.
OAK CR.
LITTLE BEAR CR.
BITTER CR.
CEDAR CR.
DEERHEAD
INMAN CR.
ASH CR.
FLOWER POT MOUNTAIN
DEADMAN CR.
OAK CR.
W. DAY CR.
E. DAY CR.
BIG MULE CR.
COTTAGE CR.
AETNA
SALT FORK RIVER
BIG SANDY CR.
HACKBERRY CR.
DRIFTWOOD CR.

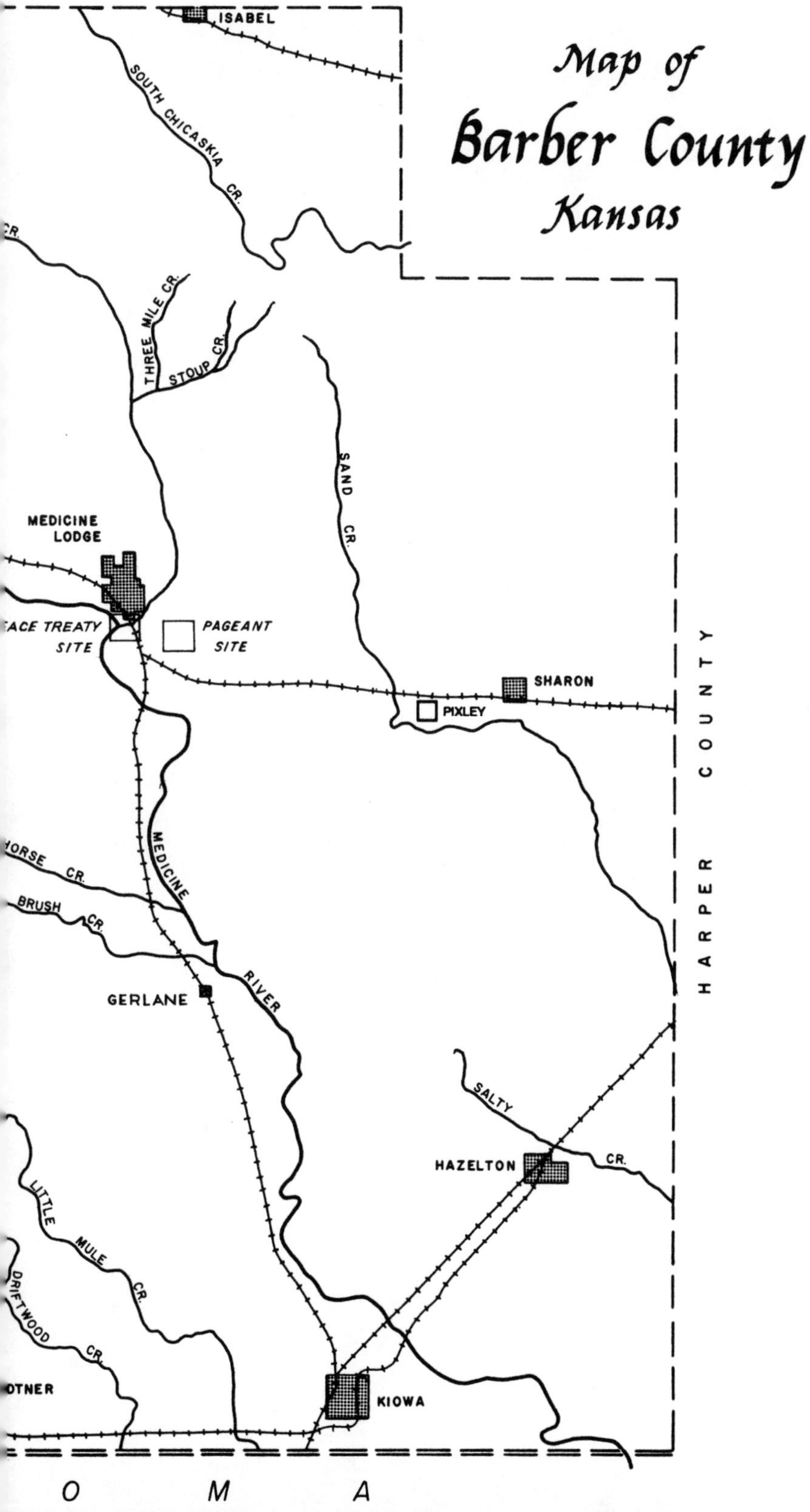
Map of
Barber County
Kansas
ISABEL
SOUTH CHICASKIA CR.
CR.
THREE MILE CR.
STOUP CR.
SAND CR.
MEDICINE LODGE
PEACE TREATY SITE
PAGEANT SITE
SHARON
PIXLEY
HARPER COUNTY
HORSE CR.
BRUSH CR.
MEDICINE RIVER
GERLANE
SALTY CR.
HAZELTON
LITTLE MULE CR.
DRIFTWOOD CR.
OTNER
KIOWA
O M A

MEDICINE LODGE

MEDICINE LODGE

The story of a Kansas frontier town

Nellie Snyder Yost

Introduction by Don Russell

MEDICINE LODGE HISTORICAL SOCIETY

Medicine Lodge, Kansas

First Printing: 1970
The Swallow Press Incorporated
Chicago, Illinois
Revised Printing: 1997
Medicine Lodge Historical Society
Medicine Lodge, Kansas

Library of Congress Catalog Number 79-132588

International Standard Book Number: 0-913507-93-8

Printed in the United States of America
by New Forums Press, Inc., P.O. Box 876, Stillwater, Okla. 74076

To the memory of my father,
Frank P. Hewitt, and my
mother, Ida L. Hewitt, and
to my daughters, Dorothy
and Marilyn, this book is
affectionately dedicated.

I. N. "Jibo" Hewitt

CONTENTS

	Introduction	*xi*
	Preface	*xvi*
1	**Legend of Flower Pot Mountain 1849-1854**	*1*
2	**Medicine Lodge Indian Peace Treaty 1867**	*22*
3	**Settling Up 1871-1880**	*36*
4	**Indians, Cattle, Growing Pains 1874-1878**	*46*
5	**The Great Cattle Pools 1879-1886**	*55*
6	**Barber County Towns 1875-1887**	*66*
7	**Frontier Violence 1873-1886**	*75*
8	**Justice in Medicine Lodge and Caldwell 1871-1884**	*89*
9	**Grand Hotel, Flood 1885**	*106*
10	**New Industry, Culture, Politics, Famous Citizens 1885-1900**	*117*
11	**J. N. "Poley" Tincher 1895-1951**	*132*
12	**Carry Nation 1899-1911**	*143*
13	**The Murder of Sheriff McCracken 1908**	*159*
14	**Cyclones, Railroads 1907-1935**	*164*
15	**More Outlaws 1927**	*173*
16	**Peace Treaty Pageant 1927-1970**	*179*
17	**I. N. "Jibo" Hewitt 1884-1970**	*192*
18	**Medicine Lodge Today 1970**	*206*
	Appendix: Treaty Text	*209*
	Notes	*217*
	Index	*229*

ILLUSTRATIONS

Flower Pot Mountain *page 45*

Indian encampment at peace council *following page 104*
Commissioners' encampment at peace council
Satanta, Kiowa chief
Ten Bears, Comanche chief
Little Raven, Arapaho chief
Black Kettle, Cheyenne chief
Peace Commissioners
Issuing clothing to Indians at peace council
Cowboy cabin, 1870's
Medicine Valley Bank
E. W. (Wylie) Payne
George Geppert
Bank robbery posse, 1884
Jackass Canyon
Bank robbers, 1884

Carry Nation, c1901 *page 142*

J. N. (Poley) Tincher *following page 172*
Lucille Mulhall, 1905
Barber County Court House
Flood damaged house, 1907
Saloon smashed by Carry Nation, 1900
Carry Nation's home
I-See-O and other peace treaty site searchers, 1926
Peace Treaty Pageant scenes
Isaiah Hewitt
Vinton Clifford Sleeper
Frank P. Hewitt and Ida L. Sleeper Hewitt
Medicine Lodge High School track team, 1923
Tokio Garden flyer

I. N. (Jibo) Hewitt *page 191*

INTRODUCTION

The purpose of an introduction to a book is to introduce the book to the reader. Publishers of a couple of centuries ago were more blunt about it. They headed this part of the book "advertisement." If you are still with us, you have already read the title and know that this book is about a place called Medicine Lodge. That may seem to you a romantic sounding name. It is my first duty to assure you that Medicine Lodge has lived up to its name. If you are not one of those viewers of television Westerns who has wondered how it really was, however, you may be turned off. This is—mostly—how it really was.

To digress a moment, there may be pedantic friends who are almost as much distressed by use of the second person vocative as they would be by the use of the perpendicular pronoun. But this is a book about the 19th century, mostly, and in those days, dear reader, it was not uncommon for a writer to back his reader off into a corner for any digression that a bit of me-to-you talk might clear up. That custom has been decried so long as to become quaint, if not camp—if that concept be not already obsolescent. Obviously this advertisement is not directed toward residents or native sons of Medicine Lodge, or Barber County, Kansas. They will buy the book as a matter of local pride, regardless of its merits—not in as large numbers as the publisher would like, perhaps, but in numbers calculable by computer. What you, dear reader, with no lodging in Medicine Lodge, past, present, or foreseeable, would like to know is why you should give a tinker's damn about anything that has ever happened in that somewhat obscure Kansas municipality.

Not being a native son of Medicine Lodge, or even of Kansas, I have no interest in the place based on local pride. However, I have been aware of Medicine Lodge since 1937. In that year one of my colleagues on a Chicago newspaper was Malcolm McDowell, whose name used to appear in the introduction of almost every book about Indians (so I like to put it here) because for a couple of generations he was secretary of the Board of Indian Commissioners. One day he slapped a bundle on my desk. "This is the largest issue of a weekly newspaper I have ever seen," he said. It was the Indian Peace Treaty Edition—Forty-eight Pages in Six Sections—of the *Barber County Index,* "published every Thursday" at Medicine Lodge. In those days of Depression a 48-page newspaper was something to be hailed, even in Chicago. I read its dozen articles by Elmo Scott Watson, later co-founder of The Westerners, an organization devoted to Western history and lore; a couple by Bliss Isley, Kansas historian; and eyewitness stories by such diverse personalities as Sergeant I-See-O, last of the Indian Scouts; George Bent, interpreter; and General E. S. Godfrey, of Custer fight fame.

Later I learned that the Medicine Lodge Treaty did not bring peace to the Plains, as some of the articles implied. Within a year or two Roman Nose, Satanta, Satank, and other signing chiefs were on the warpath; among those present both Black Kettle and Major Joel Elliott were killed at Custer's Battle of the Washita; Generals Harney, Terry, and Augur are remembered for Indian campaigns before and after the peace making. Just why it failed is a question too involved to be settled in this introduction or in this book, but it was an important and sincere effort to bring peace to the Plains, involving all these important personages, not overlooking one of the correspondents who wrote about it, Henry M. Stanley, some years before he found Dr. Livingstone, I presume, in Darkest Africa.

The Indian part of this book is not, all of it, that important. There is a bit of lore and legendry, topped off with a ghost story; a most remarkable ghost story, for I cannot recall any other ghost who kept a diary, printed here in full text. This ghostly, and sometimes ghastly, diary sounds a bit like it might have been cribbed from a Dime Novel by Colonel Prentiss Ingraham (who cribbed some of his stories from Dumas), but the Pilgrim Bard's yarn of Flower Pot Mountain merits rating as Americana.

Eventually Medicine Lodge became settled and civilized, and inevitably there was a bank holdup. Just as inevitably Medicine Lodge would have no ordinary bank holdup; it had to be the classic of Hollywood tradition with the bandits led by the respected city marshal of Caldwell whose citizens had presented him with a gold-plated Winchester rifle, attesting his valuable services for law and order. His name has come to us as Hendry Brown. There are those who maintain that Hendry is a typographical error, heedlessly carried on, but if so, it was an inspired typographical error, for who would remember Henry Brown? It is as Hendry that we associate him with Billy the Kid and the Lincoln County War; it is as Hendry that he was gunned down in Medicine Lodge by lynchers who hanged his companions in crime.

As we get on with tales of a duel, murder, violence, flood, cyclone, and other disasters, I began dreading the dull part, for few local histories lack long stretches of dull part. But how could Medicine Lodge be dull while one of its residents was Mrs. Carry Nation, battering saloons with a hatchet—an arguably legal method of violent dissent, as saloons were illegal in dry Kansas!

Still looking for the dull part, we are bucked off in the main street of the modern-day city and find that it has a mayor who is interested in history—and to find a mayor who is interested in history, dear reader, is almost as curious as finding a ghost who kept a diary. Many a mayor has signed his name to a ghost-written history, or introduction to same, but that is something quite different. Mayor Hewitt collected the documents, did the research, and then set out to find a professional writer to do the job right. For a real master of as-told-to historical reminiscence he picked well in Nellie Snyder Yost.

Nellie Snyder Yost was born in Nebraska and makes her home in North Platte, a couple of hundred miles from local pride in Medicine Lodge. Her first book in 1951 was *Pinnacle Jake*, a biography of her father A. B. Snyder, an old-time cowhand. My high opinion of that book was reinforced by receiving, while writing this, a catalog from a dealer in rare books offering a signed copy at more than four times the original cost. Nellie then got her mother to tell her another book, *No Time on My Hands*, and amazingly there is almost no crossover between the two. Now any girl who can write two books without leaving home should go far, and she has. John Leakey camped on her doorstep until she would let him tell his tale of chasing cattle from Texas to Montana in *The West That Was*. More like the Medicine

Lodge job was *Boss Cowman: The Reminiscences of Ed Lemmon,* for here she had to make a narrative from a meandering lot of newspaper articles, notes, and letters. Nellie Snyder Yost is also author of *The Call of the Range: The Story of the Nebraska Stock Growers Association.* Here she has made what might have been a house-organ book of routine propaganda into a lively history of the cattle industry in Nebraska.

That is how I see this book and its author, dear reader, and I hope you find it good reading.

DON RUSSELL
Elmhurst, Illinois

PREFACE

A year ago now I knew nothing of Barber County and Medicine Lodge, except that they were names on the map of Kansas. Then, one evening in August 1969, I had a telephone call from the mayor of Medicine Lodge, I. N. "Jibo" Hewitt. Jibo told me who he was and what he wanted. Briefly, would I write the story of his home town? A mutual friend, he said, had recommended me. When I understood it was to be a book-length job, I told him I couldn't, that I was already under contract to do another book and wouldn't have the time.

But the mayor is persuasive. He said he had much of the material all at hand, that all I'd have to do was organize it into a book. I found myself agreeing to look at the results of his many years of accumulated history of his home town and county. The huge package promptly arrived, and by the time I had finished reading its contents I was "sold" on Medicine Lodge.

In September I spent a week in Jibo's beautiful Gyp Hills. The mayor took me to see strange Flower Pot Mountain and Carry Nation's old home. We stood on the site of the original peace treaty talks and visited the great natural amphitheater where the famous pageants are held. He introduced me to Orrin Ash, and his son Dillman Ash, who retraced with me the route through the hills by which the outlaws fled after the attempted bank robbery, and showed me the box canyon where they were caught. I talked with elderly people who, as children, had known Carry Nation and many of the other folks who fill these pages. Among these good citizens who helped me so much, I wish especially to thank Orville Pfost, Mayme Griggsby, Alice MacGregor, Delilah Spriggs, Mrs. Mickey Crutchfield,

Mrs. A. I. Grigstead, W. Luke Chapin, Chester B. Fullerton, and the staff of the *Barber County Index.*

Altogether it was a fascinating week, and I came home on fire with enthusiasm to tackle the writing of the book. Of course a good deal more research had to be done, some of it at Jibo's end of the line, but the energetic mayor never once failed to answer my calls for help. After three months of furious work we had a book, *and* an interested publisher who was willing to see that it was between covers by October 1, 1970.

So, barring tornados, fire, flood, or Indians on the warpath in Barber County, I plan to be in Medicine Lodge on October 9 for the opening day of the great 1970 Peace Treaty Pageant of Medicine Lodge, and for the introduction of *Medicine Lodge: The Story of a Kansas Frontier Town.*

In conclusion I wish to state that most of all this book came into being because of the untiring efforts of "Jibo" Hewitt, the one-of-a-kind mayor, and to him of course is due the honor of dedicating the story of Medicine Lodge, for, after all, this *is* the story of his country, his town, and his people.

NELLIE SNYDER YOST
North Platte, Nebraska

Publisher's note: As this book was going to press, we received word of the death of I. N. "Jibo" Hewitt.

ONE

Legend of Flower Pot Mountain

1849-1854

Late in January, 1871, there came a white buffalo hunter to the junction of Elm Creek with the Medicine Lodge River in southern Kansas. Orange Scott Cummins, the Ohio born "Pilgrim Bard," was deeply impressed by the country he saw there, by the wild beauty of its deep canyons and its red hills, carved by erosion into towering mesas and buttes.

Long, long ago a tribe of Indians known as the Kiowa had chosen that part of North America for their own. Probably one of the most scenic and beautiful regions in Kansas, it was all that an Indian could want, for no other part of the state is so plentifully supplied with swift running streams, with sweet native grasses, or with such abundant natural shelter in the form of timber, hills, bluffs, and canyons. The beautiful river that flowed from the northwest to the southeast supplied many miles of living water. Numerous creeks emptied into the river, and the banks of all were bordered by thick stands of red cedar, elm, cottonwood, hackberry, and walnut trees. Vast herds of buffalo, elk, deer, and antelope grazed the valleys, and bear, turkey, and other animals and fowl inhabited the timber.

In addition to all this, the Kiowas had discovered that the waters of the river were endowed with healing properties; and so they came yearly to the river, to a lovely spot in the angle made by the confluence of the river and a creek. Here they pitched their tepees, bathed in the river, and drank of its laxative mineral waters. In time they also discovered the healing properties of many of the herbs and plants that grew on the banks of the streams. The better to use them, they built a great "medicine lodge" on the bank of the river, setting slender logs on end in a circle, bending the tops to the center, and covering the whole with rushes and earth. There in the tight lodge they heated big rocks and placed their healing herbs on them; then they poured on the water, thus filling the enclosure with clouds of aromatic steam. Bathed in the steam, the red people sweated and soaked away their ills. And who is to say those early sauna baths were no less effective than those of our day?

And so the years passed. The main stream came to be known as the Medicine Lodge River; the creek which joined it, due to the great groves of elms that lined its banks, was called Elm. Other streams draining the hills of the region bore such descriptive names as Bear, Cedar, Antelope, Spring, Turkey, Cottonwood, Elk, Hackberry, Bitter, and Big and Little Mule Creeks.

Whether or not a sacred medicine lodge stood on the banks of the river when Coronado and his host passed that way in 1541 is not known. By 1806, when Zebulon Pike led his expedition west to determine the boundaries of the Louisiana Purchase, it may have been there. Other white men later visited that good land in the Medicine Lodge River valley and some of them dealt unkindly with the Indians, turning their early friendliness to hate and fury, so that, by 1849, no pale skin was safe in the land of the Kiowa. Or so the legend goes.

The Pilgrim Bard listened to strange tales, told and retold around wilderness campfires, and, in time, recorded some of them, including the tragic "Legend of Flower Pot Mountain."[1] And even today, when one stands on the Barber County prairies and gazes across the miles toward the strange flat-topped butte, the Flower Pot Mountain, it is easy to believe that the story happened, and that it could have happened here.

One morning, wrote the Bard, *I left camp, afoot and alone, unarmed except for a Spencer rifle and two Colt 44's. I struck out in a westerly direction, through canyons so covered with trees as almost to exclude the light of the noonday sun. I wandered along until I came in full sight of a table-top mountain which so impressed me that I resolved to visit it and explore its lofty summit.*[2]

The mountain was so much farther away than it looked that it was well into the afternoon by the time I reached it and climbed its rugged side. When at last I came to the top and pushed through the dense thicket of trees that rimmed the mountain, I was surprised to see a huge buffalo grazing peacefully on the rich buffalo grass that covered the little plateau. I couldn't resist killing a buffalo in such a romantic place, so, though I could not use so much meat, I laid him low with one shot from my Spencer.

Since it was too late to return to camp that day, I decided to skin the huge animal, cook some of his flesh for supper, and spend the night on the mountain. I roasted choice bits of the meat over a bright fire of cedar faggots, then spread the great hide beside the coals and lay down upon it. Lighting my pipe, I rested for a time, delighting in my strange situation. I had never believed in ghosts, or that departed souls ever returned to earth again, so I felt no fear in this dark and lonely spot. After awhile, wrapping my shaggy fur mantle about me, I fell asleep.

It must have been near midnight when I was suddenly awakened by the most unearthly cries. The entire summit of the mountain was radiant with a weird light like a continuous glare of lightning. All was ghastly to look upon, and near the center of the plateau I saw a scene that froze the blood in my veins. About a score of hideously painted savages were dancing wildly around a blazing fire, and in the midst of the flames two human beings, bound to a stake, were roasting alive. Even above the howling of the Indians I could hear the despairing cries of the doomed victims.

It was too awful to look upon and I closed my eyes. Then stillness came over the mountain again and I lay in the darkness, wondering if it had been only a feverish dream. But suddenly a hollow voice spoke at my side. "Stranger," it said, "you are the first of my race to put foot on this mountain since my husband and I were burned alive at the stake. Rest here until the sun rises, then repair to the eastern edge of the mountain. There you will find a cedar tree with a dead limb pointing northward. Beneath it you will find a large, flat stone. Lift it, and be governed by circumstances. What you have seen and heard tonight actually took place here, many years ago. Farewell. I shall never again speak to you."

All was quiet again and I waited for the morning. Dawn came at last and I went at once in search of the tree with the dead limb pointing northward. It was there, just as the spirit voice had described it, but at first I could not find the stone. When I finally scratched into the earth at the base of the tree, I found it, covered with the dust and needles of the years. In all my life I had never felt such a strange sensation as the one that came over me as I stood under that ancient cedar, looking down on the stone and wondering what mystery it covered.

When I lifted it I found a small tin box neatly fitted into an earthen hole. I removed the box and slowly opened the lid. A faint musty smell arose from it. I first took from the box an ear of Indian corn and then a handful of wheat, all as fresh as when plucked from their stalks; a marriage certificate and a roll of papers, yellow with age. The certificate showed that on November 12, A.D. *1832, Evan Day and Lenora Blackwood were joined in the holy bonds of matrimony at New Orleans by the Reverend David Green. A note, attached to the roll of papers read: "To anyone who may discover these treasures. I have been told that only one more sun shall rise before my husband and myself, the last survivors of our ill-fated colony, must perish in the flames on this mountain. You will find enclosed a full and true account of events from the time we left St. Louis up to now. I cannot but believe that these valleys will some day be peopled by my race. Therefore, in the face of the dread angel of death, I ask that whoever shall find this manuscript will publish it and let the world know what happened here. Farewell forever. Lenora Day."*

LENORA DAY'S JOURNAL

St. Louis, Mo. March 13, 1849.

We are all ready to start to California, the fabled land of gold. Our company consists of 16 men, 7 women, and 9 children—32 souls in all. We have 13 wagons, made especially for the overland route, each drawn by 3 yoke of oxen and driven by experienced men called "whackers." The most prominent man in our train is the old Mountain Trapper, who has agreed to guide us as far as the mountains. There, he says, we can get a friendly Indian for the rest of the journey. He is a queer looking specimen of humanity, about 45 years of age, a little under 6 feet tall. His long hatchet face is covered with a grizzly beard and his iron-grey hair hangs far below his shoulders. He is minus his right ear and his left one is slit in several places. He is clothed in buckskin from head to foot and a tail-like fringe hangs from his cap to below his waist. His pantaloons, or leggings as he calls them, are fringed on the outside with human hair, black as a raven's wing. He carries a long rifle, a pair of pistols, and a long knife. He goes by the name of "Old Drab" and rides a lean, wiry grey pony. We are to travel on steam boats to Independence, and from there take the Santa Fe trail, as it is far enough south to afford good grass for our animals, our guide says.

Independence, Mo. March 15.

We reached the town at 9 o'clock this morning, disembarked and moved out on the trail. At 4 p.m. we camped on a beautiful stream of clear water, the banks of which are heavily timbered.

March 30.

Since the last entry in my diary the weather has been so rough that we have made little progress on our journey. We are camped near a village of Pottawatomie Indians and they are holding some kind of a gathering. Old Drab says one of them has died and they are fixing to plant him. These are the first Indians I have seen and I am not favourably impressed with them. They have low brows and coarse black hair in two braids down their backs. They are all dressed alike. Each pant leg is a separate garment, tied with a string around the waist. A piece of cloth hangs down from the waist and a blanket finishes the costume. They have been singing and dancing around the lodge of the dead one, but now they cease and four of them go in and come out, carrying the copper colored corpse in a kind of chair, sitting up, his features rigid and his eyes open and staring. A blanket is thrown over his head, so his spirit will not see the direction it is borne. As soon as the pall-bearers are out of sight, half a dozen squaws tear the lodge down. The trapper tells us this is so the spirit cannot come home but will keep on to the "Happy Hunting Ground."

The grave is a shallow hole on a knoll where others of the tribe have been buried. They put the body in the hole, still sitting up, and all his earthly effects are thrown in after him. He is covered with another blanket, then with earth, and *then* his pony is led up to the grave. As its front feet touch the grave its throat is cut from ear to ear and it sinks with a groan onto the fresh earth. The trapper says this is so the brave will have a pony to ride to the happy hunting ground. The dead brave's squaws then bring food, supposed to be enough for the spirit's journey, and put it on the grave, after which each Indian returned to the camp from a different direction.

Back at our own fire, the old trapper tells us about the Indians' happy hunting ground, a place where game of all kinds abounds, where the grass is forever green, the leaves never fall from the trees, and springs of pure, clear water flow forever. We then asked Old Drab to tell us how he came to lose his right ear and to get his left one so badly cut up.

This is the story he told us: " 'Twas nigh about 8 years ago and I waar trappin' in the Wind River Mountains. I had made a pretty good haul and waar only waitin' fer it to git warm enough to git on the trail. I waar in the Flat Head and Shoshone country, camped in a hole in the mountain, pretty well up toward the top. I had to keep a sharp lookout, for the rascals knowed I was around and wanted to wipe me out and git my furs. One night they waar a campin' on a sort of a bench about a quarter mile below me. The side o' the mountain waar mighty steep, but seein' their light I crawled out and was sorta listenin' to 'em. I was holdin' onto a weesach bush, and when the bush come loose; in spite of all I could do, I slid down and down until I landed plumb in the middle of the red varmints.

"We was all surprised. To jump the game waar out o' the question, so I sorta made myself at home. They surrounded me and began askin' questions, or so I took it, as to whaar I come from. I pointed to the moon, high and white in the sky, but I guess they didn't believe me, fer they tied my hands behind me and began torturin' me. First they took a red-hot iron and run it through my right lug [ear], but I never as much as batted my eyes. This seemed to make 'em mad, so a big son-o'-a-gun walked up and drew the edge o' his scalpin' knife across my cheek, whaar ye see these here scars, and then he cut my left hearer off close t' my head. But I never so much as grunted. Then he went to carvin' on my remainin' lug, and then he stopped as a new idee struck 'em.

"I could see by his motions he waar orderin' a fire, an' I knowed I waar to be roasted alive. So whatever I done must be done immedgitly, so I gathered my strength and made a leap, I knew not whaar. For 'twaar all the same price whether I broke my neck or got roasted. Down I went, slidin' and rollin', till finally I fell full lenth in a little crick at the foot o' the mountain. By the time I wallered out o' the crick, the water had loosed up the thong that tied my hands and I waar agin a free community. My head waar a solid clot o' blood but I made my way around the base o' the mountain and soon crep up into my own manshun, whaar I greased my wounds with taller and went to sleep."

So ended the trapper's story, and one look at him would convince one of its truth.

April 28.

Since the last entry in my diary we have been progressing slowly. The weather has faired up and the grass is quite green, game is abundant and we are having a splendid time. We have passed through several villages, but all the red people seem friendly. Tonight we are camped on the big Arkansas River, near the point where the great bend throws the stream farthest to the north. Though at low water now, it is from one-quarter to three-quarters of a mile wide and, but for quicksand, is everywhere fordable. Unlike most of the streams we have crossed, its banks are entirely destitute of timber, and for fuel we must burn what is called buffalo chips. The old trapper tells us the river is rising a little, and that we must cross it in the morning; for the snow in the mountains is melting now and it could get very high. He says he has seen the entire valley submerged. He has already crossed several times, looking out the best way to take the wagons over.

April 29.

The sun rose clear this morning, but was soon obscured by a dark, ominous looking cloud which Old Drab, being superstitious, considers a bad omen. The river had risen nearly two feet during the night, but he says we must cross, or else lay up no telling how long. So he has the cattle pushed into the stream and driven over and back twice, to settle the bottom. Then they are yoked, 12 yoke to a wagon, and so on until all but one wagon is safely across. This one was about mid-stream when it suddenly sank out of sight. The old trapper, who had crossed every trip, was riding alongside the wagon and in some mysterious manner was caught and taken down beneath the water and sand, never to rise again.

With no small amount of labor the cattle were unhitched and driven out. By then it was dark, so our weary and despondent little band encamped on a knoll on the second bottom. The river is still rising and we wish ourselves back on the other side, with our trusty guide alive.

We were still sitting around our campfire, studying over the events of the tragic day, when we were startled by the sudden appearance in our midst of a strange looking man. We did not see him until he stood among us, with uplifted hands and eyes, invoking the "Keeper of Hosts" to rest his blessings upon our little band. His weird, unearthly appearance, his hollow sepulchral voice, together with the earnest manner in which he spoke, caused us to wonder what manner of man he was. He wore a long black robe with a heavy binding of bright red and a large red Roman cross on the back. His head was uncovered and his long hair and beard were white with the frost of many winters. After his benediction he shook hands with us all, and then said, "Pale faced brothers and sisters, I was warned in a dream, three nights since, of your perilous situation and have made my way hither in order to help you, if it is in my power, to pass in safety from this tangled net into which you have fallen. The red savages know you are in their country, and have known it for several days. Your guide was a traitor of the basest kind and you have been on the wrong trail ever since you started on your journey. It was his intention to deliver you into the hands of the Indians, as he has done many others. But the Lord has dealt with him as he richly deserves and his black soul has gone to its reward. Brothers, it would take too long to tell you my story, and moreover I must not be seen in your camp at any time, unless at the last moment.

"I am the mighty medicine man of three tribes, known among them as 'White Spirit of the Whirlwind,' and I come to save you from torture. But I must be careful, else I, too, shall die a horrible death. Every full moon I go up on the summit of the Flower Mountain to learn the wishes of the Great Spirit for his people. The mountain is sacred and not one of them dares ascend it except at my bidding. Even now I am supposed to be on the mountain in a trance. Brothers, you cannot go back because of the river, so you must follow my directions and, with the help of the Lord, I will strive to bring you through the perils that surround you. If the Indians discover you, never appear uneasy, for they will not attack as long as they think you are going farther into their toils.

"And now take heed. I will leave you as I came, yet I will always be nearer than you may think. In five days travel you will come to the Great Medicine Village of three tribes. To guide you I will lay, at intervals along the way, cedar boughs. The tops will be pointing in the direction you must go. And every night I will put a light like this (here he drew a phial from his pouch and poured a few drops of fluid on a stick which, on being lighted, sent forth a bright red blaze) on the highest point near your camp. If you have gone to the right or the left, the light will always appear on the side you must bear to. And now, farewell." In a moment he had vanished into the night.

Before we sought our couches we agreed, with heavy hearts, that on the morrow we could do no bettter than to follow the directions given us by the stranger.

May 7.

After a toilsome journey over a waste of prairie, we are at last encamped on the west side of a river much smaller than the Arkansas. There are beautiful groves along its banks and all the ravines are lined with trees in the glory of full leaf, elm, cottonwood, and now and then a cedar. It is called by the Indians "River of Lodges," also "White Medicine River." The surrounding country is rough, almost mountainous, and the streams are swift and clear. The soil looks like the dust of our burned brick at home, and to me it seems to be the fabled land of enchantment, where we might well expect to find the fountain of youth. In all my life I have never beheld a lovelier picture than the one presented to our desert-worn eyes this May evening. High, rugged hills to the west are like castles of the feudal ages, and as I look over the bonny landscape I am led to wonder for what purpose God created this lovely land.

After leaving our camp on the Arkansas, we followed the directions given us by our mysterious friend, the cedar boughs and the promised light reminding us of the children of Israel. Occasionally we saw bands of Indians but they never came near us, leading us to believe that, in truth, they would not attack us as long as we were going farther into their toils. Game has been plentiful and we have had as many as five kinds of flesh at one meal.

We have a bright campfire tonight, for it is quite chilly; and dark, sullen clouds are rising in the north. Muttering thunder and bright streaks of lightning warn of an approaching storm, so we take to our wagons.

May 9.

The rain fell in torrents and the night was so dreadful I could not sleep. It must have been near morning when we were startled by a voice, the voice of the mysterious White Spirit of the Whirlwind. The rain still fell as if all the windows of heaven had been thrown open, but above it we heard the Voice crying, "Fly for your lives! A terrible flood is upon you."

The warning came none too soon, for the roaring waters were almost instantly upon us. Except for lurid flashes of lightning, all was darkness and my husband and I clung together. Then, swept out into the roaring blackness, we caught hold of the branches of an elm tree and lifted ourselves above the water. But no matter how high we climbed the water followed us, and when we could go no higher the angry torrent still rose about us. Dawn came at last, lighting the place where we clung to the treetop, in water up to our waists. But the rain was abating and the water had ceased to rise. As far as we could see in any direction there was only water, a vast ocean of water, but finally we saw some of our companions, like ourselves, clinging to tree tops. Nothing of our train was in sight. Cattle, wagons, everything was gone.

Late in the afternoon we were able to come down, and we were not surprised to find that, in the lovely grove where we had camped the night before, the water had been 15 feet deep. Soon all the survivors of our train came wearily together on a high rise of ground and we counted our losses. All of the 9 children had perished, and 3 of the women and 4 men.

Dark clouds still hung on the horizon and we presented a sorry spectacle that gloomy day. But it seemed that one woe is not passed until, behold, another cometh, for even as we huddled there a band of hideously painted Indians came yelling and screeching upon us.

To resist was useless and to attempt to fly was madness, so we were seized and dragged off in a westerly direction for about 6 miles, where we were taken into an Indian village of about 75 lodges. We were hurried to a large white lodge made of bleached skins, and there, to our joy, we found our mysterious friend, White Spirit of the Whirlwind.

He stood in the door of the lodge but gave us no sign of recognition. For a long time he stood looking toward the heavens. Then, his gaze still fixed on things above, he spoke to us softly in our own tongue. "Brothers, the Indians are resolved on your destruction. They think the Great Spirit is angry because they have not already destroyed you, and that that is why the great flood came. I have done all in my power to save you, but unless some unseen hand interposes you will be burned at the stake. The braves have gone to prepare their votes for life or death, and each will bring an arrow and drop it at my door. If the arrow points are red, you will die, if green, you will stay with the tribe, never again to leave it. But be of good cheer. The Lord may yet deliver you. Now, be careful you do not seem to recognize me, and again, farewell!"

Still the old man stood motionless, his gaze fixed on the rolling clouds that grew blacker and blacker. The wind had now lulled until hardly a leaf moved on the trees, as if nature itself held its breath for what was to happen next. The council ended and the warriors came, filing past the door of the lodge, where each dropped an arrow with a crimson point. So now we were all to perish at the stake, and the knowledge made us envy those who had so lately found a grave beneath the angry waters of the White Medicine.

We were seized and bound to nearby trees, as many as four to a tree, and dry faggots were piled high around us. Then we saw the fiendish executioner coming toward us with his lighted torch. But he never reached us, for, like Abraham of old, his hand was stayed—this time by a terrific wind, striking suddenly and tearing its way through the village, the trees, and everything in its path.

More than half the lodges were swept from the face of the earth, and the Indian with the blazing torch was caught up in the mad gale and dashed to pieces before our eyes. The hurricane was gone as quickly as it came, but a pitiless rain then poured upon our benumbed, half-clad bodies.

By the lightning flashes we could see that the big white lodge still stood, and in its doorway the venerable White Spirit of the Whirlwind, still gazing into the threatening heavens; while prostrate on the ground, face down, lay the survivors of the village. Then, without looking at us, the old man spoke again. "Brothers, you have been miraculously saved. The Indians think the Great Spirit is angry with them for planning to put you to death. They believe I stilled the hurricane and that I am now talking to the Great Spirit. Now you will be released from the stake, and I shall threaten them with other plagues unless they obey me. You will be brought to my lodge, but do not appear to recognise me and all will yet be well."

Then, looking down on his prostrate congregation, he made them a long harangue, whereupon they arose and cut the thongs that bound us. We were then taken to the white lodge, where a comfortable fire was blazing, and we were warmed and fed, after which buffalo robes were spread for us to lie down on. The old man told us that night that the Indians had decided we should stay in their country, and that we would be safe as long as we didn't try to escape. He advised us to go in the morning to look for the bodies of our lost friends, and for any of our wagons and possessions that might have survived the flood.

At first light in the morning we set out. Half a mile below our camping place we began to see evidence of the awful catastrophe—the running gears of some of the wagons, and dead oxen still in their yokes, for we had seldom unyoked until after midnight. Two miles farther on we came upon a yoke of cattle, trapped on top of a high pile of drift, but still alive. We gladly untangled them and brought them down to grass and water. Still farther down, where the river bottom on the west side of the stream is about a mile wide, we found three wagon boxes, including our own, with the contents but little damaged. Then, as the day was far spent, we made camp for the night.

May 10.

This morning, while one of the men went back up the river after the oxen, the rest of us searched for bodies. By sundown we had found all but one—a woman whose heart-broken husband refused to be comforted and wandered all night by the river, calling her name. To keep away wild animals we have kindled a bright fire beside the place where the bodies are laid, and the men take turns watching over our lonely morgue. When morning comes we will bury the bodies on a knoll beside our camp.

May 11.

This morning we dug a grave, long enough to hold all the bodies, and lined it with fresh boughs from the elm trees. We covered them with more boughs and then with earth. After the burial we went on searching for the missing woman, but though we closely scanned the river banks for many miles, we found no trace of her, nor of any more of our effects.

May 12.

Today we started looking for a suitable place for a permanent camp. All nature seemed glad, this lovely spring morning, and after breakfast three of the men, with rifles and ammunition we had recovered, started off toward the west. The rest of us overhauled and counted what remained of our earthly possessions. We found that we had a good supply of powder, lead, and flints, some writing material, clothing, a box of assorted field and garden seeds, part of a set of carpenter tools, flour, salt, a supply of Lucifer matches, and many minor articles.

Night brings no tidings of our men but we do not worry, for they said they might be gone three days. Not a single Indian has visited us since we left their village, though we have seen them at a distance and know that they keep a constant watch on our movements.

May 13.

Last night as we were about to retire we were startled by a strange cry, like that of a human in distress. We looked at each other in fear as it came again, "Help! Help! For God's sake help. I am sinking in this horrible water." The voice had hardly died away when the missing woman's half-crazed husband leaped to his feet, shouting " 'Tis my own lost Nora. Living or dead, speak to me again, Nora." But only the echo of his own pitiful voice answered. After awhile the rest of us retired, but morning found the lonely husband still sitting by the dying fire. We did not speak of the voice we had heard in the night.

About five o'clock this afternoon our men returned. Two of them carried the ham of a buffalo between them on a pole. Seven or eight miles to the west, they told us, they had come to as lovely a little valley as ever the eye beheld. It had an abundance of timber and pure water and they had determined to locate there.

May 14.

At daybreak we started for the beautiful valley. About noon we reached a winding stream and halted for dinner on its grassy banks. Truly enough, it was a lovely land. Hills small and great lay to the north and west, and in the distance we saw the Flower Mountain, looming like an evil portent, reminding us that Paradise and its counterpart were uncomfortably close together.

Just at sunset we reached the spot selected for our homes in the wilderness.[3] Here there is a rise of ground entirely surrounded by timber. The main creek, 4 to 6 feet in width, runs on the east of us, while a branch, furnished with several springs of clear, cold water, runs on the south. Game of all kinds abounds, from the stately buffalo down to the timid hare, and the woods are alive with wild turkeys.

May 15.

For breakfast we had a dainty dish, water cress, gathered from a pond near one of the springs. While some of the men went back with the team to bring up the rest of our effects, the rest of us made a garden. On a suitable spot south of the trees that lined the creek bank we dug up a good sized patch and planted some of our seeds, wondering all the while if we should ever "gather where we had strewn." This evening we sat for hours around the fire, discussing plans for the future. We decided to build cabins in the form of a village, and to name it "Day Vista," for my husband and for the beautiful view.

May 28.

Nothing worthy of note has happened since my last entry. The seeds we planted are up and I have never seen a finer prospect for a garden. The men have made a kind of plow from the fork of a tree and have commenced farming on a larger scale. They will plant turnips, as we have an abundance of the seed. We have built two cabins of cottonwood logs at Day Vista, each with a big fireplace built of stone from the nearby hills. We will build more house room as soon as we have time.

While we were sitting in front of our cabins this evening we were startled by the sudden appearance of the White Spirit of the Whirlwind. After shaking hands with us all, he said he was anxiously awaiting the coming of the full moon, as he had much to say to us. He told us that he was well pleased with our progress, and that the Indians seemed pleased, too, for they told him all that we did. Then he asked us if the last body had been found. He wanted to know because, two nights before, while the braves were holding their Spirit Dance (always held two days before the moon was made) they were terribly frightened by the appearance in their midst of a half-clad woman with long, shining auburn hair. They had prostrated themselves, face downward, and the woman, crying "Help! Help! For God's sake help, I am sinking in this horrible water," had disappeared in the darkness. He said he had told them they had seen the wandering spirit of one who had perished in the flood.

We talked it over and decided the poor woman had been cast ashore from the flood, a raving maniac. And all the while the poor woman's husband sat motionless, but suddenly he sprang to his feet, shouted, "Nora, Nora, I am coming," and fell to the ground. Blood was gushing from his mouth, nose, and ears, and though we raised him tenderly in our arms, his spirit had forever flown.

Then the White Spirit of the Whirlwind spoke again. "Brothers, some time I will tell you my story, but for now you have sorrow enough of your own. If I can I will visit you when the moon is full. In the meantime when I wish to talk to you I will raise my crimson light on the summit of the hill one mile west of this spot. When you see it, go to it quickly, for it will only appear when your lives are in jeopardy and I have news of great importance. Farewell." And with a wave of his hand, he was gone.

May 29.

What a glorious bright morning. Far different from our feelings as we prepared the body of our friend for burial. We buried him on a hillock south of Day Vista, and above him we raised a headboard, inscribed by my husband as follows: "In memory of Joel Raymond. Died May 28, 1849, aged 21 years, 6 months. Psalm LXXX."

January 1, 1850.

My supply of writing material is nearly exhausted and henceforth I shall write only the most important events. The White Spirit of the Whirlwind has visited us at each full moon. We reaped an abundant harvest in proportion to the limited amount of seed, except for turnips, we had to plant. Of turnips we have a great supply, but most of our corn, wheat, potatoes, etc., are carefully put away for seed for next spring. The oxen are sleek and fat, although they have had nothing to eat but grass, which still seems as nutritious as in midsummer. We have had no snow and little frost and the streams have not yet frozen over. We have built 3 more cabins, one for a storehouse, and have fenced our garden, as the buffalo come up from the valley in such vast herds that they almost overrun our village.

Four of our men became homesick in November and decided to try to escape to civilization. They started soon after dark, but were overtaken before daylight and taken to the Indian village, where the braves voted five times before agreeing to let them come home. They were told that a second attempt to escape would mean the death of the entire colony, for they believed that our men intended to bring help to free us all. Last night we gathered in our largest cabin to hold a meeting, as it was New Year's Eve. Today we enjoyed a New Year's dinner which, but for the absence of bread and pastry, could not be excelled.

September 16, 1852.

With a heavy heart I resume my diary. For almost 3 months I have been ill, knowing little of what went on around me. And now I find that the death messenger has entered our fold and taken from us 5 men and a woman. We were all stricken about the same time with a fever and, but for the medicine given me by the White Spirit of the Whirlwind, I, too, would have died. The first thing I ate, on my recovery, was part of a fine, large watermelon, of which we have many. We also have a good supply of almost every kind of vegetable.

September 17.

Today my husband and I walked out north about 3 miles, and from a high hill looked out over the surrounding country. In all my life I have never looked upon a grander scene. But as we gazed across the land we heard again that terrible cry, "Help! Help! For God's sake help, I am sinking in this horrible water." We turned to look, and to my dying day I will not forget what we saw. Two hundred yards away, the poor woman sat on a huge rock, combing her hair with her long, bony fingers. She was wrapped in the skin of a buffalo and she looked more like a wild beast than a human being. My husband took my arm and we started toward her, but she sprang to her feet, sent forth her wild, despairing cry again, and vanished behind the rock. As night was coming on, we slowly retraced our path homeward. Supper was waiting, and *bread*, the first I had had in many months, was smoking on the table. Our people had made a grater from a tin pan and grated the corn meal from some of the crop of almost 200 bushels they had raised.

September 21.

The night after our walk I dreamed that I was dead and in the land of perpetual sunshine, and there I talked with the departed members of our little colony. Strangest of all, I saw Nora Raymond. The wild maniac look was gone and her angelic face was wreathed in smiles as she came with open arms to meet me. Then she told me she had been in that bright land since the night of the flood, but that her poor body had ever since been wandering the earth—why, she did not know.

When I awoke that morning the sun was shining in my face and all the people of our village were gathered round my bed. For more than an hour my husband said, they had been trying to waken me. When they could not, they feared my spirit had flown. I was unable to rise and it was thought I had overdone and the fever had returned.

Come what might, my husband said then, he would visit the White Spirit of the Whirlwind and get help for me. With two of our men, all unarmed, he set out, carrying a flag made of a bleached fawn skin. Each man also carried a melon as large as he could handle. On his melon my husband had scratched, "Wife sick again. Give me more medicine."

When they reached the village they were taken at once to the white lodge, where they laid their presents down. The old man told the Indians their white friends had come in peace, bearing gifts that were good to eat. Then he cut the melons and ate a piece to show his people it would not make them dead, after which they all ate greedily until not a mouthful was left. While they were eating, the medicine man went into his lodge and came back with a curiously fashioned purse, which he gave my husband as a present in return for the melons. Inside the purse were several packets of whitish powder, with directions written on each. By bedtime I was so much strengthened that I could walk without assistance.

September 23.

Last night we sat in front of our cabins on Main Street, talking over the work of the day. The moon had risen but gave little light as a kind of fog overspread the valley. We were about to retire when we suddenly saw a red gleam on the hill to the west. We knew it at once for our friend's signal and my husband and two others repaired at once to the hill. When they were near to the light it went out and they heard these words, "Brothers, I fear your time has come. The Indians have just returned from an unsuccessful attack on an emigrant train on the main trail beyond the Arkansas River. Two of their chiefs and many of their best warriors were killed and now they are holding a fearful mourning dance, wailing and slashing their own persons to appease the wrath of the Great Spirit.

"They believe this has happened because they let you remain here, so now they have decided to burn you at the stake on the Mountain of Sacrifice. They have commanded me to have all in readiness by the time the moon is straight over the Mountain, which will be by the time I return. But be brave, for the One who has delivered you out of so many perils yet liveth. Now, farewell."

When the men got back they found the rest of us with our hands already bound behind our backs. They, too, were seized and bound. The Indians had already set fire to one of the cabins, and were about to fire the rest—when there appeared on the roof of the burning building a terrible sight: a wasted female figure, her face haggard, her eyes burning like coals of fire. Her long auburn hair, streaming in the night wind, almost touched the flames that climbed around her. She made frantic gestures with her hands and screamed her wild call for help. But while we stared in horror, she disappeared, still shrieking. And when we finally looked about us, we saw that the Indians were gone, too.

Then there came a voice from the darkness, saying, "For He hath looked down from the height of His sanctuary. To hear the groaning of the prisoner, to loose those that are appointed to death," and the White Spirit of the Whirlwind, knife in hand, cut our bonds. The Indians, he told us, thought he was still on the Flower Mountain, but when he returned to them he would tell them all that had happened here. This, he said, would frighten them so much that they would obey when he told them not to harm us more, lest they incur the anger of the Great Spirit in still greater measure. He said we were to go ahead as if nothing had happened, and then he added, "How strange that the poor demented creature lives so long in these wilds, but is so seldom seen."

September 24.

Today I was out alone, gathering wild grapes and plums. Presently I entered a ravine where the shrubs and vines were so dense as to cut off nearly all sunlight. It was so shadowy that I almost turned back, but I am no coward, so determined to go ahead. So I pushed through the foliage, and came upon a sight I shall never forget. In a little natural clearing, in the shade of a mulberry tree, lay our poor maniac —and for companions she had a she bear and two cubs. The cubs seemed as affectionate toward her as toward their mother, and the poor creature fondled and played with them as though she really loved them. Yet we all knew Nora Raymond was a timid, nervous woman, frightened of even her own shadow.

October 13, 1853.

This morning five Indians, including a head chief, came to our village. They brought us a present of 5 buffalo robes, the insides painted in the most beautiful colours. They also gave us a bow and arrows, the points all green, which we understood meant we would be allowed to stay without further trouble, at least for the present. When they were ready to leave us we gave them all the vegetables they could carry, and they made signs asking us to visit them, something they had never done before.

May 3, 1854.

Last night we had one of the most terrific thunder storms I have ever witnessed. It seemed as if the elements were at war and the continuous glare of the lightning lit up the countryside like day. And while we stood in our open doorways, watching the awful scene, a still more terrible sight chilled our very blood. For up in the branches of a huge old cottonwood tree we saw our poor maniac. Standing erect on a limb that swayed beneath her, she seemed to look toward us, then threw up her arms and shrieked her familiar cry, "Help! Help! For God's sake help. I am sinking in this horrible water." Her last words were swallowed up by a blinding flash that shivered the tree, and when we could see again we ran to it, for at its splintered base lay the body of the poor crazed woman.

We tenderly carried her into one of the cabins, where we sadly closed her staring eyes. Then one of the women and I made ready to prepare her body for burial, but she suddenly sat straight up and looked about her, and even more startling—the light of reason had returned to her eyes. She recognized both of us, then quickly asked for her husband. And when we told her he was no more, she lay down again, folded her hands across her breast, closed her eyes and died. This morning we buried her beside her husband. On a simple headboard we carved these words: "Nora Raymond. Lost in the flood May 7, 1849. Died May 2, 1854. Gone home at last."

July 30, 1854.

We are all alone, my husband and I, and only God in Heaven knows what the end will be. I would gladly pass over the soul-trying events of the last few days, but it is my duty, perhaps my last one, to finish the record.

On the night of the 26th all our little colony, except my husband and myself, started for the settlements. Knowing it would end in disaster, we refused to go. They took the oxen and wagon, and enough provisions for the journey. But, alas! They were scarcely started before the Indians were upon them. The White Spirit of the Whirlwind was with them and they instantly killed him. The rest were taken to the village, and last night we could plainly see the light of the funeral fires on top of the Flower Mountain.

So now it is only a question of hours before the same fate befalls us. There is nothing we can do.

I do not know if it is possible for the spirits of the departed to visit the earth again, but if it can be done I shall certainly return to harass these inhuman wretches. Yes! If it be God's will, I shall return to this valley I have loved so dearly, this paradise that has come to mean so much to me. Now I must stop. My heart is too heavy and sad to go on.

A final sheet of paper recorded the names and birth places of the fourteen people left alive on that New Year's Eve in 1849, when the little group celebrated together. From England, Ireland, Scotland, Brazil, Buenos Ayres, Kentucky, Indiana, Pennsylvania, Louisiana, and New York, they had come to that legendary village on the Kansas plains.

TWO
Medicine Lodge Indian Peace Treaty
1867

Of that vast area that makes up the Great Plains section of our United States, Daniel Webster once declared, "I will not vote one cent from the public treasury to place the Pacific Ocean one inch nearer to Boston than it is. What do we want with this worthless area—this region of savages and wild beasts, of shifting sands and whirlwinds of dust, of cactus and prairie dogs? To what use could we ever hope to put these great deserts . . . ?"

But far out near the center of Webster's "great deserts" there lay a green oasis, a lovely land, timbered and well watered, the Medicine Lodge River valley of the ancient Kiowas. The illustrious statesman could, however, be forgiven for his summation of the worth of the country; for to reach the sightly spot one had, in frontier times, to travel by wagon or on horseback across miles and miles of treeless prairie. And so, upon cresting any rise overlooking the valley, "the groves of cottonwood and elm, with here and there through rifts in the wooded fringe a glimpse of the swift flowing waters of two converging streams, glistening like ribbons of silver flecked with gold," the weary traveler must truly have thought he had come upon the Garden of Eden.[1]

Until near the end of the 1860s, this beautiful, well grassed valley, where the two streams came together, belonged to the Indians, the Kiowas and their neighbors. But white men had seen the land, and coveted it. And as soon as the great war between the states was finished, the eyes of restless people to the east, and even across the Atlantic, turned to the Great Plains of the West. Railroads were pushing outward, too, and settlers were following their lead. Already buffalo hunters were shooting continuously into the enormous herds that had roamed the valleys and water courses for centuries.

Alarmed and hostile because of the increased encroachment on their hereditary lands, the major Indian tribes of the whole area, from Canada to the Rio Grande, from the Missouri to the Rockies, went to war in earnest against the whites. The United States government from time to time attempted to pacify the tribes with various peace treaties, such as the one at Fort Sully in 1865, and at Fort Laramie in 1866, but little was accomplished and the hostility continued.

Some of the Indians, however, did attempt to move toward peace with the whites. Black Kettle was one who tried. He, with his Cheyennes after requesting a meeting with U. S. authorities, went into camp on Sand Creek, near Fort Lyon, Colorado, in November, 1864. While awaiting the meeting, it is said, the chief flew the flag of the United States from his tallest tepee pole. And there, early in the morning of November 29, Colonel J. M. Chivington, a former presiding elder of the Nebraska Methodist Conference, with his Third Colorado Cavalry, fell without warning upon the unsuspecting and peaceful Indians. Black Kettle and a fellow chief, White Antelope, stood beneath the flag, protesting friendship, until they saw it was useless. Black Kettle then escaped, but White Antelope, with arms folded and singing his death song, was shot. The ruthless slaughter was terrible; fleeing men, women, and children were shot down without mercy. Chivington himself proudly reported 500 Indians killed. The number was probably considerably less.

With relations between Indians and whites at an all-time low, largely as a result of the Sand Creek massacre, the United States government determined to seek some means for putting an end to the "Indian menace" on the plains. The question, of course, was how: by war or by negotiation? There were plenty of loud-voiced proponents of both.

By the spring of 1867 the whole country seemed caught up in the discussion. Congress, the newspapers, the man on the street and behind the plow, all were telling how it could, or should, be done. Whatever the method, everybody agreed that the Indian question must be settled.

On July 14 of that year, John B. Henderson, Missouri senator, presented a bill in Congress creating a peace commission to negotiate a treaty with the plains Indians. The bill set up a plan for establishing a "system for civilizing the tribes," something that had not yet been tried. The bill was passed, sent to President Andrew Johnson, and signed by him on July 30.

The President then appointed Lt. General William T. Sherman, commander of all troops and installations west of the Mississippi from Canada to Mexico, to take charge of the planned negotiations. While the newspapers made much of the upcoming meeting, the members of the Peace Commission and Sherman, from his office in St. Louis, set in motion the plans that were to culminate in the Medicine Lodge Peace Treaty.

First, the site of the treaty had to be decided, and here, it seemed, the Indians had something to say. Not about to be caught in another Sand Creek trap, they consistently rejected any and all places anywhere near to white forts or settlements. In the end, the Kiowas' sacred Medicine Lodge valley, a good one hundred miles from the nearest white settlement of any size, was agreed upon. And the first full moon in October was the time set for the assembling of the tribes and the Commissioners.

Early in October the members of the Commission gathered at Leavenworth, Kansas. They were: Senator Henderson; N. G. Taylor, Commissioner of Indian Affairs; Samuel F. Tappan, who had headed a military investigation of the Sand Creek massacre; John B. Sanborn, who had served for the Department of the Interior at the Treaty of the Little Arkansas in 1865; General William S. Harney, retired Indian fighter; General Alfred H. Terry, commander of the Department of Dakota; and General Sherman.

Before the Commission left Leavenworth for the south, General Sherman was called to Washington, and so did not go to Medicine Lodge, although he remained in overall command of the Peace Commission.[2] General Harney was thus left as the ranking military man in the field with the Commission.

Boarding Union Pacific cars at Leavenworth, the officers and civilians proceeded to Fort Harker, near the end of the rails. By this time they had been joined by nine newspaper men: George Brown of the *Commercial* and H. J. Budd of the *Semi-Weekly Gazette*, both of Cincinnati; S. F. Hall of the *Chicago Tribune*; Solomon Bulkley, the *New York Herald*; James Taylor, artist for *Frank Leslie's Illustrated Newspaper*; John Howland, *Harper's Weekly* artist; Milton Reynolds,

Lawrence *State Journal* editor; William Fayel, *Missouri Republican* of St. Louis; and Henry M. Stanley of the *Missouri Democrat*, who later achieved fame in Africa with the stilted words, "Dr. Livingstone, I presume." The size of the press party and the papers represented indicated the importance of the peace negotiations to the country at large.

Thomas Murphy, head of the Central Indian Agency Superintendency, also joined the party at Harker. That night the Peace Commission company camped by the Smoky Hill River, with campfires flaring in the windy darkness. It was a varied group. Kansas Governor Samuel Crawford and Senator E. G. Ross had lately joined the officials, and in addition there were a host of secretaries, aides, ambulance drivers, cooks, and interpreters. In the nearby wagon park teamsters sprawled around their own fires, hard by long lines of picketed mules and wagons loaded with supplies for the comfort of the Commissioners and with gifts for the Indians.

Early on the morning of October 9 the party broke camp and took to the trail, escorted by about 200 mounted troops of the Seventh Cavalry,[3] for the way lay across one hundred miles of Arapaho and Cheyenne hunting grounds. The Commissioners and the reporters rode in ambulances, followed by the long line of wagons, with three span of mules to each wagon.

Soon after leaving Fort Harker, trees, ranches, and farms thinned out and disappeared, giving way to the vast, empty, windswept prairies. By evening of the second day the travelers could see the flare of prairie fires, burning far out on the barren plains. One of the reporters surmised that the fires had been set by the Cheyennes to protest the coming of the Peace Commission. The glare of the flames against the night sky made many in the party uneasy, and mounted guards rode slowly around the camp all that night.

At Fort Larned, on the Arkansas River, Satanta, the Kiowa war leader, Little Raven, an Arapaho chief, with other chiefs and tribesmen, joined the train for the ride on to the Medicine Lodge. That night, too, the fires burned against the skyline, this time south of the Arkansas.

On the morning of October 12 the Indian agents, Colonel Jesse Leavenworth and E. W. Wynkoop, accompanied by thirty additional wagons loaded with Indian gifts and by two companies of infantry riding in ambulances, joined the Commission. The column which then took to the trail was now two miles long and consisted of 211 vehicles of various kinds and, by Stanley's figures, 1,250 animals and about 600 men. The rolling prairie over which they traveled that day was thickly thatched with buffalo grass which, along the small streams, gave way to grass belly deep on the horses. And that afternoon a large herd of buffalo was sighted.

A hunt was quickly organized, amid intense excitement in the party. Some of the hunters took only the tongues, others stopped long enough to cut hump steaks, some simply shot the animals and rode on, still shooting. Satanta, furious at the senseless slaughter, told General Harney what he thought of it. Harney then stopped the shooting and ordered Major Joel Elliott to arrest some of the hunters. That night, however, they all ate hump steak and roast tongue—and that night, again, flames lighted the southern skyline.

Later, after the camp had bedded down, General Christopher Auger, commander of the Department of the Platte, rode into camp, having traveled from Harker on horseback. The General carried a letter from President Johnson, appointing him to serve on the Peace Commission in Sherman's absence. The party was now complete, and Medicine Lodge would be reached before the end of the next day.

To Thomas Murphy, who feared the sight of armed riders might upset the Indians, the military escort had all along seemed unwise. He argued that the warriors would stay friendly as long as the peace party did not come with soldiers and guns, but Taylor had refused to leave the army behind. As the column neared the Medicine Lodge on that last day, however, Harney agreed to move the troops to the rear. Outriders, too, were called in and the infantry ambulances dropped back. The Commission was coming in unguarded, its protection all behind it, hoping to appease the Indians, nearly 5,000 strong, encamped on the stream ahead.

Although they saw numerous herds of buffalo that last day on the trail, there was no shooting. And so, quietly, and no doubt with a good many long, uneasy thoughts, the leaders of the long column crossed the last rise and entered the natural valley, or basin, where Medicine Lodge River and Elm Creek joined.

On the left rose the wooded slope that gave the place its Indian name, Timbered Hill River. A small band of painted Indians awaited the whites there, and when Harney and the other Commissioners dismounted, the chiefs shook hands and embraced them. Interpreters for both sides hurried up and the welcome got under way in earnest. Chief among the welcoming Indian leaders was Black Kettle, the Cheyenne whose camp had been almost wiped out by Chivington only three years before.

The Commission had come into the valley from the northwest. At the base of the timbered hill the Arapahoes had made camp. Ahead of them, near the Medicine Lodge River, was the ration camp, a great store of food, brought in beforehand, to feed the Indians during the negotiations. Across the creek a small band of Cheyennes was camped. Beyond the Arapahoes, on the near side of the Medicine Lodge, were the Plains Apaches. The Comanches were across the creek from them, and on down stream was the Kiowa camp. Everywhere that the whites could see, out in the open and through and beyond the trees, the place was covered with tepees, horses, dogs, and Indians.[4] It was a sight well calculated to make the whites feel uneasy as to the security of their hair.

General Harney lost no time in setting up his own camp, ordering the ambulances driven into a hollow square formation, inside which the cook fires and tents were arranged. The wagon train corraled nearby, while many Indians stood round about, watching, as the darkness came down on the Medicine Lodge and the jittery reporters tried to compose reports for their papers back home. They well knew that it would be all too easy for the hordes of Indian warriors to wipe out the few hundred palefaces, in spite of the two Gatling guns hidden somewhere in the camp. The fact that the famed scout, Kit Carson,[5] wise to the ways of Indians, was with them in camp may have soothed their qualms a bit. The night passed peacefully, however, and the next morning the reporters dared to leave the protection of their hollow square and look about them. To Stanley the treaty site was a "vale of paradise." "Viewing the encampment from the distance," he wrote, "the white tops of the wigwams could be discerned from the verdant umbrageous foliage of the groves of timber, the white forming a pleasing contrast with the vivid green."

Though it seems that no attempt was ever made to take an actual count of the Indians assembled for the treaty making, the total number at any given time was probably well over 5,000.[6] Small bands continued to arrive at the site all during the proceedings, while several tribes that took no part in the conference camped round about, just to watch. Several accounts, written long after the colorful affair had passed into history, have given the total number as 15,000, and even 20,000, but such was probably an exaggeration, though the gathering is often referred to as the largest peace treaty ever held between native Americans and white men. However, the Horse Creek Peace Treaty, held on the stream of that name in northwest Nebraska in 1851, is said to have included 10,000 Indians.[7]

At any rate, Medicine Lodge was an event of tremendous importance, and the simple fact that so many thousands of hostile and uneasy Indians could be induced to come together at one place was amazing in itself. For not only did the Indians have good reason to mistrust the whites, who came to the treaty grounds with armed soldiers and Gatling guns, but some of the tribes, particularly the Cheyennes and Comanches, did not get along with each other. To add to the mutual unease was the fact that most of the Cheyennes had stayed away, encamped on the Cimarron, a short day's ride to the south. If they chose, these warriors could fall upon the treaty camp, almost without warning, and this knowledge seemed to bother the other Indians almost as much as it did the white men.

On that morning of October 15, however, all seemed in order and the newspaper men scattered to visit the Indian camps. Each of them found special points of interest to write about for his paper. Stanley left one of the best accounts: "Some fanciful notion arose in our minds at the beautiful prospect, but on arriving at the village the charm which the fancy had woven in our minds was entirely dissolved. Within and around the Arapaho village which we first visited all was corruption and filth. Dressed in dingy buffalo robes which swarmed with vermin were the warriors, squaws and papooses. . . . The camp was strewn with the most miscellaneous articles that could be conceived. Dogs, half eaten up, tanned buffalo robes, axes, pots, kettles and pans, beadwork, old moccasins, chunks of lately killed buffalo, stews cooking in kettles, dog skins, antelope and elk hides, pipes, tom-toms, war clubs, bone grubbing hoes, stone hammers, headless arrows and broken bows, dolls, bone saddles in heaps, wicker cradles by the score, and howling and barking dogs."

After describing the architecture of an Indian wigwam, and its size, "50 to 75 feet in circumference by about 12 feet from base to apex," he listed the "furniture": a saucepan, camp kettle, three or four horn spoons, two or three wooden dishes. Half a dozen buffalo robes, "the whole forming an accumulation of filth and vermin," comprised the bedding for each lodge.

That afternoon Taylor called a meeting of the chiefs and the Commission members. Tappan was there and Senator Henderson and Generals Harney, Terry, and Augur. A goodly number of chiefs represented the various tribes, and Taylor ordered gifts of clothing given to each to start things off. Each of the chiefs then made a speech of welcome.

The first question to come before the meeting concerned the calling of the Grand Council. The Comanches and Kiowas wanted to wait until the Cheyennes were ready to come up from the Cimarron, but Black Kettle explained that his people were making medicine there and could not come for several days. Ten Bears, an old Comanche who dressed up in gold-rimmed spectacles when he spoke, stated that his tribe was friendly and would talk whenever the Kiowas did. In the end, four tribes, the Arapahoes, Apaches, Comanches, and Kiowas agreed to meet on October 19. The Cheyennes would wait.

That evening reporters Fayel, Hall, Howland, and Stanley were invited to visit a dance in Little Raven's nearby Arapaho village. Little Raven himself, a fat, friendly chief, met them at the edge of the village and escorted them to a large tent, filled with smoke and Indians. When he had seated his guests and given the signal, the festivities began, with men and women dancing around a fire in the center of the tent. Uttering shouts and cries, the tempo of the dance increased until the near naked bodies glistened with sweat and the noise was all but deafening.

Stanley found the dance fascinating, and all the more so when Fayel and Hall joined the circle, dancing until they, too, ran streams of perspiration. Finally Howland also leaped into the frenzied circle, or so the reporter wrote—but he may only have been taking advantage of an opportunity to have a little fun at the expense of his fellow newsmen.[8]

While the four reporters were enjoying Little Raven's hospitality, a bit of excitement prevailed in the Commission compound. As twilight was settling on the Medicine, nearly one hundred Cheyennes, painted and well armed, crossed the river, trotting their mounts and chanting as they came. While the camp watched this scene of barbaric splendor, wondering, no doubt, if it might be the last sight some of them would ever see, the head chiefs, Grey Beard and Tall Bull, pulled their horses up sharply in front of the camp, where General Harney stood waiting to receive them. The chiefs and a few others dismounted and greeted the General in friendly fashion, but the rest of the band sat on their horses, their arms much in evidence. Tension among the whites was high.

Harney, however, took the chiefs into his tent and talked with them for some time. When they came out, the General ordered rations issued for the visitors from Black Kettle's camp and the Cheyennes rode away, leaving a good many white men wondering if the warriors had come to look over the camp with the intention of attacking it later.

During the following two weeks there were other tense times, one when a large body of mounted men came dashing in from the west. Fear and confusion spread through the camp, for both Indians and whites thought it was a Cheyenne attack. But the party turned out to be Comanches, a band that had just learned of the treaty and had hurried in to join relatives already encamped on the Timbered Hill River.

Immediately after the first day's meeting, preparations got underway for the Grand Council meetings. In the big cottonwood and elm grove about a mile downstream from the Peace Commission camp, across the river from the Arapaho camp, the underbrush was cleared from a large space and a brush arbor built. Tables and camp stools were set up under the arbor for the Commissioners and the press party. Farther out, logs were arranged for the Indians to sit on, facing the Commissioners.

On the day set for the first meeting, the white men took their places, after which the Indians, wearing their best blankets and bone, quill, and elk teeth jewelry, moved in to sit on the logs. The whole must have been an unforgettable scene: the very tall, impressive Harney, the very broad and equally impressive Taylor; officers and civilian members of the Commission in dress uniforms and suits; the chiefs in all their colorful regalia; and the whole surrounded by a mass of Indians of all shapes and sizes, their black eyes shining with interest and curiosity.

The interpreters, sitting near the chiefs they represented, were striking too. Phillip McCusker, a plainsman married to a Comanche woman, interpreted for the Comanches and Kiowas. The two Bent brothers, half-Cheyenne sons of William Bent, and their fifteen-year-old sister Julia, interpreted for the Cheyennes. Mrs. Margaret Adams, thrice married half-Arapaho daughter of the French-Canadian trader John Poisal, wore a scarlet satin dress and bonnet and sat on a folding chair in front of the Arapaho chiefs for whom she translated.

Representing the Comanches were Chiefs Silver Brooch, Dog Fat, Horse Back, Iron Mountain, Painted Lips, Standing Feather, Ten Bears, Gap in the Woods, Little Horn, and Wolf's Name. Talking for the Kiowas were Chiefs One Bear, Stumbling Bear, Woman's Heart, Satanta, Satank, Crow, and Kicking Bird. For the Apaches, Chiefs Bad Back, Iron Shirt, Poor Bear, White Horn, Wolf Sleeve, and Little Bear.

The Cheyenne chiefs would not be in for several days, and the Arapahoes had elected to wait for them.

Both sides made many speeches, the chiefs listing the complaints of their people at length. They told of all the promises of food, clothing, arms, ammunition, knives, and the like, made by the agents of the Great White Father, and of how little of the goods they actually received; of the many times they had been tricked and attacked by the whites; of the treachery and dishonesty of their agents. They declared they did not like all the talk about putting the tribes on reservations *in houses.*

The old Comanche chief, Ten Bears, was especially eloquent. He began with a poetic greeting: "My heart is filled with joy when I see you here, as brooks fill with water when the snow melts in the spring; and I feel glad, as the ponies do when the fresh grass starts in the beginning of the year. I heard of your coming when I was many sleeps away, and I made but few camps until I met you. . . . My people have never first drawn a bow or fired a gun against the whites. . . . It was you who sent the first soldier and we who sent out the second. Two years ago I came upon this road, following the buffalo that my wives and children might have their cheeks plump and their bodies warm. But the soldiers fired on us, and since that time there has been a noise like that of a thunderstorm and we have not known which way to go.

"So it was upon the Canadian. . . . The blue dressed soldiers came out of the night when it was dark and still, and for camp fires they lit our lodges. So it was in Texas. They made sorrow come in our camps. . . . You said you wanted to put us upon a reservation, to build us houses and make us medicine lodges. I do not want them. I was born on the prairie where the wind blew free and there was nothing to break the light of the sun. I was born where there were no inclosures and where everything drew a free breath. I want to die there and not within walls."

The Kiowa chief, Satanta, was in full agreement, as were most of the others. Said Satanta, "When a Kiowa is put in a pen he dies. My people want to remain on the prairies as long as there are buffalo. When they are gone we will be ready to live in houses."

The reporters were much impressed by the diplomacy and fine manners of the chiefs.

On October 21 the Peace Commission brought a treaty to the table, ready for the Indians to sign. Ten Comanches and nine Kiowas "touched the feather" (quill pen) that day, signing away 60,000 square miles of plains and rivers that had been their homes for generations, in return for some 5,000 square miles of reservation land in southwestern Oklahoma, with hunting privileges south of the Arkansas in the Big Bend country of southern Kansas, *for so long as the buffalo may range*. The Indians also agreed to stop all raiding and attacking of white settlers, travelers, and military personnel. The United States agreed to build certain warehouses for storing goods for the Indians, to furnish agents, doctors, carpenters, etc., and housing for same, to build and staff a school for Indian children, and to provide land and tools for any Indians desiring to farm.

The treaty paper was long and involved and the red men probably understood little of what they were agreeing to. Certainly they did not expect the buffalo to be gone so quickly from the face of the prairies, thus putting into effect the treaty provision they had resisted hardest—that they live in houses.

The signing done, the time had come to distribute gifts and annuities. Great piles of blankets, army coats, cloth, beads, baskets, hats, powder and ammunition, knives, and a few firearms were presented to the excited Indians, who quickly loaded them on ponies and headed for their tepees.

The Apache signing took place on October 25, and then the camp settled down to wait for the medicine-making Cheyennes to get through and come in, so that treaty talks with them and the Arapahoes could begin. During this time there was much socializing between the Indians and the white men, although uneasiness as to the real intentions of the absent Cheyennes never did abate.

The red men and the white smoked and drank whiskey together, and some of the tribes staged splendid exhibitions of their horsemanship. Of these the Comanches were undoubtedly the best, proving their right to the title of the "finest horsemen on the plains."

During this period, Stanley, from his camp stool in the hollow square, wrote vivid descriptions of all that went on around him. Of the Commissioners' camp scene, he recorded, "Commissioners, officers, soldiers, bull whackers, mule drivers, Indian chiefs, squaws and papooses pass in and out all day long." Many of the small children, he noted, wore little clothing, or none at all.

On Saturday evening, October 26, Little Robe rode into camp to report that his people, the Cheyennes, would be in the next day. Their medicine was made, he said, and they would come in peace, but they would also come firing their pistols into the air. That night, too, the newspapermen drank the last of their whiskey.[9]

The next morning several of the correspondents and others from the Peace camp, with the interpreter McCusker as guide, rode down the Medicine Lodge River about twelve miles to a clearing where the Kiowa Sun Dance lodge stood. Apparently they had not put much stock in Little Robe's promise that the Cheyennes were coming in, or else they thought they would have plenty of time to make their little trip and return before the Indians could come in from the camp on the Cimarron.

They found the Sun Dance lodge to be a large, circular pole shelter, much like the Medicine Lodge at the forks of the river. Its walls were gaily decorated with beads, gourds, feathers, arrows, and such like. The visitors helped themselves to some of the ornaments as souvenirs of the expedition, then headed back toward their own camp. As they neared the treaty site the men, uneasy because of their pilfering, were thrown into a state of near panic when they heard shots from the direction of the Peace camp. Spurring their horses into the river, they threw their souvenirs into the water and rode at top speed for the protection of the troops at camp.

When Indians encamped along the river began running from their lodges, shouting that the Cheyennes were coming, the guilty men spurred all the harder. And so it was that the sightseers rode full tilt into the forefront of the Cheyenne warriors. Besides being badly frightened, they were also highly embarrassed.

By noon that Sunday the long column of Cheyennes had come into the camp. In spite of the warriors' grand display of horsemanship and the pistol firing, they had come in peace, stopping their racing ponies a scant few feet in front of tall, impassive General Harney, who had come out to meet them. Although fully armed and painted, they were soon laughing and shaking hands all about. After their grand entry, the tall, handsome Cheyennes were content to take their places on the logs before the treaty table, beside their friends, the Arapahoes.

The chiefs who spoke for the Cheyennes were Bull Bear, Curly Hair, Heap of Birds, Lean Bear, Little Bear, Little Robe, Roman Nose, Slim Face, Spotted Elk, Whirlwind, White Horse, Black Kettle, Buffalo Chief, Grey Head, and Little Man. For the Arapahoes, Little Big Mouth, Spotted Wolf, Tall Bear, White Rabbit, Yellow Bear, Young Colt, Storm, and Little Raven.

The Cheyenne-Arapaho council began soon after noon, and before day's end the chiefs had signed an agreement similar in most respects to the Kiowa-Comanche-Apache treaty. Eight Arapaho and ten Cheyenne chiefs had touched the feather when Little Robe, who seems to have been a rather contrary Indian, refused to sign. The treaty paper already had enough marks on it, he said. Bull Bear and White Horse sided with him and also refused. After much futile persuasion by the Commissioners, the interpreters, George Bent and John Smith, finally talked them into making their marks, although no white man ever knew what argument they used.

The usual distribution of treaty gifts and annuities followed, and so ended the historic Medicine Lodge Peace Treaty of 1867, said by many to have been the greatest peace agreement ever consummated between red and white in the United States.

Many of the other tribes had already left the camp on the Medicine, and old Satank, the Kiowa chief, had said goodbye to the Commissioners. After a sadly moving speech, said by Stanley to have been the best speaking heard at Medicine Lodge, the old warrior said, "And now the time has come that I must go. You may never see me more, but remember Satank as the white man's friend."

And truly it was time for all to go. The year was far advanced and the Indian leaders must be seeing to winter shelter for their families and pasture for their ponies. Neither did the whites, many of them city men, fancy getting caught in a prairie snow storm. Accordingly, the day after the final signing was taken up with the orderly confusion of breaking camp and packing the army wagons and ambulances with baggage, furniture, and supplies. Along the creeks squaws were hurriedly loading ponies with lodges, camp stuff, and the gifts and new supplies passed out by the Commissioners.

On that last night on the Medicine, while clouds gathered and lightning flashed, the Arapahoes, in ceremonial dress, gathered in a great circle around the still standing tents of the Peace camp and danced in farewell, the sound of their singing almost lost in the howling winds. South of the river lightning set fire to the prairie, and the flames lighted the last rites of the historic meeting with a fantastic glare. The shriek of the wind grew louder, and then the rain came, putting out the fires and all but blowing the tents from over the heads of the uneasy whites. On a dreary and muddy camp site, the last tents were struck next morning and the wagons headed north into the cold wind.

THREE

Settling Up

1871-1880

That the great treaty of 1867 was not more successful was not the fault of any of those who took part at Medicine Lodge River. Rather, the blame must rest on Congress, for that body took no action to ratify the agreement for many months, nor to make funds available to improve and staff the reservations, nor even to furnish the provisions, rations, and goods promised. So the Indians, hungry, homeless, and angry, again took to the warpath against the whites. The year of 1868, and those immediately following, saw bitter warfare in Kansas, for white travel and settlement were growing apace on the wide prairies and the tribesmen were fighting for their homelands and for their lives.

However, according to a tale told in later years by Scott Cummins, the Pilgrim Bard, not all of the Indians were hostile all of the time. "In the winter of 1871," he wrote, "our party of seven men was on a buffalo hunt. We had had good luck and our wagon was loaded with choice buffalo and venison meat when we went into camp for the night on Spring Creek (near the present town of Medicine Lodge). After we ate supper and had our pipes going, I said, 'Boys, what day of the month is it?' No one knew, so I said, 'Boys, it's Christmas Eve. So hang up your stockings, tomorrow will be Christmas.' Then everyone seemed suddenly to remember Christmases at home in days gone by, and we spent the evening telling stories around the camp fire.

"In the morning we decided to separate and every man hunt on his own hook until time to come in and cook dinner. I went west across the river and was walking up the canyon when I looked up the side of the bank and saw three full-grown bobcats watching me. They didn't try to escape, so I fired one barrel of my shotgun at them. It was loaded with double 'B' shot and I got all three with the one shot. So I went right back to camp and had two ovens of biscuits baked by the time the other boys rounded in. Each of them brought two or three wild turkeys, which we soon had dressed and in the ovens. For Christmas dinner we had coffee, turkey, and biscuits. As no one seemed to hanker for bobcat dessert, we just took off the pelts and added them to the other spoils of our chase."

The Bard went on to describe a spot nearby, where, in the bend of the river, stood three tall cottonwood trees. There "wild turkeys came in to roost after feeding all day in the canyons, and the roar of their wings sounded like distant thunder as they flew in at night. And that evening a band of Cheyenne Indians, out hunting the same as we were, camped near us and several of the bucks came over to our camp and played Seven Up with us. And so passed a Christmas in the wilderness."

Probably most of the white men who first visited the valley at the forks of the Medicine Lodge, after the peace treaty had passed into history, were also buffalo hunters. But some of them saw other opportunities and that same winter, about the same time that the Cheyennes and the buffalo hunters were socializing on Spring Creek, a man named Griffin located a ranch on another branch of the Medicine, about eighteen miles to the northwest.

In the spring, E. H. Mosley and two others, Lockwood and Leonard, settled on the river about the same distance to the southeast. Mosley set up an Indian trading post, and also hunted buffalo and bought hides. The other two built a stout stockade around their cabins, then broke and planted a few acres of prairie.

On July 30, when their crops showed verdant promise, a roving band of Indians came down on the tiny settlement at dawn. About the middle of the forenoon Mosley went outside the stockade to try to parley with the attackers, and was there wounded by an Indian sniper. The attack lasted all day and neither of the other men dared venture outside to try to help the wounded man. At nightfall, after shooting all the livestock on the place, the Indians left. The two farmers then hurried to the aid of the trader, but due to the severity of his wound and many hours of exposure to the boiling sun he was near death. Though it is known that he was buried near the river the next day, his grave has never since been located.

That same summer, Griffin, the upper Medicine ranchman, went down into the Indian Territory and was killed. But that fall another settler, Eli Smith, came to take his place. And still another, R. M. (Dick) Woodward, set up a camp on Bitter Creek on a mound which soon came to be known as "Dick's Peak." Woodward hunted buffalo until the shaggy beasts were all gone, and then became a freighter.

About the same time, a frontiersman, Derrick Updegraff, packed up his family, left eastern Kansas because it was becoming "too civilized," and pulled out for a new frontier. In December, 1872, he topped a rise northeast of the valley at the forks of the Medicine Lodge River and Elm Creek and looked down on the beautiful timbered site of the peace treaty, still marked by the beaten earth of the Commission compound and a scattering of whiskey bottles.

Updegraff was looking for a place to establish a trading post, and here, he knew, was the likeliest spot one could hope to find. By spring he had set up a sawmill on the river and built himself a one-room log house which doubled as a hotel. And none too soon, for that spring and summer of 1873 droves of people came and went in the Timbered Hill country. Some were hunters and some were settlers, looking for locations, and the little hotel, the Medicine Lodge House, was said to have sheltered as many as forty men in a single night.

That year, too, Reuban Lake settled on the upper Medicine Lodge, near Griffin's ranch, and the place was at once called Lake City. The new "city," which never became more than a small village, almost failed to reach even that status, under that name at least, for its founder nearly came to a strange end before the year was out.

Young Lake enjoyed buffalo hunting and at that time many buffalo wintered in the nearby Cedar Mountains. With several settler friends, the homesteader planned a big hunt late in the fall. There was snow on the ground the morning they set out with a wagon and camp equipment, and dark storm clouds promised more before the day was done. It was so cold that the hunters walked a good share of the time to keep their circulation active. Late in the afternoon of the short, dark day they shot and wounded a buffalo. The animal took off for the brakes, leaving a trail of blood on the snow, and Reuban jumped off the wagon, rifle in hand, and took after it. It took longer than he had anticipated to come up with the crippled buffalo, but when he did a well placed shot brought it to the ground. The chase had ended in a sheltered canyon and the young hunter hurried to skin his prize, a truly huge animal.

Reuban had expected the rest of his party to follow his trail and overtake him by dark and he was pleased with himself, thinking what a fine robe he had taken and what a good supper they'd all have when the wagon arrived. In the last of the day's murky light he climbed to the top of the ridge above the canyon and scanned the country round about. He could see no moving thing. Though he fired his gun to attract his friends' attention, no answering shot came back to him.

The hunter went back to his kill and built a fire. If his friends were still looking for him they might see its glow and come on it yet. But the land was twisted and broken into deep canyons and steep ridges, so he gave up and broiled himself some buffalo steaks, threw more wood on the fire, and went to bed. For covering he had the big buffalo hide. Rolling himself into it, like a bug in its woolly cocoon, he felt cozy and safe, even though the cold outside was deepening rapidly and it was beginning to snow.

He was awakened by the snarling and fighting of coyotes. He knew in an instant what had happened. The raw carcass a few yards away had attracted the prairie scavengers and they were making a full meal on his buffalo. This thought Reuban, would be a fine chance to take a few coyote scalps. So he attempted to throw off his buffalo robe, snatch his gun, and fire into the pack—and that was when he discovered an awful truth. The hide had frozen solid around him and he could no more move it than he could have pushed back a rock wall with his bare hands. His snug bed had become a prison.

He lay there, listening to the snarling coyotes and thinking some long, deep thoughts. If the cold spell lasted for awhile, and his friends didn't find him, he could very well perish in his snug fur bed. And with the new snow covering the trail he and the buffalo had left, would the other hunters find him in time to save him? And the coyotes—when they had finished the buffalo carcass, tomorrow night or the next night, would they then choose him for their next meal?

Before the gorged scavengers went off to their dens toward morning, some of them came to the rolled hide and pushed at it, but Lake shouted as loudly as he could in his furry bedroll and frightened them away. If he was not found the next day, he had no doubt but what the pack would be back that night, and if so he expected it would be his last on earth. By another morning only his bones would be left in the canyon.

Hours later, from within his prison, he could tell that the sun came up, so doubtless the storm was over. The hours passed, but apparently the temperature stayed below freezing, for the hide remained rock-hard, immovable. Struggling did no good. There in the deep canyon, where the sunlight faded fast, he knew that another night was nearly upon him. If the coyotes didn't finish him off there were other dangers—an Indian or a bobcat or a panther.

He had all but given up when he heard sounds, the most welcome sounds in all the world, the voices of his friends, shouting that they had seen his camp. A few minutes later they were working on his rescue, building a big fire to thaw out his frozen wrapper and finally break him free, hungry, but otherwise undamaged.[1]

In February, about two months after Updegraff's arrival at the forks of the river, a town site was laid out by Bemis, Hutchinson and Company on 400 acres of land recently pre-empted by the hotel keeper at $1.25 per acre. The town was named for the river, and for the ruins of the old Kiowa medicine lodge a little farther downstream. The town site company put up an office beside the hotel, and a bit later a D. E. Sheldon opened a general store with a twelve-foot shelf of goods and a counter made of two boards laid on flour barrels.

Very shortly a livery stable, a drug store, and three dwellings were added to the village, and a doctor, C. T. Rigg, and two lawyers, W. E. Hutchinson and M. Sutton, had come to town. Under stress of the boom, Updegraff hurried to build a new hotel in front of his old one. A two-story frame, of native lumber, it boasted six rooms upstairs, an office and a big dining room downstairs—and from its opening day it was overloaded, with guests sleeping in the hallway during rush season nights.

At this period there were a few other settlers scattered along the river and its tributaries. For example, down the river, near where it flows into Oklahoma and close by the former site of Mosley's trading post, a German, August Hegwer, had set up a new store early in 1873. But there were still not nearly enough settlers in the area to legalize the formation of a county. This fact, however, did not seem to bother a small group of men who saw an opportunity to carry out a unique get-rich-quick scheme on the sparsely settled plains of Kansas. The plan involved organizing a county, and building—or rather, *not* building—a courthouse; one historian said of it, "If ever there was a municipal organization conceived in sin and brought forth in iniquity it was . . . Barber County."[2] The state statute governing the organization of new counties at that time required at least 600 bona fide inhabitants within the territory to be organized. In 1873 there were scarcely more than 200 persons living inside the proposed boundaries, a fact that did not at all deter the predators who planned the looting of the new county.[3]

Their first step was to appoint a census taker who would go along with the scheme. From the hotel register in Medicine Lodge he copied the required number of names, and swore they were all residents of the territory outlined for the county. By mid-year the swindlers were ready to proceed with the organization of a county thirty-three miles wide by thirty-six long, to which they gave the name of Barber. A rich and beautiful region, watered by many well timbered streams, it enclosed over 1,000 square miles of richly grassed prairie and scenic bluffs. Most of the land was made up of beautiful rosy sandstone, capped by vast fields of gypsum along the Medicine Lodge River. But the beauty and natural productivity of the county concerned its organizers not at all. The rich harvest they sought lay in a different field. But the few bona fide residents of Medicine Lodge town and its immediate environs seem to have been well enough pleased, for their village was to be the county seat, a distinct advantage to any budding frontier metropolis.

The first recorded meeting of the Board of Commissioners bears the date July 7, 1873. The Commissioners were: S. H. Ulmer, L. H. Bowlus, and J. C. Kirkpatrick. According to historian McNeal, these men were not the master spirits, but they were willing servants and helped to carry out the big steal. Their first business, as shown by the "Record of Board of Commissioners," under the date July 8, 1873, was the granting of a "Dram Shop" license to Dawes & Rhian of Medicine Lodge township. The license fee was fixed at $150.00 per year, payable quarterly. The second record of business, dated August 4, was like unto it and the license was granted to D. E. Sheldon, the store keeper, on payment of the fee. The next day the Commissioners "ordered that a calaboose or jail for the purpose of confining criminals be built ten feet by twenty feet by eight feet high, and that the chairman of the board, S. H. Ulmer, superintend its construction."

In the days of early settlement, every prairie town and county thirsted for a railroad, that magic means of priming business pumps and bringing throngs of new settlers into empty territories. Barber County longed for a shining steel link with the settled east as ardently as any of the others. Therefore, when the canny Commissioners proposed voting $100,000 to the Nebraska, Kansas and Southwestern Railway Company, the enthusiastic voters came to the polls on August 27, 1873, and voted ninety-one to thirty-six in favor of the measure.

The proposed railroad was all that any resident voter could ask for. The rails were to extend from the east county line through Medicine Lodge, Lake City, and the newest town, Sun City, two miles farther west. A depot was to be built in each town, and the whole job was to be finished in three years. It was only a paper railroad, owned by the Commissioners and their cohorts, but the Barber County folk, happily unaware that they had been swindled, were ripe for further plucking.

With their railroad assured, as they thought, the people readily approved the Commissioners' proposal to enter into a contract with C. C. Bemis, one of the townsite owners, "for the purchase of a site and building thereon a courthouse in the town of Medicine Lodge. The said house and site to cost the sum of $25,000." The building was to be completed by September 1, 1874, and scrip was ordered issued to Bemis for the full amount.

"It showed great confidence in Mr. Bemis to issue him the entire contract price before he had furnished a brick, a board, or a nail," wrote McNeal. And indeed it did. Especially in view of the fact that no part of the building was ever built; but the citizens, still innocent of the manner in which they were being "taken," went merrily along when their Commissioners approved a payment of $6,000, supposedly for advertising to encourage immigration into their county.

On November 10 the County Board ordered the $100,000 in bonds paid over to the paper railroad company. And then, not quite finished with the easy picking of their golden goose, they dared to try to reach into the county till once more. On January 22, 1874, they called a special election to vote $40,000 toward building a courthouse suitable for a prosperous county that was soon to have a railroad.

But this time the voters, still wondering what had happened to their $25,000 and the courthouse it was supposed to build (and wondering too, no doubt, why not a single rail had yet been laid in Barber County), turned the proposition down by a majority of forty-two votes.

But even then they couldn't win, for on March 7 the state approved a law allocating County Commissioners to set aside votes in such matters. The board then went ahead and issued the bonds.

State law also required that a report of all County Commissioner meetings and the business transacted therein be published in the county newspaper, but such reports of Barber County business stopped suddenly in April, 1874. For the next year no reports are to be found. It was probably during this period that the Commissioners took care of such matters as issuing "forty or fifty thousand dollars in warrants to build bridges" that were never built.[4] And during the interim the voters must have taken a good, long look at the situation: thousands upon thousands of dollars gone, and not a brick or a board or a nail, nor a tie nor a rail to show for them.

When the entries began again in April, 1875, they showed that James Kirkpatrick had resigned, and that Bowlus had suddenly become a non-resident, leaving a vacancy in his district. The county clerk and his deputy and S. H. Ulmer, chairman of the County Board, had also resigned.[5] McNeal, however, does not put such a tame ending to the Great Swindle.

The fury of the settlers had at last been aroused, he wrote, and they formed a "vigilance committee with the avowed and laudable purpose of hanging the thieves." He reports that they rounded up part of the gang, but made the fatal error of allowing them to bargain. When the spokesman for the swindlers offered to restore the loot and leave the county forever, they let him go. Also, it is said, cooler heads argued that it would look bad for the county to hang its first Commissioners, and so soon after organizing besides.

So the thieves left the county all right, but they took with them the money, the county warrant books, and the county seal.[6]

A new slate of county officers was elected, men who, perforce, inherited a sizable morass of trouble and debt, as well as the by now built-in distrust of most of the citizens. Investigations into the fraudulent deals were promptly begun, investigations that dragged on through the courts for years. They ended at last in the Supreme Court and in a "valid lien against the county."[7] In the meantime the firms and individuals who had bought the bonds were suing for their money, and interest and court costs were piling up. The debt the Barber County folk finally had to pay was an almost unbearable burden, fastened leech-like to the backs of every man, woman, and child, a debt they would be sixty years in liquidating.

As for the existing minutes of the old Board of Commissioners for those early years, they seemed to deal mostly with entries of dram shop licenses, issued to numerous saloon keepers of Medicine Lodge and Sun City. Of the few other entries, one had to do with the only county seat election ever held in the county. On February 29, 1876, the citizens voted as follows: Medicine Lodge, 103; Defiance, fifty-eight; Lake City, twenty. The county seat remained at Medicine Lodge.

On June 13, 1877 the new Commissioners approved plans for a county jail twelve by sixteen feet by eight feet high. Presumably the calaboose ordered in August, 1873 had never been built. The plans for the new jail were given in detail, from the foundation to the roof, and ordered advertised for sealed bids. In May, 1878, it was recorded that the "Board of Commissioners proceeded to the jail to view said jail." The building was accepted.

December 19 the board agreed to purchase a safe for D. E. Sheldon, store and saloon keeper. In return Sheldon was to turn over $500 in County warrants to the commissioners and agree to let the county have the use of "one lock box and two pigeon holes for the term of one year." But on January 7, 1879, the board ordered cancellation of the contract. Through the troubled years the county officers had kept their books and records in their own places of business, and so, presumably, they continued to do so for a few more years.

The county records show that on April 8, 1879, the new township of Elmwood was established, and that there were "about 200 inhabitants." At a special election held in May, Scott Cummins, the Pilgrim Bard, was elected a trustee of the township.

On January 5, 1880 the commissioners heard a petition for a night herd law in Lake City and rejected same. On August 2 the sheriff of Barber County was ordered to "purchase one set of hand cuffs and shackles at the expense of the county." (Such thrift was later to be regretted.) The record for the first ten years of the county's existence closes with the entry that "Standiford, Youmans and Rogers presented a proposition to allow the county treasurer the use of their safe for keeping the county funds for $1.50 per quarter for one year, which proposition was accepted by the board."

Flower Pot Mountain.

FOUR

Indians, Cattle, Growing Pains

1874-1878

The year 1874 was one of much unrest in Barber County, not only because of the tangled political and financial situation, but because of drouth and grasshoppers. In addition, the hungry Indians, completely at outs over broken treaty promises, the non-arrival of annuities, and increased settlement within their favorite buffalo grounds, had taken to raiding and burning across southern and western Kansas.

According to one account, the Osage Indians on June 17 swooped down on the farms of John Martin and Elijah Kennedy, two-and-one-half miles southwest of Medicine Lodge. Both men were killed. The Indians then swung around to Cedar Creek and killed Isaac Kein at his place, three-and-one-half miles west of the town. Some sources assert that the Indians were led by white men in disguise. Other stories agree, even adding that the raiders had been hired by white "higher ups" to drive out the white population and cover up for the Barber County swindlers, whose activities were about to be uncovered. "Old citizens don't like to say much about that raid, preferring to let the dead past bury its dead—the dead Indians being already buried."[1]

At any rate, the attack, along with others in the besieged territory, caused Governor Thomas Osborne to organize the Kansas State Guards. Sun City and Medicine Lodge each furnished a company. A Captain Ricker commanded the Barber County Guards, and John Mosley, son of the E. H. Mosley killed on the lower Medicine two years earlier, was second in command. These men were to guard the territory from Dodge City to Caldwell and on south to the Cimarron River, and keep it clear of Indians.

To aid in protecting the town of Medicine Lodge, the guards, with the help of the frightened citizens, built a nine-foot-high cedar log stockade around the village, which at that time was located where the main business district is today. Sun City, too, was stockaded, and so was Forest City, a long-ago village northwest of Medicine Lodge.

R. M. (Dick) Woodward's wife and son, until the Indian threat drove them to the Forest City stockade, had tended the hide camp at Dick's Peak while Dick hunted. But Dick spent no time inside any stockade. Instead, he supplied buffalo meat for those who did, both at Forest City and Medicine Lodge. That year, the only year in which he kept track of the buffalo he killed, his take was 1,700; a good year, what with hides bringing seventy-five cents to three dollars apiece.

At times there were as many as 200 people inside the cedar walls at Medicine Lodge, together with their teams, cows, and dogs. The refugees ground corn with a coffee grinder to make meal for bread, and drew their daily ration of buffalo from a "meat wagon" located at a handy spot in the stockade. During prolonged danger periods the town's saloons went dry, but dancing and card playing whiled away the hours. Most of the dancers, it is said, "tripped the light fantastic in their bare feet." A man stood guard at all times on the top of the stage barn, and if an alarm was given every man inside the walls ran to the place assigned him in case of an attack. Drills and target practice were held frequently outside and to the southeast of the stockade, and the young, unmarried men were put on scout duty, patrolling more than one hundred miles of territory along the state line.

The only encounter the men of Medicine Lodge had with the Indians that year came on a summer morning. Barney O'Connor, a tall, skinny lad of seventeen, carried the mail, Pony Express style, from Medicine Lodge to Wichita. Only a few miles from town, on one of his regular trips, he spied a good sized band of Indians encamped on Sand Creek. Whirling his pony, he sped back to the stockade. "What brings you back so soon?" he was asked by the first man he met. "Indians," Barney gasped. "Well, that shouldn't scare you," the man said. "It would be as easy to shoot a well rope as to hit you." When the lad finally convinced the populace that he really had seen some Indians, thirty-five of the militiamen, under Captain Ricker and Lt. John Mosley, headed northeast. With Barney leading the way, the troop charged down on the camp. The Indians, taken by surprise, jumped on the nearest ponies and fled. Firing after them, the guards killed six or seven out of an estimated fifty, captured one fat squaw, fifty-four ponies, six mules, and all the camp stuff. Not knowing what else to do with the squaw, the men put her on a pony and headed her out after her fleeing kinsmen. And that night Medicine Lodge celebrated with a feast and a dance.

Another cause of Indian discontent was the wholesale stealing of cattle from tribal owners. Most of the cattle under Indian ownership belonged to the Five Civilized Tribes of the Indian Nation: the Cherokees, Choctaws, Creeks, Chickasaws, and Seminoles. Although these Indians ranched and farmed south of Kansas in what is now Oklahoma, their cattle ranged the unfenced prairies well into Kansas. During and following the Civil War, numerous white men built up a highly profitable business based on theft from these herds, and all Indians, whether cattle owners or not, resented such activities.

On complaint of the Indian agents, the United States Congress passed laws imposing heavy fines and imprisonment on any rustlers caught and convicted. But in Kansas powerful influences in the state, benefiting from the nefarious business, successfully protected most of the thieves. The traffic had actually become so profitable and popular that its higher ups were known as "cattle brokers" and considered quite respectable. Even the civil authorities and some of the courts were in league with the brokers, and the Indian agents were powerless to cope with the widespread thievery.

In his report to the Commissioner of Indian Affairs, Superintendent Sells wrote: "There are two classes of operators connected with cattle driving from the Indian country. The first are those who take the risk of driving from the original range. They are generally men of no character and wholly irresponsible. They drive the cattle to the southern border of Kansas, there the second class are waiting, through their agents, to receive the stolen property.

"These 'cattle brokers,' claiming to be legitimate dealers, purchase at nominal prices, taking a bill of sale, and from thence the cattle are driven to market where numerous profits are made. These 'brokers' have met with such success that the mania for this profitable enterprise has become contagious. The number directly and remotely engaged is so numerous and the social standing and characters of the operators so secure, that it is almost fatal to interpose obstacles in the way of their success."

A Seminole agent, George Reynolds, writing to Sells on July 23, 1865, reported that his life had been threatened for trying to carry out his instructions to stop the thieving, and that a man in Emporia had publicly threatened to kill him on sight because troops, acting on his orders, had taken a lot of cattle while in transit from the Indian country.[2]

It was estimated that over 300,000 head of cattle, valued at upwards of $4.5 million, were stolen from the Indians and driven out of the country while the business flourished. To stop it, the Department of the Interior was forced to ask for the cooperation of the War Department, with the result that government troops were sent to the aid of the Indian Agents, and even then it was several years before the thieves were finally driven out of the country.

Meanwhile, legitimate cattle owners were taking advantage of the rich grass pastures on the Kansas plains. The first such cattle to come into Barber County had been a through Texas herd brought in during the fall of 1872. The owner, Solomon Tuttle, wintered the Longhorns on the Medicine Lodge River, then drove them north the next summer and sold them. Better cattle came in the spring of '73, when William Carl and Judge Shepler brought in a herd of "grade cattle" and put them on the river twelve miles above the little town. From then on the plains were rapidly stocked.

To the men who had first noted the country's great potential as cattle land, it seemed for a time that the stock raising business could not fail. Cattle did as well on the fine grasses as the lately vanished buffalo had done. Buffalo wallows, made by the big beasts stamping and wallowing in natural depressions where rain water stood, had been widened and deepened through the years until they held goodly quantities of snow and rain water for quite long periods in summer: nature's water tanks. For the rest of the year the region's many streams furnished abundant water.

Some good-sized ranches soon headquartered in the eastern part of the county, among them Standiford and Youmans, Will Kelley, Ewell and Justis, and a man known as "Barbeque" Lemon (from his brand Bar-B-Q). West of them were the Hunter and Evans outfits and the ranches of Dick Phillips, J. B. Doyle, and others. Annual spring roundups were held, and in the fall market cattle were trailed to the nearest railroad.

By 1876 the Indians were quiet, most of them on Oklahoma reservations by that time, and a few of the better things of life were coming to the plains every year. On Mule Creek, when Horace Pardee came there in the fall with his family and a small herd of cattle, there were close neighbors: the Ewell-Justis cow ranch, B. C. Lottin's sheep ranch, the Durbins, Wyats, and Maxons, and another cattle ranch belonging to Schluppe and Ballinger of St. Joseph, Missouri. The Mule Creek settlers got their mail from Medicine Lodge every week or two, or whenever some one made the trip to town, until 1878, when Pardee secured a post office, named Lodi, which he kept at his ranch. Medicine Lodge got its mail direct from Hutchinson by means of a stagecoach, described as "a long buggy with only slats for springs and bed."

Although the county had never gotten its railroad or its courthouse (and was still fighting in court to keep from paying for them), it still had, by 1878, its towns: Forest City, Defiance, Sun City, Lake City. In addition to Lodi, an unknown number of post offices had been established in outlying districts, and the county had eight schoolhouses, six log and two frame. In Medicine Lodge the first newspaper, *The Barber County Mail*, had printed its first sheet in May.

Everybody in the country not sick abed regularly gathered in the settlements to celebrate the Fourth of July with picnics, speeches, and dancing on outdoor platforms. Christmas and other holidays were observed with programs and dances in schoolhouses and ranch homes. In winter, oyster[3] stew made in wash boilers was the popular refreshment for such affairs; in summer, all the watermelon everybody could hold.

The tide of immigration was still running strong, but many of the newcomers were poor, arriving with little else than the team and wagon they came with, and maybe a milk cow tied on behind. These pioneers found a strange readymade harvest awaiting them, a way to earn the cash they would so desperately need in the months ahead. Whole families took to the prairies around their homes to reap this harvest—bones, the bones of the hundreds of thousands of buffalo that had died before the hunters' guns of the past few years. Like drifts of snow, they whitened the swales for miles on end. Some men became bone haulers: men like Dick Woodward, erstwhile buffalo hunter, and Orange Scott Cummins, the Pilgrim Bard, who could, and did, address his mules in anything but poetic language. The Bard had set up a little trading post of his own on Mule Creek and named it "Last Chance" because it was the last chance for pilgrims heading farther west to get a meal under a roof.[4] The Bard and Woodward hauled bones to Wichita, said to be the greatest bone market in the world at that time. There they unloaded them in huge ricks beside the railroad tracks to await shipment east by the trainload, where they would be used in fertilizer, or for the processing of sugar. The bones brought six to twelve dollars a ton at the pile, but it took an awful lot of bones to make a ton. The freighters collected the cash, deducted their freighters' fees, and took the rest back to the ragged pickers. As an added bonus for themselves, there were always loads of goods to be hauled back to the settlement stores: food, clothes, whisky, guns, and ammunition.

The bone picking business, and the necessity that mothered it, led some tuneful soul to compose the following ditty, once popular all across buffalo land:

Picking up bones to keep from starving,
Picking up chips to keep from freezing,
Picking up courage to keep from leaving—
Way out west in "no man's land."

Cutting and hauling cedar posts to Wichita and Hutchinson, cities of the treeless plains, likewise supplied early Barberites with cash money. Most of the timber in Barber County grew on land held in trust by the government for the Osage Indians, and no white man had a legal right to cut and haul it away. But a small technicality like that bothered few of the hardup settlers. Consequently, countless loads were taken away, all but denuding the beautiful wooded canyons by the end of the settlement period.

This comparatively calm state of affairs was rudely interrupted in September, 1878, when a horseman raced his lathered horse down the valley of the Medicine, bringing news of an Indian massacre on the Salt Fork of the Cimarron in the southwest part of neighboring Comanche County. The Cheyennes, under Dull Knife, were on the loose, burning and raiding, the rider said.

The northern Cheyennes, hating the dry, desolate region for which they had been forced to trade their wooded mountains of the north, had asked repeatedly to go "home." When the government paid no attention to their requests, some of the homesick Indians set out anyway, striking a direct course for their old hunting grounds in Wyoming and Montana. Their first attack, the messenger said, was made on the Sheets cattle camp near the state line in Comanche County, where two people were killed and some others wounded before the Indians went on. At the E. W. Payne ranch Mr. Payne was shot in the neck, Mrs. Payne in the thigh, and their baby fatally wounded by a shot in the breast. Next a lone cattle herder, Tom Murray, was killed by the band, and it was high time for the fighting men of Barber County to arm and take after the marauding savages.

Within a few hours forty or fifty mounted and well-armed men had taken the trail.[5] About forty miles south of Dodge City they met a force of U.S. regulars and put themselves under command of the officer in charge. Toward evening the combined forces intercepted and surrounded Dull Knife's band in a canyon in what is now Clark County. The Barber County men were eager to attack, but the commanding officer said they would wait until morning. Pickets were thrown around the canyon, but the "wily savages" slipped away in the night, leaving the troops carefully guarding an empty canyon, to the deep disgust of the volunteers. In referring to the failure of the regulars and the guards to stop Dull Knife's northward dash for home and freedom, M. J. Cochran wrote that the Indians "outgeneraled the U.S. Troops and Dull Knife has shown himself entitled to a name among the great warriors of the red braves."[6]

Other scouting parties likewise took to the hills, hoping to locate the Indians. One of these was organized by Gene Pardee, from the head of Mule Creek on the western edge of the county. At the same time all the surrounding families gathered at the Pardee ranch to wait for things to settle down. So, also, did settler families band together at the Last Chance home of the Pilgrim Bard, but there a casualty occurred when one of the defenders accidentally shot "a Miss McWilliams, a cousin of Nina Cummins Dyer."

Although that was Kansas' last Indian raid, the residents of the border counties were uneasy for some years to come. Life went on, however, if not as usual, at least at a commendable pace. By the next year, 1879, Medicine Lodge had achieved a population of 250, plenty big enough to incorporate, the leading citizens said; and after due preliminaries it became a City of the third class on May 21.

But despite its upgraded status it still had no barber shop, at least in the accepted sense of a reasonably clean space, smelling of tonic and lotions and sporting an adjustable chair. No, when a stranger inquired for the town barber he was directed to the livery stable. There a big man, "chamber maid" to assorted mules and broncs, leaned his pitchfork against the wall, wiped his hands on his overalls and led the way to a boarded off corner of the stable. Seating his customer on a kitchen chair, he stropped his razor on his bootleg and splashed a handful of lather, well mixed with mule hair, over his victim's face. Then, placing another chair behind the first, the barber put his foot on it and bent the seated man's neck back over his knee and went to work. The job done, he anointed the shaved face with horse liniment and levied a charge of fifteen cents.

The following winter some of the citizens of Medicine Lodge decided to dispense with the editor of their weekly newspaper, *The Barber County Mail*. From this distance in time it is difficult to determine the exact reason for this decision. Whether it was personal dislike for the owner, M. J. Cochran, or, as has been hinted, that he was of too "flirtatious" a disposition, is now unknown. But on a chilly night in February the self-appointed "regulators" visited the editor in his office, stripped him of his clothing and applied a warm coat of "tar and feathers." But with this difference: there was no tar in town and, apparently, no dispensable feather bed. However, the ingenious fellows were not hampered by so small a matter. The sorghum crop had done well that year and the supply of molasses was ample, as was the annual crop of sandburrs. Accordingly, a gallon of molasses, mixed with an equal quantity of the burrs, made an entirely satisfactory coating for the bare body of the unhappy editor. Next in order was a ride around town on a cedar rail, and when his tormentors tired of their spc they invited him to leave town within twenty-four hours, and to st away henceforth.

By this time some other citizens had armed themselves and banded together to take sides with the editor who, they claimed, was no worse, morally, than some of his persecutors. When the late comers heard the sentence of banishment they told the editor he could stay in town if he wanted to, and they would be responsible for his safety. Cochran thanked them, but thought he'd better go. He asked only that they help him sell the paper so he could get away.

On March 10, 1879, J. W. McNeal and his brother-in-law, E. W. Iliff, bought *The Barber County Mail*, and at once changed its name to the *Cresset*. The unusual name was given the little frontier news sheet by Iliff, who was an admirer of Milton. Those who have read *Paradise Lost* will remember the description of Satan's palace, which was lighted by "cressets," or brilliant lights. The new name aroused considerable curiosity in the vicinity, and soon a cowboy jingled into the newspaper office to ask, "What's the meanin' of this here name, Cresset?" When its origin had been explained to him, he took a good look at the small, inky news-sheet and exclaimed, "Damned fittin' name, I would say. It is a hell of a paper, ain't it?"[7]

FIVE

The Great Cattle Pools

1879-1886

As the decade of the seventies drew to a close, the cattlemen of southern Kansas saw the necessity of organizing cattle pools. Their herds had ranged freely over all the region for several years, but as ranges in southern Oklahoma and Texas became crowded more and more cattle were pushed north. To keep cattle numbers within reason on their own ranges, the Kansas cattlemen had to join forces and take action.

Before these cowmen had turned their herds onto the Kansas prairies, no one had ever used them for anything except buffalo hunting and, contrary to popular belief, no special effort had been made to keep settlers from taking homesteads there. In fact, it hadn't occurred to anyone that the land would even be wanted for *farming*, but they did try to prevent other herds coming in by proving up most of the permanent water springs. For the man who controlled the water also controlled a sizable chunk of the range around it. But to hold their grazing lands, the Kansas ranchers saw that they would have to fence them, a job far too big for any one, or even a few, of the owners.

These, then, were the reasons for organizing the great cattle pools of the region. The Eagle Chief Pool was the first. Its members included Ewell and Justis, Sherlock and Mills, Schluppe and Ballinger, and the Geneseo Cattle Company, an outfit made up of owners from Geneseo, Illinois. The men, in 1879, leased a huge chunk of range in the Cherokee Strip, just south of Kansas. The range was watered by the three prongs of Eagle Chief Creek and by a good many miles of the Salt Fork Creek. During the first five years of the lease, the pool paid one cent per acre direct to Bushy Head, the chief who held the headright to the lands. When the lease expired, Bushy Head raised the rent to two cents an acre, to be paid to Chief Maize, the new headright holder. The Eagle Chief partners agreed to the raise, but by then the days of free range in the Plains states were numbered.

The organization of the great Comanche Pool soon followed. Hunter and Evans, Dick Phillips, Major E. B. Kirk, J. B. Doyle, Colonel W. L. Colcord, E. W. (Wylie) Payne, W. F. Flato, J. M. Rawlins, Tom Doran, William Blair, C. D. Nelson, John Wilson, C. W. James, and J. A. McCarty were its chief members. Ranging west of the Eagle Chief in the Cherokee Strip and Barber County, it included the west half of Barber County and parts of Clark and Kiowa counties, and was probably the largest cattle pool in the United States. Its headquarters were at the one-time town of Evansville, on the Salt Fork in Comanche County.

As fast as they could get to it, the pools arranged to fence the enormous tracts of land. W. F. Flato, a Comanche Pool partner, ordered enough wire laid down at Harper, in Harper County, then the end of the railroad, to fence that pasture. The wire was freighted to headquarters by ox teams and the fence, when finished, was 250 miles long. M. S. Justis, of the Eagle Chief, records that it took five carloads of wire to build 120 miles of four-wire fence around their pasture. Posts for all the fencing were cut from the cedar canyons in the bluffs. Each pool member stood the expense in proportion to the number of cattle he intended to run inside the fence. A few of the owners were cowboys or small cattlemen who worked out their shares of the expense for the big owners, Hunter and Evans, Phillips, Payne, and others.

Justis wrote that the Eagle Chief men ran about 25,000 head of cattle in their pasture. The Barber County *Index* of January 6, 1881, states there were 26,000 head, representing fifteen owners and twenty brands, in the Comanche Pool, and that every six months a balance sheet was struck and a settlement made with each member.

Another reason for the pasture fence was to keep the vast herds from drifting east into Harper County, where the settlers had banded together and passed a law making it mandatory for the ranchmen to keep their cattle off the farmers' land. But as soon as the fence was in, a great howl went up in the eastern states. The cattle barons, those greedy "range hogs," the papers fumed, had built the fences to keep honest homeseekers off the public lands.

Even though that was not the primary purpose of the fence, it may have been a deterrent to settlers for a little while. At any rate, time has proven the ranchmen right, for they were our first prairie conservationists, men who knew or perhaps merely sensed that the land was good only for range, that the settler's plow would ruin great areas of it for decades to come, making it unfit for either grazing or farming.

Both cattle pools prospered for a few years and the herds inside the fences grew in number. The roundup of the pool lands in the spring of '84 was the largest ever held in Kansas and the Strip, with a record number of calves branded. That fall, after beef shipping, it was claimed that 80,000 head still ranged the great Comanche pasture. If so, it was too many, as most of the cattlemen knew. An open winter was a must if the herds on the overcrowded ranges were to survive until spring.

That fall, too, the Eagle Chief partners divided their range, and Schluppe and Ballinger, with Nat Lane, "fenced off a little pasture of 100,000 acres for their range."

So far, in the range history of the region, winters had been comparatively mild and cattle had wintered well under the practice of reserving plenty of winter range; that is, pasturing a part of the range in summer and holding the herds off the rest. The buffalo grass, several inches in height by fall and bearing rich seed heads, cured where it stood, making a balanced ration that actually fattened cattle turned on it for the winter.

But that fall of '84, with the whole range overstocked, there was no reserve of winter pasture. But maybe it wouldn't have made any difference if there had been, for, from January 6, 1885, until spring, what forage there was was buried deep under frozen ice-crusted snow. And in those days oil cake, which has since saved the hides of thousands of cattle (and their owners, as well) had not yet come into general use.

Some historians, T. A. McNeal among them, claim that fully 80 per cent of the cattle on these ranges did not pull through that winter, and M. S. Justis records that of the 80,000 head in the Comanche Pool only 7,000 were on their feet come spring. "Down in the big timber on the Cimarron," he wrote, "I could have walked across 200 acres without stepping on the ground, so many dead cattle were piled up."[1]

The *Cresset* of April 2, 1885, observed: "The spring of '85 will long be remembered as the hardest on stock the country has ever known. Sunshine, rain, snow, freezing winds, then sunshine—and all over again. Losses will be very heavy and bad reports are coming in weekly from ranch operators. The hide business is very lively, even though many ranchers are refusing to admit to heavy losses." Poor fellows, they didn't want their bankers to know how few cattle were left to cover their loans.

The hide business was very good, indeed, that spring. So good that the Pilgrim Bard was moved to write some verses about it, featuring Simon Lebrecht, a Jewish merchant of Medicine Lodge.[2]

SONG OF THE HIDE MERCHANT

I gather them in, said Simon the Jew,
As he stood surrounded by hides, not a few,
Hides of heifers and hides of steers,
And hides of cows well up in years,
Arkansaw hard heads and Texas straight,
Were piled around by the hundred weight,
While the Dutchman stood like a spectre grim,
And he smiled as he said, "I gather them in."

I care not though the fierce winds roar,
Each blizzard adds a few hides more;
Their hideless frames line every stream,
And the sun witholds its friendly beam.
'Tis an adage old that long has stood,
Ill is the wind that blows no one good.
When one man loses another must win,
Their loss is my gain, I gather them in.

This winter has been a harvest for me,
(And he rubbed his hands together in glee).
Cattle die in the ditch, they die by the way,
They die by night and they die by day.
Where once they roamed mid pastures green,
Their hideless frames line every stream.
The coyote feeds on the carcass thin,
Their hides are here, I gather them in.

Let warning be written on parchment of hide,
Peeled off a poor brute that has famished and died;
Sow millet and cane, provide shelter and care,
No longer depend upon prospect and air.
The lines on the wall you may read at a glance,
The range is o'ercrowded, the grass is too thin,
The Dutchman is certain to gather them in.

It was said that Mr. Lebrecht bought $40,000 worth of hides at a dollar a hide that spring and summer; but after the "Song of the Hide Merchant" was printed in the *Cresset*, the hide-buyer charged into the editor's office in righteous indignation, demanding satisfaction for the damage to his reputation. The editor, T. A. McNeal, was equal to the situation. "Why, Simon," he said, "that was the greatest free advertising I ever gave anyone. By rights you should pay the Pilgrim Bard the profit from a load of hides for writing those verses."

Seeing the whole affair in a different light then, the merchant departed, satisfied. And sure enough, the first time he saw Mr. Cummins, he put out his hand in friendly fashion and declared, "Scottie, dat vas all right, I just don't like you calling me a damn Yew."

Bone picking was good the following winter, too, along with hide buying; and not only in Kansas but over the entire Plains area from Canada to Texas. For the winter of '85-'86 was another bad one. Grover Cleveland's presidential edict that cattle must be removed from the Indian lands had pushed the herds north, many of them onto the Kansas ranges, setting the scene for the next big die-up.

The weather stayed fine all through the fall months, even December, and cattlemen were beginning to hope again. An open winter, and all might yet be well. But on December 31, in the evening, the famous blizzard of '86 swept down on southwest Kansas. The Norton Hulpieu family, northwest of Barber County, over Garden City way, would long remember the date, and not because their cattle were dying in the storm.

The Hulpieus had come from Iowa that spring to a Kansas homestead, and so thought it a good idea to celebrate their first New Year's Eve in their new home with a watch party. The invited guests arrived early in the evening and the party began in high style. Some verses, written soon afterward by William S. Bothwell, tell what happened.

'Twas at a New Year's party
  Not very long ago;
And the whole assemblage
  Was blockaded by the snow.

The guests that were assembled,
  Were Miss Titus and her beau;
Rilla and Mr. Dutton,
  Tillie and her darling Joe.

The next was Plummer Ramsel,
  Erve Melick and Miss Hays;
Miss Earp and Ellis Titus,
  And McGrath who brought Miss Day.

Mr. Stephenson and Sarah Hulpieu,
  Miss Adney and Mal Bell;
Mr. and Mrs. Hulpieu,
  John Hulpieu and Bothwell.

The party then was opened
  With playing of tin, tin;
And the kissing they indulged in
  Was next thing to a sin.

Supper then was ready,
  And partners chose by chance;
The gents then cleared the room
  And got their ladies for a dance.

But ere the hour of midnight
  The howling winds did roar,
And the snow began a drifting
  Around the dugout door.

But then they kept on dancing
  Until the early morn,
With but a bull chip fire
  For to keep them warm.

Thus we were held prisoner
For hours thirty-four,
Not daring for to venture
Outside the dugout door.

It was on a Sunday morning
The prisoners were set free,
And thus the party ended,
On their New Year's jubilee.

"It was 32 below zero," Joe Hulpieu later said of the blizzard, "and the snow was so dry and fine it went wherever air could go." When the party finally broke up, two days after it started, Charley McGrath's wagon was buried so deep under a drift of ice-hard snow that he had to leave it where it was and take Miss Day home on one of his horses. Although the poem and story of the party, published in a newspaper many years later, relates what eventually became of all the other guests, no one knows "what became of the party's poet."[3]

The watch night party guests had no more than gotten home when the second blizzard of the winter blasted out of the north. And from then on storm followed storm until the pastures and streams lay deep beneath a solid blanket of ice and snow.

And when the winter was over, the range cattle business was finished; it was said there were hardly enough cattle left in all of southern Kansas to give milk for the settlers who were swarming in from all directions, taking up the land in the Eagle Chief and Comanche pastures, land pastured by thousands of cattle only three summers back.

The storms of those two winters taught the cattlemen they would have to provide something more than grass and spectacular scenery for their cattle to live on. And that spring of '86, under the double pressure of incoming settlers and the President's order to take down all fences enclosing public lands, the word had gone out across the Kansas range, "roundup and move out."

The last roundup on the great Comanche range was finished in the Comanche County valley where Coldwater stands today, and the cattle were put on the trail for Wyoming, where free range could still be found.[4] Cattle raising would again be a thriving business in the state, but under far different conditions. The industry would be carried on within smaller fenced areas on deeded land; and the cattle would be a far better breed than the rangy Longhorns that, tough though they were, could not withstand the tougher Kansas winters. But this new kind of ranching was still in the future.

In the meantime there were the homesteaders, digging homes into the bluffs and hillsides and, no matter how rough, rocky, and dry the land, breaking out little fields on every reasonably level spot, and then hoping for rain. The trail herds were still coming up through Kansas, though, bound for ranges in Colorado, Wyoming, and Montana, and Gus Hadwager, an attorney of Alva, Oklahoma, who came north with a herd from Texas to Hugo, Colorado in 1886, told of coming up with a ten-year-old boy in western Barber County. The boy, afoot and alone, was driving a lone old cow. He carried a coat and a tincup, nothing else. Gus asked him where he was going, and he said to Clark County (second county west of Barber) where his father had taken a claim. The lad and the cow had already walked from Cowley County (southeast of Wichita) through Sumner and Harper counties, making ten or twelve miles a day. Gus then asked, "Son, what do you live on?" And the boy said he milked the cow.

Yes! Those were desperately hard years for the homesteaders. Even less rain fell than usual, the little corn patches dried up, and one by one the discouraged, disillusioned settlers pulled out, leaving behind their blowing fields and their mortgages. The range was empty again, waiting for the new breeds of men and cattle to move in and build again the business that is today one of the great mainstays of Kansas.

The story of ranching in Barber County is not complete without the tale of old Two Toes, the big grey wolf that "single handed" set cattlemen in the region back a good many thousand dollars in the few years he ranged on their pastures. There may have been two big lobos known as "Two Toes," or the one killer may have ranged over a very wide area. At any rate there is a story of a wolf that hunted the southern part of Meade County and along Crooked Creek in the Neutral Strip. After committing a long series of costly kills, Two Toes was killed by a Negro, Willis Peoples, and his body delivered to cattlemen in the town of Meade.[5] Another Two Toes, the arch killer of the tale told by John D. Seeger of Hardtner,[6] ranged in the Gyp Hills north of that little town in the southern part of Barber County, near the Oklahoma border.

Some fence riding cowboys came upon a freshly killed yearling steer one morning. A hind quarter had been torn from the still warm body and the cowboys knew it was the work of a lobo wolf. They followed the trail three miles before they came to the den, in which there were five pups. While the he wolf raged and howled on a mound half a mile away, trying to draw the men away from the den, one of the boys crawled in and managed to snare a pup. The boys then rode over to the mound and saw that it was regularly used as a lookout from which the wolf kept watch on the family den.

The cowboys set a string of twenty-four traps in the dust around the mound, covering them well and driving the stakes deep into the ground. The next morning, when they came in sight of the mound, they saw the wolf in one of the traps, but when they reached the spot he was gone. Two of his toes remained behind in one of the traps. He had been gnawing at his trapped foot when the men came in sight, but had then jerked free, leaving the toes.

Livestock losses dropped off sharply the rest of that summer, while the wolf's badly injured foot healed. Meanwhile the cowboys had captured three more of the pups, and kept one alive to use as bait to catch the mother. Tieing the pup up at night, they set traps around him. Each morning the tracks of the mother and of the one little wolf that had escaped their raid were plain around the tied pup, but neither was caught for quite awhile. Then the boys saw signs of a wolf trail, or runway, along a fence, so they set the traps there, and one morning found the freshly killed young wolf in the trap. The signs showed how desperately the mother had tried to free the pup, attempting to dig up the stake that held the trap, and even to gnaw through the steel chain itself. When she knew she could not free him before the men arrived, she had killed him herself. A week later they caught the mother, too.

The next spring old Two Toes returned to his range with a new mate, and the battle of wits began all over again. The mate was caught in the den that summer, but Two Toes still ranged widely. The men then brought dogs into the battle, and one dog often met up with the wolf. The dog always came home badly chewed up and Two Toes went on killing cattle.

Two Toes showed up with still another mate that third spring, and again the she wolf and pups were caught, but the big grey killer remained at large, killing so many cattle that the cattlemen's association upped the reward for his capture considerably.[7] Affairs on the range became critical when old Two Toes suddenly moved to a new location, nine or ten miles west of Aetna in the southwest part of the county, and brought three females with him. The loss of mules and cattle on that range soon became so serious that all the cowboys of the region held a "drive." More than twenty dogs were brought in from Medicine Lodge and Coldwater, but the only results of the drive were some badly chewed up dogs.

The dread of Two Toes was now so great that two Kiowa men, Jack Middleton and Pearl Bunton, took to the hills for the express purpose of killing the big wolf. They took with them eight dogs, one the old veteran that had already battled the wolf so often. The men stayed all night at Aetna, then began the hunt the next morning. They had not gone far when they saw the wolf on the far side of the Salt Fork, carrying something so heavy that he often had to stop and rest. Besides the crippled foot, the old wolf was now hampered by a broken shoulder, acquired some months before in a fight with a buck deer. The combination of injuries slowed him up considerably. The hunters tracked him to his den, where they discovered he had carried, or dragged, the front quarter of a full-grown mule all that distance. On hearing the dogs, Two Toes had dropped the meat at the mouth of the den, then dashed along a ridge trail and jumped to the gyp rock some eight feet below. There he ran into some brush and lay down. When the dogs found his trail again he ran out of the brush into full view and headed for a canyon. Although the men shot at him several times, he escaped. Again the old dog sniffed him out and the two fought again, a wild, snarling battle that left both exhausted, but gave the men time to come up with them. One of the hunters then drew a bead on the played-out old killer and shot him squarely between the eyes.

Whether or not the hunters took the wolf, or even the mutilated foot, to town to prove they had put an end to the famous old killer wolf is not recorded. But the tale ends with the statement that the $1,000 reward offered by a Texas cattlemen's association and some of the local ranchers was never paid, partly because "there was dissension about the identity of the wolf," and partly because the hunters made no particular effort to collect it.[8]

SIX

Barber County Towns

1875-1887

Down on the Medicine, near the Oklahoma border, August Hegwer carried on at his trading post for about two years before A. W. Rumsey, a freighter and trader, moved in beside him in 1875, opened a general store, and stocked a cattle ranch close by on the river. A few weeks later Hegwer, Rumsey, and a man named George Male platted a town which they called Kiowa, an Indian word meaning "Great Medicine." Since the proposed town was on the bank of the Medicine Lodge River, a few miles below the sacred medicine lodge of the ancient Kiowas, the name was appropriate.

Although the plat of this Kiowa was never recorded at the county seat, the town continued to grow. A hotel was built in 1877, and other businesses, including several saloons, were established.

Now no prairie town of the settlement years could rightly expect to amount to anything unless it owned a lively newspaper to boast its advantages over those of any and all surrounding towns. In some recorded instances a printing press and an editor were the first assets hauled onto a new townsite. Henry King, "an early Kansas journalist of some renown and a lover of colorful exaggeration," said that Kansas was probably the only place on earth where a newspaper was started before there was any news to print.[1] Less colorful but more statistical statements have suggested that "Kansas has had more newspapers per capita than any other state."[2]

Kiowa, however, for some reason, struggled along for a decade without a newspaper. Finally, to rectify this lack, a red-headed Irishman, D. T. Flynn, was invited to town to look over the prospects. He arrived on a cold, drizzly day in April, 1884, after crossing the red waters of the Medicine and driving up the hill to the scattered, muddy collection of buildings that made up Kiowa. There he was soon squatting beside a pleasant fire in Rumsey's store, chatting with practically all of the townsmen. After securing some "guaranteed advertising," he returned to Kansas City to buy a Washington hand press "on time."

While Flynn was in Kansas City, putting an outfit together, word came to the town site officials that the Atchison, Topeka and Santa Fe Railroad was about to build on to Kiowa from Harper, nearly forty miles to the northeast, and that officials of the company were on the way to talk to Hegwer, Rumsey, and Male about station facilities and a right-of-way through the town. The town fathers met them with open arms and listened to their proposition—a request, or more like a demand, for a donation of eighty acres of land for a depot and yard facilities, plus a fifty-fifty share in the town site proper. Even then two of the board were willing to accept the terms, but the third, arguing that there was no other logical route for the road, held out for a larger slice of the town pie.

Meantime D. T. Flynn, arriving in Harper by train, there reshipped his printing press to a freight wagon and, on May 10 sailed out of that town under flying colors behind an ox team. On the evening of the third day the outfit was stuck for three hours in the Medicine River, delaying its entry into Kiowa until nine o'clock that night. And then, wrote Flynn long afterward, "No sooner had we unloaded the press than a hushed rumor of Kiowa getting a railroad could be heard."[3]

To please his friends, who wanted the news kept under cover until the deal with the railroad company could be completed, Flynn delayed release of his first paper until June 10. The young editor's description of the room where his paper first "saw the light of day" is interesting. It was very light indeed, he wrote, having neither doors nor windows. In fact, there was so little shelter that he and his "devil" were almost completely at the mercy of the sun and wind.

But the Kiowa *Herald* staff did not have to put up with the deficiencies of their quarters for long, for the railroad did not come to Kiowa after all. Instead, the company found a good route that missed the town by three or four miles, and the railroad officials came to an agreement with another land owner, W. E. Campbell, to establish a new town where today's Kiowa stands.

By early August, 1884, the town, named New Kiowa to distinguish it from the old town, was laid out and platted. And then, of course, most of old Kiowa was in a frenzy to get packed up and moved to where the action was. Even the Kiowa House, the good sized hotel that had served the old town for seven years, was hauled across the prairie to the bustling new town.

Flynn had his printing press transported to New Kiowa on November 4, and early in December ran off 5,000 copies of the New Kiowa *Herald*, listing all the advantages, real and imaginary, of the new town, which on that date could claim only two merchants, a livery stable, a lumber yard, and a handful of residents. The papers, of course, were for mailing "back east" to prospective settlers.[4]

That same winter New Kiowa's first bank, organized a few months earlier in the old town, got off to a good start. Its building was ready and the foundation already laid for its new safe, which had been ordered from a safe company in the east. The 7,000 pound steel safe came by rail to Anthony, the new "end of track town" and was hauled from there to New Kiowa by ox team. The outfit was almost a week making the trip, as the wagon sank in the Medicine and it took several days to get it out.

As soon as the safe was installed, the bank was ready for business, except for its stock in trade—money. M. S. Justis, prominent cattleman of the vicinity, was delegated to bring in the cash. Mr. Justis, an old-timer, had been in Kansas since 1872, when Indians still roamed the hills. He was riding alone and far from any white habitation when, in those early seventies he first met up with some natives of the plains. "There were about 150 in the bunch," he said, "and I was so scared I had to hold my hat on with my hand."[5]

Now, over a decade later, with the bank's $8,000 in his hip pocket, Justis was uneasy all over again, but less this time about Indians than his fellow white man. He rode the train from Harper, where he picked up the money, to Attica, the end of the line in that fall of 1884. From there it was twenty miles southwest to New Kiowa via M. J. Lane's stagecoach. Arriving safely in the new town, he wasn't long in hustling the bank's capital over to the cashier and the big safe.

Late that same December a young hardware merchant from Missouri came to the new town and found it a lively place. The merchant, A. Gregory, likewise came by rail to Attica where, in the midst of a heavy snowstorm, he boarded the stage about four in the afternoon and set out for New Kiowa. The storm forced the stage to stop for the night at Hazelton, only seven miles short of its destination, and the snow was a foot deep on the level when they pulled into town the next morning.

Gregory and a fellow passenger, another young man looking for a location, put up at the New Kiowa House, ate a venison dinner, and then set out to see the town. In the saloons they saw scores of men playing cards, four to a table, and each with a revolver at hand. Presently, when some cowboys took to making a "tenderfoot" dance by shooting at his feet, they left in a hurry, not being good dancers themselves. They next visited a grocery store, likely the quietest place in town, or so they hoped. But two armed cowboys soon rode their horses into the store and watered them from the merchant's water bucket. While the young men were wondering if they had better make a quiet dash for the door, the cowpunchers whirled their mounts and rode whooping and shooting out of the store, smashing the low-hanging chandelier as they went. "They came back in a short time," Gregory said, "ready and willing to pay for the damage done."

At the end of a week's visit, young Gregory decided to locate in New Kiowa. Accordingly, he bought a lot and hired a carpenter to build him a house and a store, and then went back to Missouri to get his family and to order his hardware stock. When he returned in March 1885, he "hardly knew the place." Two months earlier there had been about forty buildings in the town, both residences and business houses. There had been four saloons when he left, now there were nine, and a new drugstore, which sold as much or more liquor than the saloons. A hotel, eighty feet square and three stories high, was going up and sixty other buildings were under contract, and the railroad was building rapidly toward New Kiowa, accounting for the frenzied boom.

On a Monday evening late in July the new hotel, the imposing Hardwick House, was formally opened, "an occasion", reported the *Herald*, that "proved to be the grandest society event in the history of New Kiowa. Dancing and feasting provided the evening's entertainment, and the hosts, Messrs. Hardwick and Cattell, spared no expense to make the evening memorable. The ladies were all in costume, the gentlemen all smiling and happy. Between dances the younger guests promenaded the balconies and strolled through the upper halls, while the older ones sat in the moonlight and talked of old times, when

Kiowa was nothing but a cow pasture and the 'lone tree' was the only landmark visible."[6]

About eleven o'clock the spacious dining room was thrown open and some 130 guests partook of a bounteous repast at a beautifully decorated table, where the choicest of viands were served. "The silver was new and shining," the *Herald* editor stated, "and such an assemblage of splendid looking ladies and average men was never before seen in our city." The feasting lasted three hours; the guests came from Medicine Lodge, Sharon, Attica, and Harper, as well as New Kiowa.

A week later, on August 6, the first passenger train puffed proudly into town, and every living soul in the realm met it with a joyous celebration. New Kiowa had arrived. That fall 150,000 head of cattle, many of them trailed up from Texas and Oklahoma, would be shipped from its new stockyards.

It is said that New Kiowa soon had twenty-one saloons, in addition to its several drugstores that also sold alcoholic beverages as medicine. Even so, it was never known as a "tough" town, though it did have at least one rousing "shoot out," involuntarily hosted by the fine new Hardwick House.

On the evening of August 13, 1886, some cowboys, celebrating at Jackson's saloon, close by the hotel, became too noisy. When the loud party ran on into the night, Marshal O'Shea had to ask them to "stop their fussing and go to bed." His request upset the boys so much that they turned their guns on him and ordered him out. He went, after telling them he'd be back. With several armed townsmen to back him up, he did go back a bit later. As the marshal and citizens entered the saloon, the cowboys opened fire and charged through the group to the Hardwick, where they forted up in the billiard room. More armed townsmen arrived, and both groups kept up an almost continuous fusilade for half an hour. The moon was very bright that night, making all parties as visible as in daylight and, what with everybody shooting through the billiard room doors and windows, that section of the hotel was thoroughly wrecked. The only human casualties, however, were the marshal with three buckshot in his face, and one of his men with a buckshot wound in his leg. The cowboys finally agreed to surrender to the mayor, after securing his promise that they would not be harmed. They were then put under guard in one of the hotel rooms, while the townspeople held a meeting to see what to do with them. "As the fight was unpremeditated, no ill feeling was held against the prisoners and it was finally decided to let them off with heavy fines."[7] The big wonder was how two groups of men, fighting for half an hour in moonlight as bright as day could keep from killing somebody, an innocent bystander at least.

The coming of the railroad did not immediately do away with ox team and wagon train freighting, for great expanses of the prairie were still far from the rails, and goods shipped in by train had to be transported on by team and wagon to those far places.

In September, 1886, a big bull train left New Kiowa, bound for Mobeetie, Texas, and the *Herald* editor described the manner in which the twenty-three wagons got on the road with their 80,000 pounds of freight. The animals, he wrote, ranged in age from "three summers to eighteen years, and many had rings far out on their horns, showing them to be well up in years, real old 'moss horns.' "

Ordinarily it would take but a few minutes for the ten men in the crew to hitch six yoke of oxen to each wagon, but this was the first experience for some of the animals and they did not take kindly to the yokes and chains. One young steer broke away, bucking and bellowing through the herd, dragging the yoke with him. The rest of the herd got excited and stampeded off across the prairie. The man holding the cattle started after them on the jump, but his horse fell and rolled on him. Another man leaped on the horse, rounded up the steers and brought them back. By that time the first rider was on his feet again, ready to take over, and the yoking went on until the train was hitched and ready to pull out.

Those years of the early eighties, all across the prairies, were rife with town and railroad building. Wherever rumor, or even wishful thinking, made a railroad probable, new towns sprang up. As a result, most of the plains counties fathered more towns that died than lived; and of those that lived, many not only never reached the heights to which their promoters attempted to elevate them, but with the passing years deteriorated to mere sleepy little villages, barely hanging onto their post offices and depots.

In March, 1884, as the railroad built southwest from Harper, an enterprising set of town builders hastened to lay out a town only seven miles northeast of where New Kiowa was to rise a few months later.

They called it Hazelton. Nearly a quarter of a century later, in 1910, it had a population of 350, two banks, three churches, a newspaper, and several mercantile establishments. By 1965 it had shrunk to 246 residents.

Other Barber County towns built on proposed or projected railway lines were Sharon (1885), nine miles east of Medicine Lodge; Isabel (1887), thirteen miles north of the county seat; Lake City (1883), eighteen miles northwest of Medicine Lodge; and Sun City two miles farther west, and almost as old as Medicine Lodge. Other towns, long since dead, whose names still cling to the communities where they flourished for a time, are Aetna, Deerhead, Defiance, Pixley, Forest City, and Custer. Mingona, platted April 2, 1885, was laid out around a pretentious public square. Sharon gave its streets high sounding names such as St. Louis and New York Avenues. Today it still has a population of 272, but Mingona is long gone.

Jacob Achenbach, desirious of a town close to his ranch out west of New Kiowa, organized a town company in 1886 and bought 640 acres of land from a Dr. Hardtner of Illinois. And there, ten miles west of New Kiowa, he platted a town named Hardtner. No town in Barber County today needs that large an area, yet the Hardtner promoters once planned to use it all for the city they hoped to build. Achenbach, president of the town company, at once secured a post office and was appointed postmaster, a post he held for the next thirty years. In addition to his ranch and the post office, he also owned and managed a general store in the town. In 1896, just before the presidential election of that year, he built a telephone line from Kiowa to Hardtner and installed a telephone in his store. On election day everybody for miles around gathered at Jacob's store to wait for the returns to come in over the phone, the only one in town. No doubt many bets were won or lost that night, when McKinley's victory was finally flashed over the line. By 1910 Hardtner's population was a modest one hundred, only a dot in the midst of its 640 acre town site.

The trade territory of each little town extended for miles on either side of the railroad. People living far out drove all day to get to town for supplies. After finding a good spot in the feed yards for the teams and wagons, the farmers headed for the stores. Most of them ate lunches brought from home, or crackers, hard cheese, and sardines, purchased for a few cents at a grocery counter, then spent the hours until midnight visiting, swapping news, and looking over the merchants' stock of goods, for stores didn't shut their doors at six o'clock in those days. A few might then go to a hotel for the rest of the night, but most bedded down under their wagons, or in the livery stable hayloft.

Next morning the merchants, clerks, and customers were out at five to begin the day. And when the settlers left town on the long drive home, their wagons were loaded with hundreds of pounds of flour, sugar, beans, coffee, dried fruit, lumber, barbed wire, and maybe a few yards of calico for the wife and a nickel sack of candy for the kids.

Little groups of Indians wandered in, too, to visit and buy a little candy or sugar and a few gewgaws, bright scarves and sashes. The men wore these articles tied around their arms or fastened into their head-dresses, and strutted around town, vain as any dude. Some of the young bucks had good ponies and ran races with each other or the cowboys down the dusty summer streets. And all day long the main streets were lined with saddle horses, teams and rigs, the horses kicking and pawing up the dirt in front of the hitching racks. Down by the depot, in the fall or early spring, long strings of wagons waited their turns at the boxcars, either to load grain and hay for shipment outstate, or to unload lumber, coal, and feed shipped in for the ranches and big outfits.

Most of the little towns were cattle shipping centers, too, where for days each fall dust clouds hung above the shipping pens, for as long as cattle were trailed up from the south. And Kiowa was for awhile one of the largest shipping points in the west, equal with Caldwell and Dodge City, according to Albert Rumsey, son of one of the town site organizers. Herds came from as far away as New Mexico, he said, to be held on the prairie, waiting their turn at the loading pens. As soon as a train of twelve to fourteen cars (all the little engines could handle) pulled out for Kansas City, another engine with its complement of cars took its place.

And as for August Hegwer, leading founder of old Kiowa, he perished with the cattle trade, lost in one of the January blizzards of the terrible winter of '86. While hunting down in the Indian Outlet, he was caught in the storm, wandered for hours, and froze to death on Mule Creek.

To conclude the history of Barber County's towns, it is necessary to tell the story of Elm Mills, the town that was never planned nor platted, the accidental town that just happened to grow up around a mill. The mill was located on Elm Creek, in the northern part of the county, simply because the stream at that place was a good source of water power.

The mill was scarcely in operation when, in 1876, Louis Frame and Schuyler Strong settled nearby and established a "gypsum plant." From the bluffs along the creek they mined fine gypsum rock and burned it by the ton in the kiln they built. The next year they made a quantity of molds in which they pressed blocks of pure white gypsum, twenty-four by twelve by ten inches in size. On the banks of the creek Strong built a home for his family of the white blocks, a home that, fifty years later, stood as strong and beautiful as on the day he finished it.

For many years the flour mill flourished, and so did the "gyp" plant, providing sturdy building materials for the plains people.

The first child born in the new settlement, on May 17, 1876, was Louis Frame's son, Clarence. Dr. C. C. Bond, the only doctor in northwest Barber County at the time, was in attendance. A few years later, when the country was fast settling up, Dr. Bond, on another call to the Frame home, pulled into the yard and threw several barbed wire gates out of his spring wagon. The cattlemen, he stated with finality, "had no right to fence up the country, anyhow."

More merchants and settlers tended to gather around the mill and the gypsum plant, and presently the place was a thriving, pleasant village of one hundred or more. But the mill stones have long since ceased to turn and the gyp plant is no more. However, a few full time residents still make their homes there and a few others spend the summer months in cottages shaded by the ancient elms on the banks of the pretty stream.

SEVEN
Frontier Violence
1873-1886

An unusual number of shocking tragedies took place in Barber County during its formative years, and most of them in Medicine Lodge. Most communities can come into being and grow up peaceably, but a few seem singled out for violence and disaster. And so it was with Medicine Lodge, snuggled in its pleasant valley between the rippling streams and the rosy bluffs. In fact it seemed the town hardly awaited its first birthday to record its first fearful bloodletting.

It happened in the summer of 1873, when the place was only a hotel, a store and a saloon. On a hot Saturday afternoon, when the little settlement was filled with hunters, land seekers, and travelers of many sorts, a man called Arthur McCluskey, and Richards, his guide, rode in from the north.

McCluskey is described as a big man, a "handsome brute in a buckskin suit," who carried both a six gun and a knife. He stopped to ask a camp crew, lazing in the shade of a tree, if they had seen a man by the name of Hugh Anderson. They told him Anderson was working at Harding's saloon that day, and he rode on to the log cabin hotel and rented space for himself and his guide. He then sent Richards to the saloon to tell Anderson that he had come to make him pay for killing his brother, Chet McCluskey. "Tell him," said the big man, "that I'll fight him with gun or knife, and I'll give him an even show."

The guide went to the rough two-room cabin that served as a trading post, bar, and gambling joint. The furniture was plank tables and empty liquor kegs, the customers were hunters, gamblers, trappers, drifters, and a few Indians. Back of the bar and stud poker table stood the Texan, Anderson, a small man with flint-hard eyes. Richards pushed his way through the crowd and delivered his message in a low tone. Anderson frowned as he listened, then talked with the guide a few minutes before he told the crowd that the game was closed, as he had "a chore to do."

The two men went into the second room of the cabin, where Harding, the huge bearded trader, was busy. Anderson told him that McCluskey had come for his hide, and that he wanted him (Harding) to serve as his second in the duel that was about to come off. Harding nodded assent.

The news of the coming showdown spread like a head fire before a high wind. By sundown seventy men had gathered on the open patch of ground picked for the fight. Excited and cheerful, the men made bets and discussed the terms of the match. The two duelists were to stand twenty paces apart, their backs to each other. A pistol shot would be the signal at which they would whirl and shoot. If the guns didn't end the match, they were to finish it with knives, or even their bare hands, for it was to be a fight to the death.

In the bright summer dusk the big man and the small one took their places, guns in hand, and at the signal spun and "shot as one." But each only nicked the other. McCluskey broke Anderson's arm with his second shot and the Texan was knocked to his knees by the force of the blow. As he fell he snapped off another shot of his own, one that smashed into the big man's mouth and came out at the base of his skull.

Still on his feet, McCluskey, though terribly wounded, came at the kneeling man with a roar. Shooting twice more at close range as his enemy came on, the little Texan hit him in the shoulder and stomach, finally bringing the big man to the ground on his face. The watching crowd thought the battle was over then, but McCluskey suddenly raised his head, lifted his gun and fired again, hitting the other in the stomach and stretching him on the grass.

Then McCluskey, almost head to head with his brother's killer, peered at him from blood spattered eyes, dropped his gun, drew his knife, and began to inch closer. Some of the watchers, sickened by the gory sight, would have stopped the fight, but the big trader told them to stand back. Let it go on, he said, on the terms the two had made.

So McCluskey kept on with his bloody crawl, and the Texan, still conscious, drew his own knife and waited, gritting his teeth as he struggled to a sitting position. When his attacker came within reach, Anderson struck, slashing McCluskey's neck. The blow was his last and the knife slid from his loosening grip. Then the big man struck, opening the Texan's side as his own breath ran out with the red tide gushing from his neck. And so the two men died together, locked in a grisly embrace.

The sobered onlookers carried the bloody pair to the saloon and laid them out on the table, then ordered up round after round of drinks, toasts to the dead men's grit, they said, but more likely to wash the sight and smell of hot blood and violent death from their own memories. Later that night they wrapped the bodies in hides and buried them in a common grave at the edge of town. No marker was ever placed at the grave but, as the poet, Richard Wheeler, wrote:

> There's a spot in the town of Medicine Lodge,
> Where a pair who fought till they died,
> Have been laid away
> Till the Judgement Day
> And are waiting it side by side.[1]

No one in Medicine Lodge today remembers the bloody duel, but this is not surprising. The village was not to have a newspaper for another five years, and of the people who saw the fight or heard of it first-hand, only a few remained long in the town, and these few have long been dead. Even their descendants are dead or gone from Medicine Lodge. So there is, quite simply, no one left who knew anything about it.

Except for the Indian raids of '74 and '78, and a near killing toward the end of the decade, affairs rocked along fairly peaceably for about six years. The near killing came about when two men grew violently angry with each other on the main street one day. Dunc Doles, a Barber County settler, and his eight-year-old son, Amp, were in town that day and saw the wrangle. One of the men had his dog with him, and the poor animal, frightened by the shouts and threatening gestures of the angry pair, ran between his owner's legs and hunkered there. Whereupon the other pulled his gun and shot the dog.

Bystanders leaped in and kept the quarrel from going any farther, but Dunc turned to his son and said, "Amp, this town is gettin' too dangerous. You're agoin' t' have to stay home til things quiet down." To the prairie youngster, the denial of those infrequent and exciting trips to town was a real blow.

In March, 1879, things livened up again in Medicine Lodge. The affair began with the report of the accidental shooting of John W. Hillman on Spring Creek, northwest of town. Hillman, a farm laborer from up Lawrence way, and one J. H. Brown had been camping together on the creek. It was Brown who came in with the body, explaining that he was taking his gun out of the wagon and it accidentally went off, shooting Hillman through the head. Since this kind of thing happened every once in awhile, and the dead man was a stranger besides, it caused very little excitement. Purely as a matter of course, George Washington Paddock, a country justice, held an inquest over the body and found the death had come about as related. The dead man was buried at Medicine Lodge where, according to the *Cresset* of April 17, 1879, "for ten days he lay at peace with all mankind."

His rest was disturbed by the arrival in town of some curious insurance agents. Why, they wanted to know, would a poor laborer such as Hillman was known to be take out $25,000 in life insurance on himself—and then so quickly meet his death? Furthermore, the agents complained, no cash had been paid on the premiums; only notes, endorsed by a man named Levy Baldwin, had been received by the life insurance companies. In search of an answer to their question, the insurance men had the body taken up and shipped to Lawrence.

And so began one of the most celebrated cases in the history of life insurance. The company investigators were certain that Hillman himself and his co-conspirator, Baldwin, had connived in a scheme to defraud the companies. The man killed on Spring Creek and buried in Medicine Lodge, they charged, was not Hillman, but a stranger whom Brown had been hired to kill and bury as Hillman.

The town of Medicine Lodge and eventually the whole eastern half of Kansas took sides in the controversy. Some of the town's residents remembered that Mrs. Sadie Hillman had not come to her husband's funeral. In fact, no relatives had turned up for the last rites. So some citizens concluded that Mrs. Hillman and Brown, owner of the gun that went off "accidentally," had conspired in killing Hillman for the insurance money.

The *Cresset* editorial for April 17 related that "divers and sundry medical experts" had examined the body, and that the insurance companies by "quack doctors, old women and hack drivers" had tried to prove that the body was not Hillman's but "some poor unfortunate [whose] soul had been sent to eternity and his body made to do duty as a dead man in Hillman's boots."

"As far as our researches have gone," concluded the editor, "we find, instead of a deep plot in blood, the mysteries are on the part of the insurance companies, who have availed themselves of some cheap testimony to disprove the identity of J. W. Hillman. The friends of Mrs. Hillman have as yet made no showing, but we predict that hundreds can be found willing to examine the body and make the necessary identification. The whole affair will be thoroughly sifted and the light of calcium[2] truth permitted to shine through the dark and infamous swindle which the insurance companies so cooly purpose to carry out."

The insurance people, meanwhile, were attempting to build their case. A man named Walters, they charged, had been hired by Baldwin and Hillman to go to Barber County with Hillman and Brown. There Walters was to be murdered and buried as Hillman, while the real Hillman disappeared. Some months later Brown, it was reported, had admitted that his statement to the coroner's jury was false and that Walters had been murdered. Only he, Brown, had not done the foul deed. Hillman, he declared, was the killer.

Mrs. Hillman, however, produced reputable witnesses who swore that Hillman had visited Medicine Lodge several weeks before the killing and that, due to a bad storm, had been forced to stay in town several days. The stormbound visitor, these witnesses declared, and the man who was shot on Spring Creek were one and the same.

"Knowing these men well," wrote T. A. McNeal years later, "I cannot doubt their honesty, and it is hard to believe they were mistaken. Pictures of Walters and of Hillman do not show any marked resemblance between the two. On the other hand, the taking out of $25,000 in life insurance by a common laborer, the burial of the body in an unmarked grave, with apparently no intention of removing it to his home at Lawrence, the giving of notes instead of cash for the payment of the first premiums on the policies, and the confession of

Brown, all tended to make a strong *prima facie* case for the insurance companies."[3]

For a quarter of a century the case dragged its way through the courts, all the way to the Supreme Court of the United States, back again to the Kansas courts, and again to the Supreme Court; and some of the best lawyers of Kansas and other states argued the case on one side or the other. Eventually politics took a hand and Webb McNall, insurance commissioner under Governor Leedy ordered New York Life to pay the Hillman policy or get out of Kansas. A compromise settlement then ended the case.

No doubt there was a conspiracy to defraud the insurance companies, but perhaps the plan failed in some way and Hillman was really killed at the lonely Spring Creek camp. If not, then why was he never heard of again? And if the dead man was not Walters, then there was another unexplained disappearance.

While the Hillman case, not yet two months old, was still the talk of the town, another and even more bizarre killing shocked the county to its very roots. One sweet spring evening in May, the twenty-third to be exact, a young Mrs. Steadman and her mother, Mrs. Champion, went out to hunt their milk cows. On their way home they came to the crossing of one of the little tributaries of the Medicine at the same time that a young horseman, John Garten, reached it.

Garten, a gawky, green country boy of nineteen or twenty, was not mean, but ordinarily quiet and law abiding. On this day, though, he had been in Medicine Lodge and had "bent his elbow" too many times at one of the bars. The quality of the whisky sold there at that time was said to be "as bad as the worst," and certainly it brought out the worst in the boy. He rode whooping out of town, bent on learning, straight away, to draw and shoot with the best of the gunmen of his day. When he overtook the two women, who stepped out of the trail to let him pass, he whipped out his gun, let out a drunken howl and fired two shots in their direction. One account of the tragedy says the gun missed fire when he shot at Mrs. Champion, and that he then turned it on the young woman and pulled the trigger again. Mrs. Steadman cried out as she fell, mortally wounded, but Garten rode on, not even looking back.[4]

The accounts also differ in what happened during the next few hours. One states that he went on home, ate his supper, and then rode back to the Parsons ranch, where he spent the evening and stayed all night. Nothing unusual was noted in his actions and he did not mention the shooting. About daybreak Sheriff Simmons rode in and arrested him on the murder charge, but Garten claimed he didn't remember anything about shooting at the women.[5]

The other story relates that after the shooting he rode on to the ranch where he worked, unsaddled his horse, and made no effort to escape. When the sheriff rode in a few hours later and said, "John, I want you for murder," the boy protested that he didn't know the gun was loaded, that he only meant to scare the women, and didn't suppose he had hit either of them.[6] The sheriff took his prisoner to Medicine Lodge and put him into the crude little jail.

The senseless murder aroused a storm of indignation and talk of hanging was soon rampant in the streets and saloons. But the sheriff, wise to the ways of frontier towns, took his prisoner quickly to Squire Wise, where he waived examination, and then left with him in the darkness of a moonless night and headed for the safety of the Rice County Jail, northwest of Hutchinson, to await trial. Before the next term of court in Barber County, young Garten broke jail and fled to New Mexico. Although he was never caught by the authorities, it is believed in the Gyp Hills country that he paid for his crime. For soon after his escape, the dead woman's father, a lean, powerful man from the mountains of Kentucky, headed for the southwest. A grim man who believed in the old hill law of a life for a life, Champion was gone for about a year. When he came back to Barber County he said little about his trip, but his neighbors always believed he had carried out his aim.

However, there were many in Barber County who, on sober second thought, placed the blame for the murder where it belonged—on the vile whisky sold in the saloons of the region. The next year at the election of 1880 a prohibition amendment to the state constitution was placed on the ballot and the citizens of the county gave it a good majority of their votes.

The settlement at Elm Mills experienced its share of the county's gory history when, in the fall of 1886, seventeen-year-old George Castine was shot down in cold blood in the street in front of Stewart's store. For some time there had been hard feelings between John Castine, George's father, and Cornelius Stewart, village storekeeper.

Stewart had accused Castine of stealing from his store, and Castine claimed Stewart had poisoned some of his livestock. Each had made angry threats against the other.

Finally David Stewart, about twenty years of age, decided one evening to put the Stewart threat into action. Knowing that John Castine, his eighteen-year-old daughter Effie, and the boy, George, regularly walked past the store on their way to church, he hid in the building where he could watch the road and await the Castines' coming. It was dusk by the time they passed, Effie and her father walking together. George, walking alone, was a hundred yards behind the others. Young Stewart, assuming the brother and sister were walking together, as they usually did, held his fire until George came by, then, believing he was firing at the father, he shot the boy down in the street. The two ahead, hearing the shot and the cries of alarm, turned and hurried back. Some men in the crowd were carrying George into the drugstore.

Leaving Effie with her badly wounded brother, John Castine hurried home to get a team and wagon to take his son away. As soon as he was out of sight, the Stewarts, realizing they had made a serious mistake, insisted that Effie go home too. This was no place for a lady, they told her, and in her fright and confusion she left. Then the Stewarts, who kept the Elm Mills post office in one corner of their store, brought some marked money from the office till and put it in the wounded boy's pocket.

Charged by Cornelius Stewart with theft of post office funds, the dying youth swore that he had not been nearer to the store than the road on which he walked, and that he was innocent of the charge. The account of the murder does not reveal what, if anything, was done to avenge the murder or punish the murderers.

The supreme tragedy of the county, one that has been told in story, song, and film for more than three-quarters of a century, is also a tale of Medicine Lodge. There, in 1884, in the space of a few hours, a strange and bloody drama was enacted.

The opening scene took place in the bank, an institution with an unusual history of its own. Under the high-sounding title of the Merchants and Drovers Bank, it opened its doors in October, 1880, with capital "borrowed on a safe that had been purchased on time," or so the story goes. The bank failed on January 10, 1882, and two days later E. W. Payne picked up the remains and organized them into the Medicine Valley Bank, and made George Geppert his cashier.

Wylie Payne was a most important man in the affairs of the town and the region surrounding it. Besides holding office as president of the bank, he was also president of the great Comanche Cattle Pool and a director in one of the largest and most successful livestock organizations in the world, the Cherokee Strip Livestock Association. Immediately upon reorganizing the bank he had put up a handsome two-story bank building and fitted it out with the latest thing in ornate furnishings. In a short time the bank "numbered its patrons and depositors from the Panhandle of Texas to the Arkansas, and from the Medicine River to the Colorado line."

Payne's history, too, is interesting. Born in poverty in Missouri, he fought his way to a position of power and wealth well before he was forty. Orphaned at the age of six, he had knocked about, going to school in the winters until he was sixteen; then he engaged in freighting for two years. At the age of twenty-eight he bought a farm of his own, and a year later was elected to the Missouri legislature.

Turning his eyes then to the new frontier, he came to Barber County, went into ranching, and soon acquired a large section of deeded range lands and considerable property in the new town of Medicine Lodge. By 1884 he also owned the Barber County *Index*, official organ of the Democrats, and was a candidate for the state legislature. Married and the father of nine children, he owned a fine home near the river and was in the process of promoting a fine hotel for Medicine Lodge.

And so, with Wylie Payne and his cashier, the popular George Geppert, in their places in the bank, the stage was set for the tragedy that was about to be played out that Wednesday morning of April 30, 1884. There are countless versions as to exactly what happened as the scene unfolded and in the few hours that followed the opening act. But probably the account printed in the *Cressett* the next day, Thursday, May 1, is as accurate as any.

"Our little city was yesterday thrown into a state of intense excitement and horror by the perpetration of a murder and attempted robbery, which, for cold bloodedness and boldness of design was never exceeded by the most famous exploits of the James gang.

"The hour was a little after nine, a heavy rain was falling and comparatively few people were upon the streets, when four men rode in from the west and hitched their horses back of the bank coal shed. The bank had just opened; Mr. Geppert, the cashier, had taken his place and begun work on settling the monthly accounts. E. W. Payne, president, was sitting at his desk writing, when as nearly as we can learn, three of the robbers entered. According to a preconcerted plan we presume, one advanced to the cashier's window, one to the president's window, while one seems to have gone around into the back room to the iron lattice door.

"Almost immediately after the men were seen to enter the bank, several shots were heard in rapid succession. Rev. Friedley, who happened to be just across the street, immediately gave the alarm, and Marshal Denn, who was standing near the livery stable, across the street from the bank, opened fire on the robber outside, who returned the fire, fortunately without effect. The robbers now saw that their game was up and broke for their horses, mounted and rode out of town, going south. It was but a few minutes until a score or more men were in hot pursuit.

"To those who remained, on going into the bank, a horrible sight was presented. George Geppert, the esteemed cashier, lay at the door of the vault, weltering in his blood and dead. A hole in his chest, showing where the ball had entered and probably severed the carotid artery, told the tale. Mr. Payne lay near him, groaning with pain. An examination showed that a pistol ball had entered back of the right shoulder blade, and ranging across, had probably grazed his spine and lodged somewhere under the left shoulder blade. Mr. Payne's wound is a very serious one, but the doctors express strong hopes of his recovery.

"Going back to the pursuing party, we got the story of the exciting chase from a participant. The pursuing party first came in sight of the robbers beyond the crossing of the Medicine, south of town. The party, seeing that they were about to be overtaken, turned and opened fire. Several volleys were exchanged. While the fight was going on, Charley Talliaferro and, we believe, one or two others, rode around the robbers and headed them off on the south. Seeing that they were cut off in this direction, they left the road and started almost west toward the breaks of the gypsum hills, but were so hotly pursued that they took refuge in a canyon some three or four miles southwest of town.

"The boys in pursuit surrounded the canyon to prevent the possibility of escape, and George Friedley and Charlie Talliaferro came in for reinforcements. In a short time every gun and horse which could be brought into service was on the road to the canyon. Before the reinforcements arrived on the ground, however, the robbers had surrendered.

"The surprise of the captors can be better imagined than expressed when, on taking charge of the outfit, they found that they were well known. The leaders of the gang were Hendry Brown, Marshal of Caldwell; and Ben Wheeler, Assistant Marshal of the same city; the other two were well known cowboys, William Smith, who has been employed for some time on the T5 range, and another cowboy who is known by the name of Wesley, but has several aliases.

"Of these men Brown is the only one who has acquired any notoriety. His history on the frontier began with his connection with "Billy the Kid" in New Mexico. It is said that he was a companion of the noted desperado in some of his most exciting adventures. Of late years, however, he seemed to have sobered down. Some three years since he was elected assistant city marshal of Caldwell, and for the past two years has occupied the position of marshal of our neighboring city. In appearance Brown does not show the criminal particularly. He is a man of medium height; strong, wiry build, wears no beard except a mustache, and his face indicates firmness and lack of physical fear. During the time he has held office he has killed several men, but was generally considered justified.

"Ben Wheeler, the man who fired the shot which killed George Geppert, is a large and powerfully built man, sandy complected and with rather an open countenance. So far as we know he has never been noted as a desperado. He has occupied the position of assistant marshal of Caldwell for the past two years and has been considered, we believe, a good officer. His action yesterday, however, showed him to be perhaps the most cold blooded murderer in the gang.

"Wesley is rather under medium size and has an evil, reckless expression of countenance and is just such a boy as would aspire to be a desperado. Smith is also undersized, with dark complexion and a rather hardened expression of countenance.

"When the party were brought in they were surrounded by a crowd of exasperated citizens, and cries of 'Hang them,' 'Hang them' sounded on every side. For awhile it looked as if they would be torn from the hands of the officers and lynched on the spot, but a somewhat calmer feeling came over the crowd, not that the feeling was any less intense, but the desire to do the job up in a more business like style was greater.

"All afternoon little knots of quiet, determined men could be seen, and all over town was that peculiar hush which bodes the coming of a storm. Little was said, but the impression was prevalent that before many hours the bodies of four murderers would swing in the soft night air.

"About nine o'clock the stillness was broken by three shots fired in rapid succession, and at the signal a crowd of armed men advanced on the jail and demanded the prisoners. This was refused, but notwithstanding their spirited resistance, the sheriff and posse were overpowered and the doors of the jail opened. The prisoners, who were in the inner cell unshackled, made a sudden dash for liberty. In an instant the moonlight was so mingled with bullets that it was a highly unsatisfactory locality for a promenade, and the fact that no one except the prisoners was seriously injured is a matter of wonder. Wheeler, Smith and Wesley were captured, Wheeler badly wounded. Brown ran a few rods from the jail and fell dead, riddled with a charge of buckshot, besides having a few stray Winchester balls in various parts of his body.

"Wheeler, Smith and Wesley were taken by the crowd to an elm tree in the bottom east of town and told if there was anything they wished to say, to say it now, for their time of life was short. Wheeler at the last showed great weakness and begged piteously for mercy. Wesley was also shaken, but managed to answer, in reply to inquiry, that he was born in Paris, Texas, in 1853, and requested that word of his fate be sent to friends in Vernon, Texas. Smith displayed great nerve and gave directions cooly, to sell his horse and saddle and some few other trinkets and send the money to his mother in Vernon, Texas.

"After the remarks the ready ropes were fastened on the necks of the robbers, the ends tossed over a limb and in a moment more their bodies swung in the wind. And so ended the most exciting and the most sorrowful day in the history of Medicine Lodge.[7]

"Mob law is to be deplored under almost any circumstances, but in this case the general sentiment of the community will uphold the summary execution of justice by the taking of these murderers' lives."

T. A. McNeal notes, "Perhaps there was never a more orderly lynching. The next morning the coroner, determined that no forms of the law be overlooked, summoned a jury who solemnly viewed the remains and rendered a verdict that they had come to their deaths at the hands of persons unknown to the jury."[8]

A week later, on May 8, the *Cresset* published the official results of the inquest as follows: "In compliance with the forms of law, Coroner Singer on Thursday empaneled a jury . . . who in connection with the Sheriff and county attorney examined the bodies of Brown, Wheeler, Smith and Wesley. On the person of Brown they found nothing of value. On the person of Ben Wheeler was found 11 cts. in money, a lady's gold ring with amethyst setting, a pair of cuff buttons and a pocket knife. On the person of Smith was found $2.60 in money, and on the person of Wesley $5.90. Sheriff Rigg testified before the jury that he was overpowered at the jail by persons so masked that he could not recognize them, and that they spoke in sepulchral tones so that he could not recognize their voices.

"The jury gave in their verdict to the effect that H. N. Brown had died from the effect of gunshot wounds at the hands of unknown parties; that Wheeler had come to his death either from the effect of gunshot wounds or from hanging or from both causes, at the hands of unknown parties; that Smith and Wesley had come to their deaths from hanging at the hands of parties unknown to the jury.

"There are some developments in connection with this examination held by the coroner's jury which are worthy of comment. A party who came over from Caldwell last Friday claims that he had loaned Wheeler, previous to his leaving Caldwell, $300 in currency and a gold watch valued at $625 and a diamond pin valued at $50 or $60. Sheriff Rigg states that he knows Wheeler had some money on his person after he was captured. He does not know the exact amount, but estimated it at $40 or $50. Two or three parties who were present at the capture of the robbers also state that they saw Wheeler take what they supposed to be a watch out of his pocket and give it to somebody, they are not certain who.

"In view of these things, it looks as if somebody had made a liberal stake at the expense of the robbers. If such is the case, we have no hesitance in saying it was a dishonorable piece of business. But we have no sympathy to waste on a man who was foolish enough to lend a man of Ben Wheeler's character a $625 watch and $300 in money."

And in the same issue, the *Cresset* added a sequel to the exciting story: "On account of the intense excitement which prevailed immediately after the tragedy last week, and in view of the fact that we had but three or four hours in which to write up the proceedings, it would not be surprising if we made some inaccuracies of statement. Among these mistakes was the statement of the position of Marshal Denn at the time the shooting commenced. As we afterward ascertained, the Marshal was standing under the awning of Herrington & Smith. He immediately ran out into the street and commenced shooting at the robber outside. While crossing the street he was in a most exposed position and showed great nerve and coolness in answering every shot from the robber's Winchester, and for which he deserves all credit.

"The parties who were actually present when the robbers proposed to surrender were Barney O'Connor, Vernon Lytle, Alec McKinney, Lee Bradley, Roll Clark, Tom Doran, John Fleming, Wayne McKinney, Howard Martin and Nate Priest. George Friedley and Charley Talliaferro had started to town a short time previous to the surrender, after reinforcements. Among those who surrendered the canyon, a remarkable degree of coolness and daring was displayed, and it took no small amount of nerve to face the music on that occasion. Another statement in the account of last week was that the prisoners were unshackled in the jail. As this might be misconstrued, we will explain that the sheriff is possessed of but one pair of shackles and one pair of handcuffs. Brown and Wesley were shackled together, while Wheeler and Smith were handcuffed together. Smith had a rather large wrist and remarkably small hands, and on this account managed to slip his handcuff. Wesley in a like manner managed to slip off his boot and then his shackle. This left all four free. Hence the sudden rush when the visitors opened the cell door to call on the prisoners."

EIGHT

Justice in Medicine Lodge and Caldwell

1871-1884

To the people of Barber County, the most shocking part of the attempted bank robbery, other than the deaths of the six principals. was the fact that it had all been planned by the respected peace officers of the border town of Caldwell, some sixty miles to the southeast.

Caldwell, a wild town almost from its beginning in 1871, became even wilder after it attained cowtown status with the arrival of the railroad in 1880. Lynchings were numerous there, no less than eight recorded, all horse thieves. The town was also hard on marshals and peace officers, accounting for four killed in the line of duty within a four-month span of time;[1] it is a matter of record that at least twelve killings occurred there between 1879 and 1884.[2]

Deputy Marshal Frank Hunt was shot down by unknown assailants while he stood at a window of the Red Light saloon and dancehall, the toughest joint in town, looking in at the dancers. Marshal George S. Brown was killed in the same saloon while attempting to arrest two drunken cowboys. George Woods, husband of Meg, proprietress of the Red Light, was shot by a young Texan, Charlie Davis, who then sped out of town and was never caught. George Flat, city marshal, and Constable John Wilson, attempting to arrest George Wood and Jake Adams, drunken Texas cowboys, in Jim Moreland's saloon, killed both of them in the shooting that followed. Flat, later dismissed for drunkenness, was shot one night as he staggered home from the Red Light.

After Flat's death his friend, Jim Talbot, a well-known Texas desperado, spent a month or more in Caldwell, drinking, gambling, and boasting that he had come to town to kill Mike Meagher. With him were six other members of his so-called gang. Meagher, four times city marshal at Wichita, and said to be far the best that town ever had, had come to Caldwell some two years before. A widely known and popular man, the big Irishman was elected mayor in the spring of 1880. He refused re-election in the turbulent spring of '81, and the following December was cut down by a bullet from Talbot's gun.

The shooting started early one morning when the Talbot gang, after an all-night drinking spree, erupted onto the main street, firing their pistols. Marshal Wilson arrested one of the drunks, but the others forced him to let him go. Meagher then went to help Wilson out. Others, including Special Officer Ed Rothbun, Assistant Marshal Fosset, and Mayor Hubbell, shortly joined in the fight. The shooting went on well into the afternoon and ended when Talbot shot Meagher with a Winchester (both Rothbun and Wilson testified to seeing the Texas outlaw fire the fatal shot), after which he and his men raced to the stable where their saddled horses waited. One of the gang was shot down at the stable, but the rest escaped.

At least twenty men had taken part in the big shoot-out that December day and at least a hundred shots had been traded. No wonder then that on December 17, 1881, the Wichita *Beacon* commented, "As we go to press Hell is again in session in Caldwell."

In the wake of all this, Hendry Newton Brown came to Caldwell in July, 1882, and applied for the job of deputy marshal. B. O. Carr, marshal of the town at that time, had done little in the way of keeping order, and there were even those who said he was in league with the desperados of the region. At any rate the Red Light, in spite of the efforts of a few of the better class citizens to close it down, was still running wide open and drunken cowboys still hurrahed the town at will.

Brown came well qualified for the deputy's job. A former marshal of Tascosa, out in the Texas Panhandle, he had also been deputy sheriff of Oldham County, Texas. Before that he had taken part in the Lincoln County war of New Mexico where, along with Billy the Kid, he was a member of the posse organized by Dick Brewer, Tunstall's foreman and a duly appointed deputy, sent to arrest Tunstall's murderers. A short time later he was included in another posse, also headed by Deputy Constable Brewer, which met Buckshot Roberts at Blazers Mill. Buckshot, a member of the Murphy-Dolan outfit of Lincoln, was killed that day, but not until he had killed Brewer and wounded three members of the posse. Brown was with the Kid, too, when he and several others made a raid on John Chisum's Seven Rivers outfit and stole seventy-five or a hundred head of horses and drove them to Tascosa, where they sold them.[3] Still later that fateful year of 1878, Brown was one of the men who tried to defend the McSween home in Lincoln against the Murphy-Dolan forces during the climatic hours of that bitter war. Billy the Kid was one of the leaders in the fighting on several of these occasions, which accounts for Hendry Brown's name being so often connected with that of the famed Kid.

Almost immediately after Brown was hired as the Caldwell deputy marshal, the town's weekly newspaper, the *Commercial*, announced on July 6, 1882: "Mr. Brown is a young man who bears an excellent reputation, and although he has acted in similar capacities for several years, has never acquired any of those habits which some seem to think are absolutely necessary to make an officer popular with the 'boys.' With Mr. Carr for marshal and Hendry Brown for assistant, we think the city has at last secured the right kind of a police force."

In August the *Commercial* reported that in Caldwell guns seemed to be giving way to nature's arms, or "bunches of fives." In church the previous Sunday, a citizen had heard for the first time that the Jews had killed the Savior some 1,800 years ago. This upset him so much that next morning he pitched into the first Jew he met. But Carr and Hendry Brown stepped up just in time to keep the incensed citizen from avenging the wrong of nearly nineteen centuries standing. A few days later two other citizens had a row over a financial matter, and again the affair was settled by the officers, and all without the use of guns, which made the editor very happy.

There were those who said, *after* the affair at Medicine Lodge, that Brown had aimed from the first to have Carr's job. Some even said he took the sheriff's star by force, yanking the badge from the other's vest and ordering him to "git."[4] At any rate, by December of 1882, Carr had resigned and Brown had been appointed marshal. Several weeks later a tall man by the name of Ben Wheeler came to town. Introducing him as an old friend, the marshal had him hired as his assistant. The two kept a sharp eye on the town and between them gave it a good dose of law and order.

Cowboys, cattlemen, men of whatever kind and business, were

required to leave off their arms as soon as they hit town. Brown even had some new ordinances passed, giving him authority to remove lewd women from the streets and to close down entertainment in the saloons. He then went after Meg Woods and her Red Light saloon and dance hall. Meg put up a spirited fight, but the decent townspeople backed the marshal and the city council declared the tavern a public nuisance and ordered it closed. As she left the place, Meg set it afire, and watched it burn as she and her "girls" pulled out of town on the train.

Hendry Brown has been variously described as "a soft-spoken, colorless, stony-faced gun fighter," as "a lean, sinewy man with thin cruel lips and cold grey eyes," as "a loose-jointed cowboy about five feet, eleven inches in his high-heeled boots and weighing around 160 pounds," and as "runty, slim, slope shouldered, with a hard round face, widely set, cold grey eyes, a bulldog jaw and tight lips that seemed stingy of words."[5] Actually, he was twenty-six years old at the time of his death, medium height, compactly built, and light complected. His eyes were blue and his mustache on the blonde order. A native of Rolla, Missouri, he left home at an early age and drifted to Colorado, then to a cow camp in northern Texas. There he killed a man by firing three shots at him. Soon after that he showed up in New Mexico, where he became an associate of Billy the Kid in the Lincoln County war.

Wheeler, on the other hand, was a big man, six feet two, and built accordingly. One of the post-robbery descriptions has him "a giant in stature with a weak and sensual face." Ben Robertson, alias Ben E. Burton, alias Ben F. Wheeler, was a native of Rackdale, Milam County, Texas, and came of a fine family. One of his brothers was at one time General Land Agent of the state of Texas.

Wheeler left home as the result of a shooting scrape. He went first to Wyoming, stayed for awhile, and then went south again with a herd of cattle. In Indianola, Nebraska, he met Miss Alice Wheeler and married her in her father's home under the name of Burton. They seem to have lived happily there from November, 1881, until the next summer when he left for Caldwell, using his wife's name of Wheeler. She followed him a few months later, but the new deputy persuaded her to go home again, promising to send her support money. In the winter of 1884 she came again to Caldwell with their eighteen-month-old child and her aged mother. Her father, she said, had died the past December and she was the sole support of the child and the old woman.

After the hanging at Medicine Lodge, as the authorities dug deeper into the pasts of the erstwhile peace officers, it was found that Wheeler "was said to have a wife and four children in Texas under the name of Robertson." As for the current wife, the *Commercial* reported that, although left alone in Caldwell with her mother and child, "she is willing and anxious to work for their support and in her brave resolution will no doubt meet with ready help from the kindhearted ladies of this city."

After the hanging, too, there were those who remembered that after Brown secured Wheeler as his assistant, several cattlemen who had headquartered at the Southwestern Hotel in Caldwell had been held up and robbed of a good deal of money. "Supposition now is," states the account, "that Brown and Wheeler pulled the robberies."[6]

Nearly every writer who later chronicled the tale of Hendry Brown, marshal of Caldwell, credited him with numerous killings. T. A. McNeal writes that "some men from the range undertook to shoot up the town. Brown killed them as cooly as he would have shot a stray dog."[7] A writer for Zane Grey's *Western Magazine* makes his tale read as if killing men was a daily chore for the marshal. Another wild west magazine tells how Brown offhandedly shot and killed a gambler, Sandy Jim, and two celebrating cowboys in the Kansas cowtown.

Chester C. Heizer, however, writes that Brown killed only one man while he was marshal of Caldwell.[8] The killing occurred in May, 1883, after a complaint was lodged against an Indian known as Spotted Horse. The Indian had entered a home in the town and asked for food. The home owner, frightened by the Indian's manner, reported him to the marshal, who located him in a grocery store. There are two stories as to what happened next. One is that Brown asked the Indian to go with him to an interpreter, and when he refused, he took hold of him. Whereupon Spotted Horse began to feel under his blanket for his revolver and the marshal pulled his gun and told him to stop. When he didn't, Brown shot him. The other story has Brown walking into the store and asking Spotted Horse where his gun was. When he reached under his blanket to get it, Brown drew his own gun and shot him in the head. At any rate the Indian was dead, an inquest was held, and a verdict of justfiable homicide was rendered.

Perhaps one of the strangest aspects of the whole Brown affair is the genuine respect and esteem in which almost the whole town seems to have held its marshal. Not only were its people grateful to him for cleaning up the town and taming its wilder element, but they actually liked the man.

He neither smoked, chewed, drank, nor gambled, and the Caldwell *Messenger* asserted, "Very few frontier peace officers were accepted socially by the leading families of the towns they policed. Hendry Brown was one of the rare exceptions. By the time he began his third term as marshal of Caldwell, no door was closed to him. He was often a prominent figure at church socials and picnics. This could have been only a role he was playing, founded on deceit and treachery, or [it could have been] the direction in which he honestly wanted to go."[9]

Quite likely it was the latter. No doubt he liked being a settled, respected citizen, a man doing well in a big job that needed doing. No doubt he really appreciated the town's sincere gratitude when, on January 4, 1883, the people of Caldwell, through their mayor, presented him with a gold-plated and engraved Winchester rifle. A silver plate on the stock carried the inscription, "Presented to the City Marshal, H. N. Brown, for valuable services rendered the citizens of Caldwell, Kansas. A. M. Colson, Mayor, Dec., 1882."

Perhaps love for a good woman played a part in it, too, for on March 25, 1884, Brown married Maude Levagood, the daughter of a prominent Caldwell family. He seems to have been happily married for one month, but during that time the plan to rob the bank of Medicine Lodge must have been born and perfected in his mind. The reason why he chose to risk all he had gained in the way of respectability in the past two years was probably that he wanted more money, the better to provide for his new wife. For the marshal's salary in a small town like Caldwell did not enable him, as a married man, to cut much of a figure. And neither did he anticipate that robbing the bank would be a very hard job. Just where he intended to use his share of the money will likely never be known. No mention is anywhere made that the men were masked; therefore, if the robbery had come off successfully, it doesn't seem that any of the four would ever have shown up in Kansas again.

It was a strange sequence of events that caused the plan to go so far awry. The heavy rain, falling on the morning of Wednesday, April 30, would seem to be just what the would-be robbers might have ordered. It practically guaranteed that few people would be abroad in the streets of Medicine Lodge, making it easier for them to enter and leave town without being observed. But it also resulted in a crew of cowboys and cattlemen being saddled and ready to ride. The men, planning to join a roundup on Antelope Flat that morning, were waiting in a livery stable near the bank for the rain to let up.

Various accounts have listed the number of men in the accidental posse all the way from twenty to fifty; actually there were about a dozen. One of them, Barney O'Connor, had left his saddled horse, a good, fast animal, in the barn while he went down the street on an errand. When he heard the shots, and the Rev. George Friedley shouting that the bank was being robbed, he turned back toward the bank and the livery stable, just in time to see four horsemen dash away from the bank, headed south. Before he reached the stable, the roundup crew raced away in the same direction. Barney ran on to the stable, but found it empty, or nearly so.

Someone else had ridden away on Barney's good horse, and the only critter left in the barn was a skinny, sorry looking nag. There being nothing else handy, he borrowed the crowbait and took off after the posse. The last man to leave town in pursuit of the robbers, he soon began to catch up with the hindmost possemen, and then to pass them, and the speedier riders as well. Presently he passed his own good horse, and before the chase was ended he was in the lead, the first man to reach Jackass Canyon, where the robbers were holed up, or boxed in.[10]

Hendry Brown, knowing he and his men would be riding hard and fast when they left Medicine Lodge, had arranged to have a man waiting with fresh horses in what was known as the "Gap in the Gyp Hills," a break or pass in the range of rugged hills some ten miles southwest of the town. Although he must have been concerned by being followed out of town by mounted men who were almost within pistol range, he no doubt figured escape was assured. By the time they reached the Gap the horses of both parties would be winded, but the outlaws, on fresh mounts, could then easily leave their pursuers behind. So Brown, who knew the country well, headed straight for the Gap.

But still another strange coincidence was about to intervene. A homesteader, three or four miles southwest of town, had set out to fence his farm, and in the day just past had built a tight barbed wire fence out across the table, far enough that the fleeing outlaws had to bear well to the south to get around it. Far enough that when they swung again toward the Gap they were off course just enough that when they dropped down off the wide table over which they were racing and headed due west across the rugged region of bluffs and canyons that lay ahead, they plunged directly into the only real box canyon in the whole country.

Still unaware of the trap, they spurred their tiring horses up the twisting, high-walled canyon, around tall, upthrust buttes of red sandstone and across deep washouts, until they came to its upper end—and there they knew the truth. Looking up at the sheer, eighty foot walls in shock and unbelief, they knew there was no way out, except by the way they had come in. Their last slim hope, then, lay in getting out before the cowboy posse got in. Wheeling their horses, they raced back down the canyon, but Barney was already inside and they saw that in another ten seconds they would be face to face with him in the narrow defile.

Barney saw the outlaws at the same instant, and all five jumped from their horses and took shelter in ditches or behind clay knobs as more of the possemen came up. Some of the cowboys stayed where they could control the canyon mouth, others went up on the rim; all were firing at the robbers, who steadily returned their fire.

The canyon bottom was well grassed and a good many shrubby cedar trees grew along its walls and inner ridges, giving rise to the suggestion that a few barrels of kerosene, with the heads bashed in, could be rolled from the rim into the canyon. The splashing, spilling fuel would make it easy to start a fire that could turn the whole inside of the canyon into a blazing inferno and "smoke the robbers out." Rev. Friedley and Charlie Talliaferro at once left for town to get the coal oil.

When some of the others explained the plan to the men hidden in the canyon, they threw down their arms and surrendered. Strangely enough, in view of all the shooting that had gone on, when the posse and the prisoners were all assembled at the mouth of the canyon, it was found that no one had been so much as grazed by a bullet.

The commotion had roused the whole countryside, though for a little while it wasn't known what the excitement was all about. Joe Wiley, who lived on a homestead about two miles south of town, saw the robbers race by his place that morning, but thought they were just a bunch of drunk cowboys running their horses as hard as they could. When the posse pounded by a few minutes later, he wondered what was going on. When he heard distant shooting he wondered still more. After awhile the posse came back by his place, taking their prisoners to town, and at last he learned what it was all about.

Back in town, two young men, Jacob Achenbach and his cousin, left the hotel about nine o'clock that morning. Jacob, a newcomer to Barber County, had driven in the day before from the ranch he was establishing near where the town of Hardtner stands today. Reaching town after dark the night before, the two had put up at the hotel and, as they stepped out into the almost empty street the next morning, they wondered why the man they saw back of the bank was standing in the rain with a gun in his hand.

A moment later the gunman fired at the marshal across the street. The bullet missed its target, hit the building behind the marshal, glanced, and smashed through a window in another building. Before the young men could move, three men ran out of the bank, guns in hand, and all four jumped on saddled horses and headed south out of town on a dead run.

All was tumult and confusion then, as news of the cashier's death and the critical wounding of the president spread across the town. A short time later two riders galloped into the town with information that the outlaws were surrounded in the box canyon. One of the riders, learning that Jacob had his team and spring wagon handy, asked if he'd help load a couple of barrels of coal oil into the rig and take it back to the canyon to burn the robbers out. Jacob agreed, but just as they were ready to load the oil, another rider dashed in to report that the men had surrendered and were on the way in.

Almost the whole town watched as the outlaws, muddy and discouraged, were taken to a restaurant for their noon meal, then marched to the jail, where their pictures were taken before they were put inside. Among the interested spectators at the jail was a young salesman from Harper, a young man who wanted to get married but didn't have the money for a wedding trip—like to Niagara Falls—worthy of his lady-love.

Just before the photographer ducked under the black cloth that sheltered his big box camera while he snapped the picture, a bright idea flashed into the salesman's head and he quickly elbowed his way through the crowd until he stood just back of Smith and Wheeler. When the pictures were ready, with his own face showing clearly, he bought one and wrote a lurid description of the attempted robbery, the murder, the flight and capture, and the triple hanging. Enclosing his story and the picture, complete with names, he sent them off to the New York *Times* with a letter explaining why he hoped the paper would buy his journalistic labors. In due time he received a letter thanking him for the illustrated story—and enclosing two round-trip tickets to Niagara Falls.

After getting the outlaws' pictures taken sheriff Riggs shackled Brown and Wesley together and put the handcuffs on Smith and Wheeler, then locked the four into the little jail, built eight years earlier of two-by-four scantlings. And there, that afternoon, Hendry Brown wrote a wistful letter to his wife of one month.

"Darling Wife: I am in jail here. Four of us tried to rob the bank here and one man shot one of the men in the bank. I want you to come and see me as soon as you can. I will send you all of my things and you can sell them, but keep the Winchester. It is hard for me to write this letter, but it was all for you, my sweet wife, and for the love I have for you.

"Do not go back on me. If you do it will kill me. Be true to me as long as you live, and come to see me if you think enough of me. My love is just the same as it always was. Oh, how I did hate to leave you last Sunday evening, but I did not think this would happen. I thought we could take in the money and not have any trouble with it, but a man's fondest hopes are sometimes broken with trouble. We would not have been arrested but one of our horses gave out and we could not leave him [the rider] alone. I do not know what to write. Do the best you can with everything. I want you to send me some clothes. Sell all the things you don't need. Have your picture taken and send it to me. Now, my dear wife, go and see Mr. Witzleben and Mr. Nyce[11] and get the money. If a mob does not kill us we will come out all right after while. Maude, I did not shoot anyone and didn't want the others to kill anyone, but they did and that is all there is about it. Now, my darling wife, goodbye. H. N. Brown."

As the news spread across the countryside, excitement grew. All afternoon men rode into town, to gather in the saloons to drink and talk, and on street corners for more talk. And when, late in the afternoon, word came that Payne had died, the talk turned grim and ugly. There would be a hanging in Medicine Lodge that night.

Out on the Bloom farm, six or seven miles west of town on Cedar Creek, fourteen-year-old Joe Bloom and his chum, Bill Aubley, listened to the story told by a neighbor going by, and they made up their minds to see that hanging. The boys well knew their parents would not approve, so they slipped away at dusk, rode hard, and got to town in time to see the three men swing from the limb of the big elm tree—and then heartily wished they hadn't.

The boys, and Jacob and his cousin, and several hundred other men and boys saw the jail door opened that dark night, and watched Brown make his desperate dash for liberty. They saw him shot down, and they saw Wheeler try to run, too, and saw him stagger at the impact of the bullet that struck him at such close range that it set his coat afire, making him easy to follow in the darkness. And finally, when the three men stood under the long limb of the hanging tree, Jacob Achenbach walked up to one of them and asked him how he felt. All he would say, stated Jacob, long years later, was "My God! My God!" "And with all the drinking and shooting," Jacob added, "I do not see how it happened that many more were not killed."[12]

The next morning, May 1, the four dead men were laid out in the yard west of the jail, where all who wished might go and view them. One who came to look was Ben Harbaugh, a settler who had a dugout home eight miles south of Medicine Lodge on Brush Creek. After one quick look at the men, he pointed at Wheeler and Smith and said, "Why, those boys had breakfast at my place yesterday morning." Then he added as he turned away, "I thought that one (pointing to the tall outlaw) was too well dressed and had too good a horse and saddle to be an ordinary cowpoke."

Still another settler, Isaiah Hewitt, newly arrived on the ridge northeast of town, came in that day for a wagon load of supplies. His twelve-year-old son, Frank, was with him and as soon as they heard what had happened, they too went over to look at the bodies. The boy listened to the talk around him, learned which of the four were Brown and Wheeler, the dead law officers, and then screwed up enough courage to touch those two—a shivery experience he never forgot.

Most accounts of the affair state that the dead outlaws were buried in the little frontier graveyard at Medicine Lodge. T. A. McNeal writes that all of them were later dug up, probably winding up as skeletons in doctors offices, but one elderly resident of the town says that Brown was never buried there. Instead, his sad, pretty wife drove into town that warm May day in a lumber wagon and claimed his body. She had it put into the seat beside her and drove away, taking him home to Caldwell.

Meanwhile, Medicine Lodge prepared to pay tribute to its murdered bankers by draping all its business houses in the black crepe of mourning and turning out in total for their funerals. Wiley Payne's funeral was held in the Presbyterian church on Friday, "the house being crowded to its utmost capacity," and he was buried with Masonic honors. Geppert's funeral was held in the same church on Sunday. Apparently he was even more beloved than Wylie Payne; the crowd that attended "was so immense that many were unable to obtain even standing room inside the church."[13] Both Masonic and Odd Fellow lodges paid him honor.

On May 8, the editor of the *Cresset*, in a full column bordered in heavy black, paid his own and the community's respects to its departed citizens. Under the heading IN MEMORIUM, he wrote, "The last act of the horrible tragedy which stirred to their profoundest depths the sympathy and indignation of our people has closed. The curtain has lowered amid the sad, solemn sound of earth falling on the coffins of the dead, and we have now to measure, without undue praise but with the fullest charity, the character of our murdered citizens."

Following extensive eulogizing of Payne, he added, "Though we have sometimes passed sharp words with Mr. Payne through the columns of our respective papers, yet our personal relations with him have always been pleasant. We have differed widely with him at times but we have always admired his promptness and courage of expression. But whatever faults he had, let them be forgotten. What good deeds he did, what noble qualities he possessed, let their memory be green forever. And may time deal gently with the widow and the orphans."[14]

Of George Geppert he wrote more warmly, "It is remarkable that even while he lived we never heard anyone speak of him in a tone of bitterness, while there was a multitude whom he had placed under obligation by acts of accommodation and personal kindness. On the morning of the tragedy strong men wept like children and when the long procession wound slowly from the church to the burying ground on the prairie it was made up not simply of sorrowing relatives and respectful neighbors but was a gathering of people who came to bury a friend and mingle their tears in common at his sepulcher."

The first that Caldwell heard of the trouble in Medicine Lodge came in a telegram to Ben S. Miller, dated May 1, and signed by Charles H. Eldred. It read: "The bank robbers were Brown and Wheeler, marshal and deputy of Caldwell, and Smith and Wesley. All arrested. Tried to escape. Brown killed. Balance hung. Geppert dead, Payne will die."

On May 14 the *Cresset* gave front page prominence to Caldwell's reaction under the heading CALDWELL'S CONDOLENCE. Stated the city fathers: "Whereas, two men in whom the government and people of Caldwell have heretofore reposed great trust and confidence have, to the unutterable amazment and mortification of our citizens proved themselves to be murderers, robbers, cowards and villains of the worst type by their criminal attack on the Medicine Valley Bank at Medicine Lodge, and the wanton murder of Mr. Payne and Mr. Geppert. . . ."

The long resolution goes on to admit that Brown and Wheeler had received a large degree of credit by reason of their employment as peace officers, therefore Caldwell deemed it due the citizens of Medicine Lodge that official notice be taken of the terrible crime, and that a proper expression of the sentiment of the community and its deepest sympathy be extended. They also admitted to the "obloquy" which the murderers had brought on the community of Caldwell, and concluded that "while our people deplore the necessity for lynch law, they do most heartily approve of the summary manner in which the men of Medicine Lodge administered justice to the scoundrels who had so rudely invaded their community and brought death and sorrow to their doors."

On May 22 the *Cresset* carried two announcements which, in a manner, drained the bank robbery story dry of its news value. The first was an account of the public sale of the outlaws' possessions.

Wheeler's saddle had been sold for $22.00, Brown's for $25.00, Smith's for $10.00, and Wesley's for $24.50. Wesley's grey horse brought $120.00 and Smith's black mare $123.50. The bidding on these was good, as both were fine animals. Brown's and Wheeler's horses had been replevined by Ed Sample, attorney for Mrs. Burton and executor of Ben Burton, alias Ben Wheeler, and so were not offered for sale.

The second story recounted one of Medicine Lodge's first encounters with nation-wide fame as a result of the attempted robbery. "There was a considerable rush for the post office the other day when it was understood the *Police Gazette*, containing a full, illustrated account of the recent attempted bank robbery had arrived. The papers went like hot cakes on a frosty morning, but an expression of profound disgust spread over the buyers when they examined the illustration which represents one of the robbers as firing through the window of the cell at a crowd of long-haired, villainous looking men, one of whom is brandishing a two-inch rope over his head, while another is shooting at the robber at the window. The account states that the crowd battered in the jail door with a heavy plank, when John Wesley, who had a revolver secreted in his boot, opened fire on the crowd, but was immediately riddled with bullets, being shot nineteen times." Ah, what price fame!

But strangest of all is the story, hinted at by some, plainly spoken by others, involving the cashier, Geppert, in the robbery that didn't come off. T. A. McNeal states that the would-be robbers said the whole thing was a frame-up to save the cashier, who was short $10,000 in his accounts.

They had set the last day of April for the bank hold-up because Wylie Payne was to be out of town, shipping cattle. If this is true, it is but one more instance of the nemesis that pursued the unlucky bank robbers; for the hard rain and a falling market had caused the banker to change his mind at the last minute and postpone the shipment. Brown and the others, seeing him at his desk that fatal morning, when they had been promised he would be miles away, must have had some serious misgivings. At any rate, according to the story published in Payne's paper, the *Index*, on May 2, the outlaws ordered Geppert and Payne to throw up their hands. Mr. Geppert did so, but Mr. Payne leaped to seize his revolver. At this, concludes Mr. McNeal, the outlaws thought they had been double-crossed and quickly fired four shots. The cashier, shot through the heart, died instantly.

At no time, then or later, did either of the Medicine Lodge newspapers make any illusion to a shortage in the bank accounts, or to any connivance between Geppert and the outlaws; nor is it known to whom the men in the jail might have told this story, perhaps with the dim hope that it might buy them some time. And so, no doubt, we will never know.

The whole affair leaves other questions unanswered, too. Such as what became of the "golden gun." Brown, in his letter to his wife asked her not to sell the Winchester. But Chester C. Heizer states that "Sheriff C. F. Rigg collected the personal effects of Brown and intended to send them to Caldwell, however, before he could do so someone stole the engraved Winchester Brown prized so highly."[15] Heizer adds that he started searching for the golden gun in 1953, and eventually located it in a collection in Texas.

Another account has the Winchester passing through several owners' hands and finally winding up with Orval Shreeves, who acquired it from a Taos Indian in 1931 and gave it to the Kit Carson Historical House in Taos, New Mexico. And the writer of a highly irresponsible tale, "The Outlaw Marshal of Caldwell," concludes his story with the convenient statement that "Barney O'Connor kept the Winchester as a souvenir."

Wheeler had guns, too, but what happened to them at the time of their owner's hanging is another good question. Tradition has it that Caldwell gave Wheeler a silver mounted revolver at the same time that Brown received the gold-plated Winchester. If so, nothing of its history seems to have survived in print. However, Colin Rickards, in a carefully researched article entitled "Tracing a Bandit's Gun," states that in the summer of 1883 Assistant Marshal Benjamin F. Wheeler bought a Colt .44-40 Single Action Army Revolver in Hulbert's Gun Store in Caldwell. On the back-strap he stamped "Ben Wheeler, Caldwell, Kansas, 1883," nothing more. Rickards, compiling the story of the robbery, makes this statement, "As I write this, Ben's pistol lies before me. It looks just like any other Colt S. A. .44-40, with its $5\frac{1}{2}$ inch barrel and its Colt grips. Battered perhaps—a heretic, in years gone by, used the butt as a hammer and the marks are still visible—but otherwise in good condition.

"It is now owned by an English gun collector, Harry Leah of Todmorden, Lancashire, who bought it from a British gundealer. How it came to this side of the Atlantic is anybody's guess."[16]

There is one more strange story about Ben Wheeler's gun, his other gun. Orville Pfost of Medicine Lodge owns a gun and here is the story of how it came to him. His uncle, Henry Peters, a blacksmith in Byron, Oklahoma, many years ago took the gun in payment of an old smithing debt from an old man who said he "got it from a bank robber." In 1927 Peters gave the gun to Pfost, who then lived in Oklahoma but later moved to Medicine Lodge. There are four notches on each upper edge of the grip, but whether or not they mean anything important is not known. The gun's most interesting feature is Wheeler's "autograph" on one of the rubber grips. It is simply a wheel, carved into the grip, with the screw head as the hub. To the right of the screw are the carved letters ER. Inside the same grip is the full name Ben, then the wheel, with the screw hole as the hub, and the letters ER. Knife-cut into the grip beside the name is the date, 1882.[17]

Today in Medicine Lodge, if you visit the First National Bank, its president, Chester Fullerton, will take one of the hanging nooses, somehow still intact after eighty-five years, from his top desk drawer for your critical, and perhaps cringing, inspection. And if you'll walk across to the office of the Ford dealer, you can still see the ornate partitions that railed off the Medicine Valley Bank office and vault from the customers' side of the room at the time of the hold up. With their brown marble bases and heavy carved posts and rails they have sturdily withstood the passage of the years.

Indian encampment at Medicine Lodge peace council. From a sketch by John Howland in *Harper's Weekly*, November 16, 1867. *Courtesy Kansas State Historical Society.*

Peace Commission encampment at Medicine Lodge peace council. From a sketch by James E. Taylor in *Frank Leslie's Illustrated Newspaper*, November 23, 1867. *Courtesy Kansas State Historical Society.*

Satanta, Kiowa chief. *Courtesy Smithsonian Institution.*

Ten Bears, Comanche chief. *Courtesy Smithsonian Institution.*

Little Raven, Arapaho chief. *Courtesy Kansas State Historical Society.*

Black Kettle, Cheyenne chief. *Courtesy Oklahoma Historical Society.*

Peace Commissioners at Fort Laramie prior to the southern treaty talks at Medicine Lodge. L to R: A. H. Terry, W. S. Harney, W. T. Sherman (not at Medicine Lodge), Sioux squaw, N. G. Taylor, S. F. Tappan, C. C. Augur. *Courtesy National Archives.*

Issuing clothing to the Comanche Indians at Medicine Lodge. From a sketch by James E. Taylor in *Frank Leslie's Illustrated Newspaper*, November 23, 1867. *Courtesy Kansas State Historical Society.*

Cabin built in 1870, near Aetna, Kansas. Used by Comanche Pool cowboys.

Medicine Valley Bank officials killed in 1884 robbery. L: E. W. (Wylie) Payne, president. R: George Geppert, cashier.

Posse members who captured the 1884 bank robbers. Top row, L to R: Tom Doran, Barney O'Connor, Alec McKinney, Vernon Lytle. Middle row, L to R: Lee Bradley, Roll Clark, Wayne McKinney. Front row, L to R: George Freidley, John Fleming. Howard Martin, Nate Priest, and Charlie Talliaferro are not in the picture.

Jackass Canyon where outlaws were captured.

Outlaws in front of jail after capture. Front row, L to R: John Wesley, Hendry Brown, William Smith, Ben Wheeler. The would-be bridegroom who wrote up the story for the New York Times can be seen between Smith and Wheeler.

NINE

Grand Hotel, Flood

1885

As the excitement of that last day of April 1884 died away and the people of Medicine Lodge had time to take stock, they began to realize to what extent the death of the bankers, especially Payne, had struck at the heart of the community. The bank, the troubled Comanche Cattle Pool, the *Index*, all had lost their leader; and even the magnificent new hotel had lost its chief promoter.

Since the days of Updegraff's little log hotel, Medicine Lodge had never had a hostelry that completely met its needs. To fill this pressing demand, E. W. Payne had proposed the construction of a hotel "worthy of the town of Medicine Lodge," and on January 25, 1884, had called a meeting of all interested persons to form an organization, the Hotel Building Association, to carry out the project. The board of directors included Payne, W. W. Cook, W. W. Standiford, D. Van Slyke, and George Geppert.

Plans were drawn for a most imposing structure, three stories above a basement, to be built of a half-million bricks of local manufacture. The building was to be fifty-five by seventy-six feet, with fifty sleeping rooms, sample rooms, reading rooms, parlors, a dining room, and a commodious office. The total cost was to be about $23,000. The association members bought stock in the company and sold shares to their friends. Standiford and Youmans donated the site at South Main Street and Washington Avenue. The fine structure was under way when Payne and Geppert were killed, and since no man is indispensable the other board members went ahead with the building. Perhaps they looked on the big hotel as something of a memorial to the two men who would not now see their dream framed in stone.

As the lofty walls went up on Main Street that summer, they looked so fine that the owners of other businesses up and down the street decided they had better do something about their own buildings. The result was a lusty boom all along the main street. Some hurried to put up new structures worthy of hobnobbing with the new hotel, others painted and spruced up the ones they had.

The Grand Hotel, slated to open very early in 1885, was plagued by the usual problem of such establishments—delays in the arrival of the necessary freight. The *Index* of February 13 carried this half apologetic announcement: "The opening of the Grand Hotel will not likely occur before the 24th or 25th instant, owing to the delay in getting in the furniture and fixtures. All of the goods have been shipped but part of the lot is sidetracked somewhere. As soon as the carpets and furniture are here it will be but the work of a few days to have the house ready for guests." The subsequent non-arrival of the silverware further held things up, but on March 4 the Grand was "formally opened." In addition to the rooms mentioned above, there was also a billiard room and a barber shop to serve the patrons.

An elegant writing desk dominated the lobby. About ten feet long, the heavy, carved desk was topped by a lofty mirrored back panel, bordered by twenty-three framed, colored glass advertisements (the Yellow Pages of Medicine Lodge). The attractive ads featured the town's most prominent business establishments: drugstores, general stores, loan agents, attorneys, lumber yards, boots and shoes, the bank, livery stables. The latter pictured fancy buggies and fine teams traveling at a high-stepping gait.

The grand opening featured a ball and supper, and any and all who cared to pay the price of admission were welcome. It is said that about one hundred couples availed themselves of the opportunity to while away a joyous evening of dancing and feasting, to music furnished by the Medicine Lodge String Band, "an organization fast gaining notoriety as first class musicians." All fashionable dinners, wedding suppers, and such like were held at the Grand for a good many years thereafter. That they were truly elegant affairs is attested by this sample menu, listing the fare to which the guests sat down one day in 1886, to help celebrate a wedding.

SOUPS
Pat a foi D'Orleans
FISH
Broiled Mackeral Tomato Sauce
MAYONNAISE
Chicken Salad Russian Salad a la Duchess
BOILED
Ham, with Champagne Sauce Buffalo Tongue
ROAST
Turkey with Cranberry Sauce Sirloin of Beef with Pan Gravy
Haunch of Venison, a la en Brochane Mallard Duck, with Jelly
ENTREES
Broiled Quail on Toast Roman Punch Saute Turkey Giblets
Tenderloin of Beef Glazed with Mushrooms, a la Blanch
Boneless Turkey
VEGETABLES
Mashed and Brown Potatoes Succotash Stewed Tomatoes
BREAD
Cream Bread Boston Brown Bread Hot Corn Bread
PASTRY
Mince Pie Apple Pie Lemon Pie
Fruit Pudding with Old Port
FRUITS
Oranges Lemons Apples Nuts Candies
BEVERAGES
French Coffee Black and Green Tea Sweet Milk Buttermilk

The first lessees of the hotel were Frank E. Lockwood, a popular train conductor, and Ben Phillips, of Wellington, Kansas. About ten years later George Horney bought the hotel, and it has since been operated continually by members of the Horney family.

Most of the town's prominent people "ate out" there on Sundays and special days at "two bits" a plate. There was even a special rate for families, making it almost cheaper to take the wife and kids to the Grand on Sundays and holidays than to feed them at home. Many a family man drove his carriage to the front door with a flourish, cramped the front wheels, and deboarded wife and progeny. When all had eaten to the point of suffocation, father walked up to the counter, paid the bill and bought a five cent cigar, feeling like he was really "living up town."

During World War I, when the cost of help rose so high that it was impossible for Mr. Horney to go on serving the twenty-five cent dinners, he closed the dining room.

Old-timers in Medicine Lodge remember how strong the smell of cigar smoke used to be in the lobby, when the men of the town gathered there by day and by night to play endless games of pitch. Today a coke machine and a TV set, almost the only concessions to modernity, seem somehow out of place among the memories of past elegance. For the big hotel, long outstanding for a town the size of Medicine Lodge, is still a noted landmark, and still in business, ornate desk, high ceilings, wide transoms, and all.

But for Medicine Lodge, disaster was only taking a brief holiday. A scant six weeks after the gala hotel opening, heavy clouds banked the northwest horizon at dusk on the evening of April 20. As darkness came on, distant flashes of lightning lit the black cloud bank and the rumble of thunder drifted over the hills. The storm came closer, with more livid flashes of lightning and crashes of thunder, but prairie dwellers are accustomed to violent storms, and the people along the Medicine went to bed as usual.

This storm, however, was different. The rain came suddenly and with raging fury, and "continued without interruption for five hours,"[1] a savage storm such as the Pilgrim Bard described in his "Legend of Flower Pot Mountain."

The early town of Medicine Lodge was built on a rise of land between the Medicine Lodge River and Elm Creek. Spring Creek, rising a little way west of Elm, ran south past the town, washing the feet of the highland town site and connecting with Elm Creek a few hundred yards below. As the town grew, new residence lots were laid out on a lower flat between the occupied site and Elm Creek and new houses were quickly built there.

Spring Creek was a clear, beautiful spring branch, scarce two miles long. Elm was a shallow stream about eighty feet wide, rippling between banks four to six feet high. A little below the flat stood a large grove of tall, well-branched old elm trees, the most beautiful spot in the county and a natural picnic and camp ground. All season long covered wagons pulled in to stay overnight, or for several days, while the travelers rested, washed clothes, renewed supplies, or looked for a suitable homestead location. On summer evenings and Sundays many a family group or gathering of young folks sought the grassy shade for picnics. On that Monday evening before the storm ten wagons sheltered in the grove and some forty people tended their camp chores, then went to bed, in tents, in wagons, and under wagons.

The land on either side of the Medicine River and Elm Creek is high, rolling prairie, gashed by numerous canyons and washouts. Down these steep-banked ravines the water dashed in a terrific torrent that night, swelling the river and its tributaries. Barber County settlers living along these streams had been careful to build their houses and corrals on high ground, well above the known high water marks, but none had foreseen such a flood as now swept down upon them in the night.

The *Index* for that week told the story. "There are different theories as to what caused the terrible rush of water. Some say it was the bursting of a mighty water spout; others that the unprecedented rain was the cause. We incline to the latter view, but at the same time can't understand how such a sudden rise could occur simultaneously on the Medicine River and Elm Creek, ten or twelve miles apart, where the rise started. And it did come suddenly. The experience of everyone who witnessed the flood was similar. A mighty roaring was heard above them, a look outside brought to view huge billows rolling in a most frightful manner toward them. Everything movable was on the waves and carried with the flood."

Big trees and debris of all kinds were rushing downstream with the torrent, crashing into houses and sheds, wrenching them from their moorings and sweeping them along with the rest of the wreckage. "Fence posts were snapped off or pulled entirely out of the ground and barbed wire was broken as easily as a man would snap a twine string in two." The water was full of heavy rolling quicksand, and "woe to the unfortunate human or dumb brute that chanced to be caught in the whirling mass of water and ruins."

The heaviest damage to property and the greatest loss of life occurred in the flat, or bottom, east of town. Until Monday evening fifteen homes stood there, "neat and tasty, surrounded by fences and gardens." By four o'clock Tuesday morning all the lowland between Spring and Elm creeks was under water, a flood three to ten feet higher than the highest water marks shown on the old trees.

"The screams of those floating down the turbulent stream could be plainly heard up in the city," reported the *Index*, "and these plaintive appeals for help from the drowning, the lowing of cattle, neighing of horses, braying of mules, squealing of pigs, crashing of timbers and the terrible rush and roar of the waters, were heart-rending and sickening. The cries were taken up by the people on shore, and soon the whole population was alarmed. Church bells were rung and in the rain and darkness confusion was everywhere. The relatives of those who lived in the bottom were running up and down the bank of Spring Creek, appealing for the rescue of their dear ones."[2]

Just before daylight, in their eagerness to help, Sheriff Rigg, Postmaster Van Slyke, and Boardman Smith launched a hastily made raft or boat into the raging creek, near the widow Payne's yard fence, and tried to cross to the homes on the east bottom. But the boat was quickly dashed to pieces and the three men spilled into ten feet of surging water. Smith struck a high spot of ground and stayed there; the other two were carried a quarter mile downstream, where they managed to climb into trees. It was several hours before the rescuers dared to leave their perches and again extend a helping hand.

Daylight came at last, revealing the extent of the disaster, making known who had survived, how many had perished, and the fearful extent of property damage and destruction: a devastation so widespread that it was several days before it could be totaled. As the day wore on many at first thought to be drowned were found in trees along the streams. Of the fifteen new homes on the bottom, four were gone, along with nearly all the outbuildings and fences.

All that morning volunteers by the hundreds engaged in the search for survivors and the dead. Lumber yards offered lumber free for making rafts, and a relief fund was set up by Standiford, Youmans, and Eldred, who started it off with a donation of $100. The district courtroom[3] was turned into a morgue, where bodies were taken to be properly cared for and dressed for burial. "Nice coffins were furnished by John Higgins," according to the *Index*, "and into these the bodies were laid as fast as prepared."

The full story of the storm was gradually pieced together, with tales of miraculous escapes and of tragic drownings. Bunk Ward, with his wife and child, had just moved into one of the new houses on Spring Creek. When the roar of the flood wakened him and he jumped out of bed, he stepped into six inches of cold water. At the same instant the outer door was blown open and pieces of furniture and drift swirled into the room from outside. Hauling his wife and baby out of bed, they climbed frantically into the attic. Moments later the house began to move. Bunk punched a hole through the shingles and stuck his head outside. By the lights in the houses on higher ground, he could see that his own house was sailing rapidly downstream, and all around him he heard the frightful sounds of the flood, human and animal screams, and the roar of the maddened waters. The house crashed through treetops, dipped and swirled, and finally struck something solid, spun around in the boiling water and stopped. By the morning's light he saw that the house had been carried nearly half a mile from its rightful site, though not even a window was broken.

Frank Shepler was far less fortunate. Wakened at four in the morning, and with the water already a foot deep in his new house on the bottom, he and his wife and baby also took refuge in the upper story. Soon afterward they felt the house moving and the walls spreading, then the structure seemed to swing to the west and a great wave knocked the east gable in. With water pouring into the room, Shepler boosted his wife and child through the hole onto the roof, but as he tried to climb up himself, a heavy piece of flotsam knocked him off and the house was carried away. Shepler swirled on with the flood, dashing into trees and floating wreckage. After awhile he was swept into the main channel of Elm Creek and carried downstream. Finally, somewhere south of town, he caught hold of two scantlings nailed together, and held onto them until they lodged in a tree. With the coming of daylight he struck out for land, swimming some fifty yards before he could pull himself out on the bank, where he lay exhausted for a time, then staggered to the nearest farmhouse. The man was frightfully bruised and one of his ribs was broken. The front part of his house was found that day, on Standiford's ranch eight miles south of town, but no one had seen his wife or the baby.

Another new house, nearly opposite the Shepler place, had been one of the first to go. Its occupants, Jerry Gibbs, his daughter, and little granddaughter, were all drowned. The bodies were found later, but no trace of the house.

The flood victims who had taken refuge in tree branches during the night were in dire circumstances by morning, for most were in their night clothes, and some had no clothes at all. A cold wind blew, chilling the wet and miserable throng. To get aid and comfort to these unfortunates, a rope was thrown across the angry stream from the Medicine Lodge site and made fast to a tree by one of the marooned men. Food and dry clothing were then passed over on the little tramway, until rescues could be attempted.

Another boat, quickly knocked together by a carpenter, E. Z. Larash, put into the still violent waters of Spring Creek at eight o'clock that morning, in the hope of picking up some of those clinging to trees above the flood. But the frail craft shattered against a tree before it had made a single rescue. Its builder managed to grab a willow and save himself. Later, as quickly as it could be done, a stout cable, tied to the original tram rope and pulled across the creek, was rigged with a pulley and seat. Soon volunteers were making the trip across to help in the search for bodies; and victims, rescued from their precarious perches in the trees, were pulled back across to safety.

Three men, Porter Secat, G. W. Baricklow, and Charles Smith, on their way home to Cowley County from a trip to Clark County to take up claims, had camped in the grove that Monday evening. When the flood struck, Secat and Baricklow stayed in the wagon but Smith decided to try getting out of the bottom on one of their horses. His body was later found in the timber south of town.

Most tragic of all was the fate of the Samuel Maddox family. With his wife and eight children, the old man was on his way from Chautauqua County, Kansas, to Montana Territory. They had a good outfit, two wagons, nine head of horses and mules, a large tent, a goodly supply of household furniture, and $1,500 in cash in a trunk in one of the wagons.

The family was sound asleep in the tent under the trees when the first onrushing wave of water struck. Wakened by water flooding into the tent, they all ran for the wagons. The older members boosted the smaller children into the wagons, and then tried to turn the rigs against some of the big trees to keep them from being swept away, but the water rose so quickly and dashed against them with such force that they had to give up and climb the nearest trees to save themselves.

The wagons whirled away in the darkness. One lodged against a cluster of trees in the grove, but the other was carried to a point just south of town, where it overturned, flinging its human freight into the flood. The oldest girl, a pretty lass with long golden hair, caught hold of a tree, climbed it, and stood high among its new-leaved branches, screaming in utter fright. Her terrible shrieks, it was later said, could be heard a mile away, bringing hundreds of people to stand on the opposite bank, helpless and sick at heart. About a hundred yards below, her thirteen-year-old brother held onto the branches of another tree, likewise crying piteously for help.

As daylight paled the darkness there were some in the crowd who insisted the screaming girl held a baby in her arms, then others said they saw her drop the child. In the frenzied excitement, some members of the crowd on the bank began to offer $500 to anyone who would try to cross the roiling stream to rescue the girl and her brother—but none dared to make the attempt.

And then came P. B. Cole, his son Sam, and Frank McAlister, all on horseback. The Coles lived three miles east of Medicine Lodge, beyond the flooded area, and had just learned what had happened in the town and along the creek. They rode straightway into the water, swimming their horses toward the marooned girl and boy. Mr. Cole took the girl onto his stout little horse and returned to the bank with her, while McAlester brought the boy out in the same manner. And when the rescue had been accomplished, the crowd let out with a cheer that could be heard for miles.

The father and his eldest son, with the two brought out on the horses, were all of the family that survived that night of storm and flood. Later in the day the mother's body was found, half a mile below the grove where her son and daughter clung to the trees, nearly buried in driftwood and sand. The bodies of the two youngest boys were recovered nearby, the other two girls were found not far away, and the body of the eighteen-year-old son was taken out of the mud at the Kiowa ford, far downstream. During the search, Sam Cole and the oldest Maddox son found the other wagon box and the trunk, still intact, with the $1,500 inside.

By Tuesday evening ten bodies lay in coffins in the district courtroom, while hundreds filed by, seeking family members and neighbors still among the missing. Not a body was free of bruises and scratches, though tender and careful handling had almost succeeded in hiding such unpleasant reminders of the horror of the flood. By Wednesday morning the graves were dug, and at eleven o'clock the first coffin was carried to the cemetery, after prayer by a minister and a song service by some of the good women of Medicine Lodge.

More than $1,000 was raised through donations, to give aid to those who had suffered most from the flood. But, as in nearly every disaster, there were a few in the community who sought to profit from the misfortunes of their neighbors by rifling boxes and trunks found in wrecked homes or carried down the river, some for many miles. Even more ghoulish were the acts of some who drove into the flooded area and loaded up scattered lumber and posts for their own use. So much of this was done that law officers had to insert notices in the local papers to the effect that a search would be made and warrants issued for the return of all property that could be identified.

As the days passed, the search for still missing persons went on, and Barber County residents began to make a final total of the damages. Even those whose buildings and fences had not been harmed found that most of the good topsoil had been washed from their ploughed fields.

And from down in the southeast corner of the county, where it hadn't rained at all, came some strange stories of the flood. Over at New Kiowa, three miles from the river, the residents could not believe the first stories they heard: that so many people had actually drowned, that damage and destruction had been so widespread. Oh sure! They knew the old Medicine was often cantankerous, like when the cowboy, Clark Bunton, and Julia Conine were married, over in old Kiowa in January, 1878. Bunton had had to swim the river, which was on one of its rampages, to get to Medicine Lodge to get his license so the wedding could come off on the day set for it. And only the past January the stage and mail hadn't been able to cross for four days due to high water and rotten ice. And even then the first stage that tried to cross upset, throwing the passengers into the icy water; and the next team put into the river almost drowned. But a flood bad enough to do all the damage they'd just heard about must have been stretching the facts a bit.

Then on Wednesday Tom Doran and Alph Updegraff came in from Medicine Lodge by crossing the river in a boat at old Kiowa and swore to the truth of the tragic story. Then Jim Van Hook, the stage driver between old Kiowa and Harper, came back from Harper and told how the morning before he had started his daily trip with a lady and several men passengers in his stage. Just as he was driving into the river crossing the wall of water came rushing down the valley. By lashing his four-horse team into a dead run he barely managed to clear the ford and drive his careening stage out of the water course ahead of the foaming water. And there, from the higher ground, while he rested his heaving teams, they watched the battered hulk of part of a house go rocking by, and from its top a woman, Mrs. Shepler, begged frantically for help. But there was nothing any of them could do, and a few days later the poor woman's body was dug out of the mud four miles below the ford. Then Mrs. Bessie Norris, of old Kiowa, came in and told her tale. Mrs. Norris, from her farm home near the river, had gone down to the stream to look at some fish lines she had set the night before, and there she was almost caught in the flood that reached the ford a little later. And even there, thirty miles or more below the junction of Elm Creek with the Medicine Lodge River, the force of the flood was still great enough to carry the Norris' old iron mowing machine several miles downstream.

Early in May, two weeks after the flood, someone found the Shepler baby's body on the river's edge. Of the victims of that dark and awful night, the baby was the eighteenth and last ever to be recovered.[4]

The six members of the Maddox family are still buried in the Medicine Lodge graveyard, and P. B. Cole's granddaughter, Mrs. Lois Cook, faithfully puts flowers on their graves every Memorial Day.

Farewell, and be a requiem said,
For one and all who perished.
Sweet be your sleep, though buried deep
'Neath sand, or in the churchyard laid,
Your memory shall be cherished.[5]

TEN

New Industry, Culture, Politics, Famous Citizens

1885-1900

Disaster and adversity of one kind or another had lived with Medicine Lodge and Barber County most of the time: the distressing county swindles, the Indian troubles, two very bad winters, a dry summer or two, the wild day of murder and mayhem at the Medicine Valley Bank, other assorted murders, and the big flood. But with the pluck and determination of most pioneers, these, too, consistently turned their backs on the misfortunes of the past and faced the future with ever renewed hope and courage.

And things *were* looking up that summer of 1885. Change was everywhere in the land; the last of the big cattle outfits were moving out, settlers by the hundreds had moved in and more were coming, bringing with them a burgeoning need for supplies of all kinds: building materials, barbed wire, food and clothing, wagons, and tools. More stores, more banks, more of everything was in demand. And, best of all, at last the railroad was coming to Medicine Lodge, bringing new industries and access to markets for the settlers' grain and produce. With business booming as it never had before, the county officials, with the blessing of most of the voters, set about building the courthouse they had twice paid for but didn't get.

The handsome brick building, finished in 1886, had no running water, either upstairs in the county offices or downstairs in the jail. When, a few years later, this luxury was available in the town, a bathtub was installed in the basement jail. Shortly afterward a man was lodged in one of the cells to await transportation to the State Insane Asylum at Fort Larned. The poor man was so filthy that one of the officers in charge remarked that he must not have had a bath since the last one his mother gave him.

That evening a drunk was shoved into the same cell. After a short period of such intimate association the second man, thoroughly sobered, decided he would never live through the night unless something was done. So he ran the bathtub full of water, put the crazy man in, and scrubbed him with the jail broom. Then he hoisted him back in bed, crawled in beside him, and slept peacefully through the night. The drunk was in good shape next morning, but the poor old crazy man was dead.

The Santa Fe rails reached Medicine Lodge in 1886, and the celebration that marked the coming was hardly over before plans were laid for a mammoth sugar factory in the town. Construction on the $100,000 refining plant began the next year. A total of 700,000 bricks and 250,000 feet of lumber went into the building of the three-story plant, which housed a one-million-gallon capacity syrup cistern and a huge ironclad, fireproof boiler. The plant's water supply came from a seven-acre lake, fed by a ditch from Elm Creek. Operating under the impressive name of the Medicine Lodge Sugar Works and Refining Company, the mill employed fifty men at a daily wage of two dollars and in 1889 turned out 511,000 pounds of sugar.

Many farmers were employed in raising sugar cane to supply the mill, and added prestige came to Medicine Lodge with the establishment, in 1892, of a government experimental station on the edge of town. There forty acres of sorghum crops were raised and tested, and in the adjacent laboratory twenty-six chemists tested all sugar made and shipped by the town plant. For two more years the business prospered, then declined and died, the last of seven such plants in Kansas to fail.

Other ambitious enterprises followed the sugar mill into Medicine Lodge. One of these was the big flour mill, another three-story plant. The mill, built by a man from Illinois at a cost of $4,000, was likewise operated by water power from the Elm Creek ditch. It had a capacity of 500 bushels of wheat per day, producing 200 sacks or fifty barrels of flour, which found a ready market as far away as Comanche County. After a life of only four years, the mill closed in 1894, due to an annual shortage of water during the busiest months, July to September, and the machinery was shipped back to Illinois.

Another short-lived big business in Medicine Lodge was the cheese factory and creamery. It was a co-operative industry and the surrounding farmers owned stock in the plant and contracted their milk to it. Although it had a daily capacity of 1,000 gallons of milk, it failed at the end of three years. There just wasn't enough milk in the area to keep it supplied.

The Tisdale ice plant, however, did a thriving business for a good many years. Tisdale's crew, filling a vast icehouse from the lake every winter when the ice was "prime," daily supplied the hotel, the homes, and the businesses of Medicine Lodge all through the long hot summer. With the advent of mechanical refrigeration, traffic in nature's product faded into oblivion.

A brick kiln and gypsum plant thrived for awhile, when the county seat and adjacent towns were racing each other to build the biggest business district. The plant's product was needed for all the stores and other buildings going up so hopefully along all the little main streets.

The cattle business was building up again in the county, too, small herds at first, in fenced pastures that a cowboy could hardly have found inside the Schluppe—Ballinger—Lane little 100,000-acre pasture of a decade earlier. But the cattle were better now, with good herd bulls inside the fences, too.

As early as 1899 O. L. Taylor of Trinidad, Colorado, established a Hereford ranch on land he bought near Elm Mills. There he built extensive improvements and brought in more than 200 head of registered Herefords, including some fine cows costing from $1,000 to $1,500 each. Taylor was soon shipping registered Herefords all over the country, to Hereford sales and to individual breeders. After five years of outstanding work with the breed, he turned the ranch over to a W. F. Rose, who soon disposed of the herd. But others, and other breeds, too, were soon to follow, gradually building Barber County herds into some of the finest in the nation.

The railroad brought another advantage with it to Medicine Lodge: culture, in the form of outstanding lecturers, fine touring stage shows, and other entertainment that had not been practical in the pre-railroad days.

The splendid opera house, seventy-five feet wide, two stories high, and fashionably ornate, had risen almost simultaneously with the Grand Hotel. George Geppert, cashier of the Medicine Valley Bank, began the structure in 1884 but did not live to see it finished the next year. Two months after Geppert's murder, his widow sold the property to Henry G. Thompson for $4,500. Thompson completed the opera house and then in 1891 sold it to G. M. Woodruff for $35,000, an enormous sum in those days, probably enough to purchase, for example, a 5,000-acre ranch in Barber County. Although the opera house was almost always referred to simply as "The Opera House," it was occasionally called, when a more formal title seemed in order, The Thompson Opera House, after its builder. Until well past the turn of the century, the opera house and the hotel were high fashion, for a dinner party at the hotel followed by a theater party at the opera house were the ultimate in social activity in Medicine Lodge. Today in Medicine Lodge there are few residents left who remember the opera house as it was in the days of its glory. Those who do were small children when its stage was in general use. Alice MacGregor recalls the Le Brein Opera Company and the fine show it staged there in her childhood. Most of the other shows, she said, were put on by stock companies, big and little, good and bad. The town's newspapers advertised the shows well in advance and commented on them afterward, and many of those pioneer reporters were pretty sharp drama critics. If the acting or the show itself deserved "roasting and basting" it got it.

After twenty-five years or so, the opera house began to be used less and less. Finally its main floor was rented to the owner of the new Ford agency and the huge upper floor was used merely for the storage of the town's unused odds and ends. The Medicine Lodge public library stands today on the old opera house corner.

Culture in other forms also, both religious and secular, came early to Medicine Lodge. The first religious service recorded in the little frontier town was held in March 1877, by a traveling Methodist preacher. The congregation met in the frame schoolhouse one Sunday each month after that whenever the circuit riding minister could get back to town. The Methodist Episcopal church building, the first in town to be used exclusively for the worship of God, was built in 1879 at a cost of $1,200. The parsonage, built in 1881, cost $300. Later, the one-room brick church was used during the week as a schoolroom, the student population having outgrown the schoolhouse. In 1907 the parsonage was torn down and a new one started—just in time to be carried away by the tornado of that year.

During those early years members of the Christian church, the United Brethern church, and the Presbyterian church also held services in the schoolhouse, each denomination having one Sunday a month. In 1878 the First Christian Church was organized; a church building was erected and dedicated two years later. The Presbyterians organized in 1880 and, after the Methodist church was built, held services there on the second and fourth Sundays of each month. They completed their own building early in 1884 and thereafter held regular services.

The Baptists organized in 1888, with W. A. Cain from Des Moines as pastor. The First Baptist Church first held its services in a three-room house, but built and dedicated its own building in 1901. The Second Baptist Church was organized in 1897. A Negro church, its charter members numbered thirty. Its first services were held in the courthouse, and then in the home of a member, Thomas Carter. This church's building was erected and dedicated in 1908 but abandoned in 1919, after which its members were assimilated by the town's other denominations.

The Episcopalians organized in 1889 and ten years later built their own building on North Walnut Street. The Seventh Day Adventists began meeting in various community schoolhouses in 1900, while the Assembly of God church was founded in 1928 during a series of tent meetings held on a vacant lot. Contributions made during the meetings resulted in the building of a tabernacle that same summer.

Other small denominations held meetings in various places in the neighborhood. The Free Methodists, under Moses Wright, first held services in the Wright schoolhouse near Hardtner. Most of its members were from Sharon but some came from Medicine Lodge.

Another organization which ministered to the spiritual needs of this pioneer community was the American Bible Society. Its chief purpose was to distribute Bibles to people who could not afford to buy them for themselves. About two hundred were given away in Barber County during the settlement years.

Lodges, too, as in most early settlements of the midwest, played an important part in the affairs of Medicine Lodge. The first to organize there was Pioneer Lodge No. 179 of the Odd Fellows. Its first meeting was held in February 1881. It had seven members and pre-dated the Masonic Delta Lodge No. 77 by only a month. By the time its charter was granted a year later it boasted twenty-two members. By 1910 the Odd Fellows had forty-one members, the Masons forty-seven, and both had their own meeting halls.

The ladies of the town reversed the above order of organization when the Eastern Stars instituted their auxiliary to Delta Lodge in 1885. The Rebekah Lodge, auxiliary to Pioneer 179 was instituted a year later but soon ceased to function. Revived in 1908, it became a strong chapter. Both auxiliaries are active today.

Antedating even these pioneer feminine societies was the W.C.T.U. of Medicine Lodge. Organized in 1884 by some militant ladies from the national headquarters, the union started out with a membership of twenty women and a few men. Mrs. Cain, the Baptist minister's wife, was its first president. Although staunchly against the state's illegal liquor traffic, the group did not really hit its stride until Carry Nation came to town and lent her belligerent support. Mrs. Cain and others of the female membership helped with prayer meetings and saloon smashings, and later kept Senator Chester Long supplied with petitions stating their stand on the question of seating or not seating congressmen-elect from Kansas and other states.

In March 1892, thirty-seven women banded together in the opera house to form a Woman's Equal Suffrage Association. Anna Shaw, a minister from New York who travelled over the country marshalling the ladies under her sufferage banner, was on hand for the organization meeting. The Medicine Lodge chapter was, therefore, officially named the Anna Shaw Equal Suffrage Association. Although the chapter was active for only two years, it, in company with thousands of like organizations, no doubt did its part in winning the vote for women. Kansas adopted women's suffrage in 1912, ten years before the nation as a whole accorded them the right to vote.

Probably antedating all other ladies clubs in Medicine Lodge was one known simply as the Monday Afternoon Club. This club was important because it was instrumental in providing the town with a library. Early in its history Senator Long offered to present the club with 250 new books if the ladies would institute a library and call it The Lincoln Library. The ladies would, and could. They immediately organized a Library Association, obtained the "loan" of an unused room in the courthouse, and installed the books. Each week one of the members served as a volunteer librarian. They operated in this manner until 1911, when the Association received a legacy from a local estate for the purpose of erecting a library building. At this point the city took over and provided tax money with which to operate the library

Barber County has produced a host of outstanding women and men. Perhaps the rough times endured and overcome by the pioneer citizens had something to do with it. In any case, David Demosthenes Leahy, better known as "Dynamite Dave," noted Kiowa editor, had this to say: "Considering its small population, Barber County in my time had a greater variety of talented men than probably any other county in the United States, certainly more than any other county in Kansas. It had statesmen and near-statesmen galore. I cannot recall any other county of equal age and size that had three of its old-timers in Congress and one in the Senate. It had a poet in Scott Cummins—the Pilgrim Bard of Mule Creek—who should have been the laureate of Kansas. It had an author and humorist in Tom McNeal whose wit is as refreshing as that of Will Rogers. It had at least two internationally famous women —Lucille Mulhall, a thrilling rodeo figure, and Carry Nation, the smashing enemy of John Barleycorn."[1]

Lucille Mulhall was the first woman in history to be publicized as a "cowgirl." Daughter of Zach Mulhall, she could put most men to shame with her speed and skill at riding, roping, and steer tying. She was the first to hold a world's championship award for women ropers. Ed Lemmon tells how she was a star roper and "tie-down performer from 1895 to 1900" and held the ladies championship during those years.[2] Will Rogers says: "You can go tell the world that . . . Lucille Mulhall was the first well-known cowgirl. She became a very expert roper, and was the first girl that could rope and tie a Steer, not only do it but do it in such time that it would make a good roper hustle to beat her."[3] For example, competing against twenty-seven men in El Paso when she was fifteen, she roped and tied her steer in the shortest time of any of them, 29½ seconds. That same spring, with her father and brother, she rode in President McKinley's inaugural parade in Washington D. C.; the Mulhall family had been invited by Theodore Roosevelt, vice-president elect. During the next two years she won various medals, saddles, and trophies. Then in 1903, at Fort Worth, she won $10,000, first money for the best time at the big show for tying three steers in one minute, fifty-one seconds, the fastest time ever made up until then for roping and tying three steers. In 1905 Lucille was a sensation at Madison Square Garden. She went on to win many other plaudits, retired at thirty, and was later killed in an automobile accident in Oklahoma.

"Dynamite Dave" Leahy was himself a colorful character. He came to Kansas in 1887 to clerk in a Caldwell grocery store. Told he had to sleep in the store, he made his bed in the front window. When he woke up that first morning and looked out, he saw three dead men in the street outside. Such, he often said, was his introduction to that wild border town. He may have been exaggerating a bit, as he sometimes did later, after he became the editor of the Kiowa *Herald*.

Once, when news was slow, he reported that a little girl had fallen into a bored well in western Kansas. When the mother discovered what had happened and that the child, though far down in the hole, was unhurt, she frantically summoned help. A desperate effort to save the child then began. According to the *Herald*, men were working in relays, day and night, digging down around the pipe. Eastern papers picked up the story and wired for details. Realizing he had opened a literary mine, Dave enlarged on the tale. When the rescuers were getting near the child he permitted her to slip down a little farther, thereby prolonging the nation's agony. In the end he let the little girl be rescued, little the worse for the suspenseful days spent in the well.

Leahy got another good idea from an account he read concerning a U.S. Consul to Madagascar who got in trouble with the French government, was arrested, taken to Paris, and imprisoned there for awhile. Leahy's take-off on the story was a report on a Frenchman down in Oklahoma who was captured by some Negroes and held in a cave, all by way of getting even with the French for holding the American. The story crossed the ocean and came to the notice of the French government. The French Department of State at once took the matter up with our Department of State. Our government didn't know anything about any such affair but, at the pressing request of the French, a special agent was dispatched to Oklahoma to investigate. The agent could uncover nothing: no kidnapped Frenchman, no Negro kidnappers, and no cave in the locality described in the story. After much urgent diplomatic correspondence, the French government was finally convinced that no citizen of France was being held in durance vile in Oklahoma.

While in Kiowa, Leahy knew Zach Mulhall, to whom Will Rogers owed his start to fame.[4] In a story written in 1934, telling something of the time he spent there in 1887-88, Dave wrote, "Zach had an eight-year-old son who used to ride a pony helter-skelter through the streets. He gave me the boy's picture and asked me to write a story about him. I had it elaborately displayed in the *Police Gazette*, which had not an excellent reputation, especially among religious people, and I thought Zach would trounce me for it. I avoided him for several days, but finally ran into him on the sidewalk. He hopped onto me, drug me into the York-Key store and dressed me from head to foot in the most picturesque suit of clothes on hand, including a ten-gallon hat."[5] Thus dressed up, Leahy wanted to go somewhere to show off. President Cleveland was coming to Kansas City with his young and handsome bride. So, with his friends, Ben Key, Oliver Ewell, M. S. Justis, Tommy Wilson, and some other Democrats, he went to Kansas City.

About his editorship, Leahy said that in certain cases he felt it his duty to "scorch, blister, roast and baste" officials who didn't toe the line according to his own opinions. So, after the custom of the time, he went after the editors of rival newspapers with every derogatory word at his command. His attacks usually began, "Our loathed contemporary," and might continue, "That unmitigated scoundrel and professional blackleg, the bilious nondescript that runs the ———," or "The *non compos mentis* journalist, the flagrant blatherskite, this audacious poltroon, this cantankerous jackass, this lunatic at large, this brainless chicken-eating dude." His "loathed contemporaries" usually returned the compliments in kind, but when Leahy referred to one as a "Brachylurous besulcanus amphibious baralapus," the poor fellow kept still, as he had no idea what Dave meant; and the Kiowa editor, not being certain either, also held his fire for awhile.

Dynamite Dave Leahy's stay in Barber County lasted only six months, but, as one of his "contemporaries" said, "he managed to raise considerable hell while he was here." From Kiowa he went to Wichita, where he was editor of the *Eagle* for many years and also wrote for the Kansas City *Times*.

Of the famous Barber County citizens Leahy mentioned, Chester I. Long and Jerry Simpson were especially outstanding. Of them, on the occasion of Long's funeral, Leahy wrote: "Last week I followed the remains of Chester I. Long to their final resting place on Fairmount Ridge, among the marble vaults of the palatial Old Mission Mausoleum.

"As the moving cortege skirted Maple Grove Cemetery I glanced at the resting place of Jerry Simpson, a few yards from the road. I stood at that grave twenty-nine years ago and saw the wasted body of the sturdy old commoner received into the fond embrace of kindly Mother Earth."[6]

He then recounted his memories of his two old friends, memories going back to the year he first came to Barber County. The Cleveland-Harrison presidential campaign was in full swing in 1888 when Andrew Jackson Jones of Medicine Lodge, editor of the *Barber County Democrat*, invited Dynamite Dave over from Kiowa to help win the election for Cleveland. Long was about Leahy's age at the time, in his twenties, the handsomest man Leahy had ever seen, and the best dressed. In fact, as he at first assessed him, he was "too darned nice" to be popular among the young fellows of the town. Simpson, on the other hand, was middle-aged but "by reason of good health and happy spirits hadn't entirely lost the ways of youth."

The Democrats lost that election, of course, and immediately after the returns were in, the Republicans decided to "jubilate." A feature of their celebration was the capture of Andrew Jackson Jones, who was to be compelled to make a public speech for the victorious Harrison. But Jones had retired to a speakeasy to help another Democrat, Tom Eads—who had bet a farm on Cleveland—drown his sorrow. And by the time the Republicans found him he was in no condition for speech making, so the jubilators captured Leahy instead, loaded him into a dray wagon and took him to his audience, awaiting him on the highest point on Main Street. Deciding to be a good sport about the whole thing, Leahy made the speech. It wasn't long, he said, but it was well padded with a "lot of pleasant bunk" about Mr. Long, who stood in the wagon beside him, "like an Adonis in modern dress," presiding over the meeting.

"There stands a man," orated the shanghaied speaker, pointing at Long, "a man of the future, a man physically, mentally, and sartorially fit to fill a seat in the U.S. Senate, or an ambassadorship at the court of St. James." After more of the same, he retired to the cheers of the multitude. His close friendship with Long began at that time, "and Mr. Long," he wrote, "has told me fifty times since then that that little fool speech first stirred his ambition to enter public life."

"Jerry Simpson," Leahy went on, "at that time and ever afterwards, was the opposite of Mr. Long in every respect. Whilst he would make but a poor showing with Mr. Long in a beauty contest, he was passably good looking, or at least attractive. He had a charming grin which generally forecast a shaft of wit or a bit of satire aimed with deadly effect at his opponent in debate. He was not a dresser, but always felt he was sartorially presentable when he wore a clean pair of boots and a paper collar. He had a treasury of knowledge but a very limited education. He was an omnivorous reader but the art of writing escaped him entirely. I have searched in vain for a letter written by him. His widow had none. When he married her he couldn't even spell, but he was strong in the spoken word."

Mr. Simpson, like Mr. Long, was not over-popular at Medicine Lodge when Dave Leahy first knew him. Neither tried to be popular, the editor noted, and he suspected that Long rather considered popularity a liability, while Simpson had a combative disposition and was fond of strange "isms." "I do not think anyone in Medicine Lodge ever dreamed, at that time, that both of them would become the most distinguished citizens of Barber County."

Chester I. Long was a lawyer, of whom Leahy remarked, "It has always been a mystery to me why Mr. Long settled in Barber County at all. But I have a theory that his legal mentor, George R. Peck of the Santa Fe Railway Company, encouraged him to do so, although the county already had a big bunch of lawyers, more than could eat—and drink—like gentlemen on the income from normal litigation."

Jerry Simpson's background was much more colorful. Born in the province of New Brunswick in 1842, he came to Michigan with his parents a few years later. Although his mind was keen and his hunger for knowledge great, he had little opportunity for formal schooling. He made up for this by constant reading and a remarkable memory. After enlisting in the army and serving for a few months in the Civil War, he was discharged for a disability. He returned home, worked in a sawmill for six months, then left the woods to become a cook on a Great Lakes schooner. During his twenty-three years on the Lakes he rose to the post of first mate on the *Summer Cloud*, and there he began to dream of "planting something in the ground to see it grow." And so, heeding the urgent call of the prairie, he made his way to Jackson County, Kansas. While fairly successful as a farmer there, he left after a year or two and came over into Barber County, where he put his money into cattle. Just in time to be caught in the disastrous winter of 1885-86, he saw his cows dying faster than he could skin them. That summer, his savings of a lifetime gone, he took the forty-dollar-a-month job of constable in Medicine Lodge.[7]

A good story teller, Jerry was soon in demand as a local political speaker on behalf of the new Union Party, and that same year was nominated its candidate for the state legislature. T. A. McNeal defeated him by a small majority. Jerry ran again in 1888, and that time was *buried* under the Kansas Republican landslide. Many thought that would end all thoughts of a political career for Jerry Simpson and that he'd never be able to make a comeback. But the next year, when Kansas turned out the biggest corn crop in its history—and the price dropped to ten cents a bushel—the farmers of the district had some second thoughts. With ten-cent corn, with forty-cent wheat, and with the backbreaking debt of '73 still to be paid, a lot of people turned against the party in power and deserted in droves to the Farmer's Alliance. As a result, Simpson, though he went to the congressional convention as a delegate, came home the party's candidate.

It was during the campaign of 1890 that Simpson acquired his nickname of "Sockless Jerry," and used it to help defeat his opponent, J. R. Hallowell. A correspondent of the Wichita *Eagle* accused him of wearing no socks. The homespun candidate not only didn't deny it but proclaimed that Hallowell wore silk hose. In a year such as that one, when most of the farmers and many other Kansans as well were down to rock bottom, Simpson, who freely admitted to his own poverty, was their man.

The Republicans had won the contest of 1880 by a majority of 15,000 in Jerry's district. Jerry won it in 1890 by a Populist majority of 8,000, an upset that catapulted him into fame. As surprised as anyone else, he went to Washington and there became one of the most talked of men in the United States. His nickname followed him and one of his fellow congressmen affectionately dubbed him "The Sockless Socrates of Kansas."

When he came home to campaign for re-election in the 1892 campaign, his opponent was his neighbor, Chester I. Long, who had made his political debut in 1889 by getting himself elected to fill a vacancy in the state senate. After Simpson's big majority in 1890, it took a brave Republican to run against him in 1892 and Long had no hope of winning. He made a vigorous campaign, however, and reduced Simpson's majority to something like 2,000.

He might have done even better if some party or parties unknown (perhaps working for the opposition) hadn't persuaded him to pass out cigars during his campaign. Now Long, who neither smoked nor drank, was not a judge of tobacco. All "smokes" looked alike to him and it was easy to palm off on him a quantity of cigars offered as a choice article by Simon Lebrecht, the Hebrew merchant, at a "reasonable price." They would be just the thing to garner votes, he was told. According to T. A. McNeal,[8] campaign cigars, at best, were bad, but these were the limit. When the first batch had been passed around and lighted, the men began to cast suspicious glances at each other and look around for the dead varmint's body. After the real cause of the vile odor was determined, Long's best friends decided to tell him, and suggested that if he wanted to win he'd better jettison the rest of the cigars.

By 1894 the tide of Populism had so far waned that Long, again a candidate, won over Simpson, the incumbent. But by 1896 the political scale had tipped again. The issue was free silver versus the gold standard, and Long, the incumbent, lined up on the side of gold. Simpson challenged him to defend his position and was nominated as the opposing candidate. The fight was on, and a bitter fight it was. "My judgement at the time was, and still is," concluded Leahy, "that Mr. Long's speeches were logical, while Jerry's were more psychological." The supporters of both seemed well pleased with their standard bearers, even though Long lost.

In 1898, however, the silver issue was dead and Simpson, without a cause to inflame his followers, came home to stay, while Long, the winner, went on to win again in 1900 and in 1902. The following year he was elected to the United States Senate by the legislature, and so did not complete his fourth term in the lower house. Senator Long was re-elected in 1904 and served until 1909. He was an advisor to President Taft, accompanying him to the Philippines.

Simpson, a radical both in religion and politics, was known as a "free-thinker," or infidel. Among his books were Payne's *The Age of Reason* and some by Huxley and Ingersoll. He generously loaned them all to a neighbor to read, but the neighbor and his family, converted shortly afterward by an evangelist, decided they could best help Jerry by burning his books, which they did.

During one of his campaigns, Simpson had to prove himself on other than the political platform, when a big blacksmith named Corson took offense at one of his statements and undertook to change his way of thinking by attacking him without warning. Simpson, though in his fifties, hadn't forgotten the rough and tumble skills he had learned in his years on the Lakes. In no time at all Corson was whipped, while the congressman wasn't even scratched. The blacksmith then became one of Jerry's most ardent admirers and political supporters.[9]

Zeal Johnson, son of a local livery stable owner, who grew up in Medicine Lodge, remembered Jerry Simpson as his leading hometown hero. As a boy, he said, he once went to Simpson's farm with a mule buyer. Jerry ran a little bunch of mules into his corral for the buyer to look at and one of the mules bumped into the barn as he went through the gate.

"That mule must be blind," the buyer told Simpson. The truth was he was locoed, but Jerry said, "Oh no, that mule just don't give a darn."

As to the many stories about Jerry and his socks, or lack of them, Zeal says it was true that he didn't wear 'em. "Us boys knew it, for he used to go to the river swimming with us, but we paid no attention. He was our friend when he was town marshal and whatever he did was right."

But when he was nominated for Congress some of the good women of the town heard the story that he didn't wear socks. They talked about it at a sewing circle meeting and some of them decided to go ask him about it and see if it was true. Someway, it seemed kind of indecent for a man in his position to go around without socks. "Mind their horror," Johnson said, "when Jerry told them, 'Ladies, I am a trader and I'll make you a deal. If you'll show me your legs I'll show you mine.' "

When William Jennings Bryan made his first race for the presidency, young Zeal rode to Wichita in a buggy to see the great man. Jerry Simpson went too, of course, and the boy rode in the parade with him. "And boy! did I think it was great, and how I spread it on when I got back home," he said.[10]

Sockless Jerry, never a moneyed man after the hard winter of 1885-86, died penniless, leaving his widow in sad circumstances. The poor woman told her troubles to Dynamite Dave and said she wanted to go to the Masonic home. Leahy, not a Mason, as Simpson had been and Long was, advised her to ask Long's help. Not at all sure her husband's long time political adversary would help her, she said she wouldn't ask a favor of him. So Leahy asked him, and Long had her in the home in almost no time.

Long, though never a man of great wealth, lived very comfortably, maintained a law office in Wichita and another in Washington, and had homes in Medicine Lodge, Wichita, and Washington.

ELEVEN

J. N. "Poley" Tincher

1895-1951

J. N. "Poley" Tincher, summed up the history of his predecessors, Jerry Simpson and Chester Long, and the condition of the country in a brief sketch of "how it was" when he came to Medicine Lodge in 1895.[1] There was one bank in the town, he recalled, and it did not have money to loan as it was a receiving bank. Times were hard, farms were being foreclosed, the sugar mill had closed down, and hogs were three cents a pound. Fifteen dollars a month was the going wage for a good farmhand.

There wasn't a bathtub in Medicine Lodge then, nor for several years afterward, nor a telephone. Simpson and Long were having a contest every other year over going to Congress and the county offices were held by the Populists. Some of the county officers could write and they had one clerk by the name of Cash Heskert who could figure. They used him first in one office, then in another. You could buy land in Barber County then for whatever you had, and if you didn't have anything you had to watch out or somebody would give you some land anyway.

There was a man named Springer that they claimed paid cash for everything he bought. He was noted for it. Hardly anybody else had any cash in those days, though Poley said he had heard of a farmer in the county who was supposed to be rich. People said he had $600 out on interest but he thought it was an exaggeration.

Chandler, the man who had the first bathtub in Medicine Lodge, also had the first automobile. But he didn't dare use it much because he had the bank, and people hated him so much for running the auto and scaring their horses that he was afraid they'd draw out their deposits. There was a Normal Institute in Medicine Lodge in the summer time then, and students could get board and room for $1.75 a week.

The campaign of 1896 between Long and Simpson was long remembered because Long had a five-dollar gold piece, a ten-dollar gold piece, a twenty-dollar gold piece and a silver dollar. He used them in his debates with Jerry—and lost the election because most people thought he was dishonest or he wouldn't have that much money.

They had lawsuits in Medicine Lodge back then, and McKay was the judge. He wasn't a lawyer and didn't know any law. Jim Titus was called on the jury once to try a case over a calf. He didn't want to sit on the jury so he asked what the calf was worth and the lawyer said about four dollars. Then he asked the court if he could pay for the calf and be excused from jury duty. Titus was ever after pointed out by the younger fellows as a very rich man.

If you got a crop in those days, which was seldom, everybody else had a crop too, and it would have no value. If you didn't have a crop, which was frequent, nobody else had a crop either and things were pretty tough.

Jasper Napoleon Tincher was born in Scottsville, Missouri, in 1877, the eldest son of Andrew and Coriene Tincher. At the age of eighteen he left his Missouri home and came to Medicine Lodge, where his aunt and her husband, Lewis Leonard, had a ranch four miles northwest of town. "Poley," short for Napoleon, had sixty-five cents in his pocket the morning he got off the train. The first thing he did was walk up to the post-office and mail a card to his mother. That left him sixty-four cents with which to face the world and launch his career. So he began by going out to the Leonard ranch and hiring on at thirteen dollars a month.

The next winter the husky young man worked at a dairy where, he said all he had to do was milk eight cows in the morning and twelve at night and, of course, feed and care for them. If he had any extra time left over he delivered milk. Soon tiring of dairy work, he decided to take the county teachers' examination and see how he came out. He passed, was given a teacher's certificate, and was hired to teach a country school. After two terms he gave up teaching as a career, came into Medicine Lodge, and found a job as janitor in the law office of Long and Noble (Chester Long and Albert L. Noble).

Fascinated by the shelves of books he found there, he began reading so hungrily that almost from the beginning he was far more occupied with reading than dusting the heavy old law books. His boss, Albert Noble, frequently found the big young man sitting in his (Noble's) chair, his feet on the desk, lost in the captivating mazes of the law. And before Noble knew what he was about he found himself spending a good deal of time answering Poley's penetrating questions and explaining the finer points of the law to him. Before much longer his eager young janitor was helping him with some of his cases.

Poley passed the bar examinations in 1899 and was admitted to the bar, after which his employer began turning minor cases over to him. The big young lawyer was so consistently successful that he soon acquired the title of "The Winning Lawyer;" when, in 1902, he ran for the office of county attorney he won that too. His salary was $800 per year and he prosecuted twenty-four criminal cases during his two-year term. None of the defendants was acquitted.

By the time his term of office ended, Long and Noble had dissolved partnership. So Poley went back into the law office as Noble's partner. The senior partner later moved to Arkansas City, leaving big Poley Tincher in full charge of the Medicine Lodge office.

Poley had a hand in numerous famous cases of the area. He secured a conviction for two murderers who were confidently expected by the whole county to go free, and so broke up a big cattle stealing ring. Early in his career he also defended Barber County's highly respected Bud McCracken (later murdered in Kiowa) in a sensational murder trial. McCracken had been involved in a range war in Chickasha, Oklahoma, many years before, killing a gunman hired by a ranchman named Campbell. McCracken fled after the shooting, finally came to Barber County, married, and built a ranch of his own. Thirty years after the killing in Oklahoma he was elected sheriff of his home county. The ranchman, Campbell, saw his picture in the paper at the time of his election and promptly had him arrested and brought to Chickasha for trial. Poley won his acquital by ferreting out an elderly cowhand witness who testified the gunman had been hired by Campbell to kill McCracken, who had escaped death by spurring his horse into a mighty leap as the gunman squeezed his trigger. McCracken had then cut his assailant down with a single shot from his own Winchester rifle.

The largest sum at stake in any of the cases that the biggest lawyer in Barber County ever tried was the $400,000 that hung on the outcome of the Achenbach, Blackstock versus Tack trial. Jacob Achenbach, of Hardtner, and Ira Blackstock, of Springfield, Illinois, were the builders and owners of the Beaver, Meade and Englewood Railroad, south and west of Hardtner. The partners had sold the railroad to the Rock Island for more than one million dollars and Jack Tack, of Wichita, then claimed a third interest and expenses. Tack seemed to have a very strong case, so strong that he and his lawyers curtly refused a $100,000 out-of-court settlement. So Poley Tincher went ahead and won the case for Achenbach and Blackstock, and Tack collected nothing.

Tincher's most famous case, however, was the Nation divorce suit in which he represented David Nation. Carry contested the divorce but Poley won it for his elderly client. More than twenty newspapermen, representing famous big city dailies all over the nation, covered the case and telegraphed daily reports on the progress of the trial.

In 1918 the big Seventh Congressional District of Kansas (thirty-two counties) sent Poley to Washington as its Republican representative. He was re-elected in 1920 and again in 1922. In 1924 he carried on a series of seventy-two coast-to-coast Chautauqua debates with-Alben Barkley, Democratic congressman from Kentucky. By the time he came home in October to spearhead his campaign for another re-election, Poley was among the best known and most popular figures in the midwest.

Always a big man, he had begun to put on weight by the time he went to Washington. By 1924 he weighed close to 300 pounds and, even if he had had no other outstanding attributes, his size alone would have made him prominent in any gathering. Huge crowds turned out to hear him that autumn of 1924, and wherever he spoke in his district he was loudly acclaimed. Women's groups staged large, enthusiastic luncheons for him and most of the newspapers gave him high praise. The Kiowa *News-Review* applauded him: "Mr. Tincher has earned a most enviable position in the House of Representatives. His rapid promotion has been almost unprecedented. His ability was immediately recognized and during his first term he attracted the attention of the big and influential leaders of his party. As a result, Mr. Tincher, who is only serving his third term, now occupies the highest position in the house heretofore held by a Kansan."[2] Poley was then a member of the House steering committee.

"Huge crowds turned out to hear him when he came home. Seldom does a candidate receive a finer audience or greeting than was given Mr. Tincher by the homefolks."[3] "The record breaking crowd that came out last Monday to hear their Congressman and fellow-townsman, Poley Tincher, deliver his campaign speech was nothing short of an ovation."[4] "Poley is a powerful speaker, a real orator."[5]

Among the state's big city newspapers, the Kansas City *Star* was not overly friendly to him and the Dodge City *Globe* accused him of lining up with "special privilege," but the Kansas City *Times* predicted that he would be floor leader in Congress after the election.

As the campaign drew to a close, Poley was speaking to standing room only crowds wherever he went and his popularity in the predominently rural areas of his district easily won the election for him. He went back to Washington in overwhelming triumph and in the Congress of 1925 was made assistant floor leader. In addition, he was still a member of the all-powerful steering committee and of the agricultural committee.

Throughout 1925 and '26 he was a prominent man in the nation's capital. "There is hardly a week that he isn't called to the White House for conferences by President Coolidge, who regards Mr. Tincher very highly, both as a man and as a leader," one admirer reported. An outstanding parliamentarian, he often served, during his fourth term, as acting chairman of the House, for whenever debates became heated the regular chairman, a gentleman from New York state, hurriedly relinquished the floor to Poley.

Consistently a staunch defender of agricultural interests and a fighter for what he thought right, Tincher was the co-author of the Capper-Tincher bill legalizing boards of trade, which prior to this were considered outlaw organizations. Against strong opposition, he dragged it through the House to victory.

A reporter for a Kansas newspaper wrote concerning a trip to Washington D. C. early in 1926: "There I saw wonderful sights—including our popular Congressman, Poley Tincher. . . . I was in Washington long enough to find out to my entire satisfaction that Kansas is very competently represented in both branches of Congress. Both senators (Curtis and Capper) stand very high there. And I came home just as proud as can be of J. N. Tincher, the Big Seventh Congressman. If you do not think that Poley is a power in the lower branch of the National Congress, all it will take to prove that he is, is to make a trip to Washington, where he is considered one of the few really brainy men in the House—and is respected by Republicans and Democrats alike. . . . I stayed a couple of days longer than I meant to in order to hear Congressman Tincher deliver a speech in the House. He aroused the ire of a number of Democratic Congressmen before he had gotten well started, and was frequently interrupted by several of the minority leaders, but in every case they found they had gotten hold of a 'red-hot poker' and soon subsided. His speech was the subject of discussion in official circles during the remainder of the day and the papers gave it much publicity."[6]

When Poley returned to Washington for the opening session of Congress in 1926 he was hailed by his fellows as "Coal Oil Johnny," due to widespread rumors that he had struck oil on his land in Kansas. Though he denied that he was a big oil man, Washington persisted in its mistaken belief that he was an "oil millionaire."[7] Then, when the big congressman almost immediately announced that he would not run for Congress that fall, turmoil broke loose in earnest.

His many friends were certain he could easily be re-elected and vociferously told him so; but he steadfastly refused to reconsider, stating that he had already served two more terms than he had intended when he was first elected.

The Kingman (Kansas) *Leader-Courier* speculated that "It is quite possible that the discovery of the new oil field at Kingman and the gas and oil showings in Mr. Tincher's well at Isabel affected his decision to retire from public life."

The Kansas City *Star*, the paper not too friendly to Poley during his campaigns, accepted his retirement gracefully by stating: "Rounding out eight years of service in the House, Representative Tincher has been an unusually successful member. Large and jovial and a splendid mixer, he knew nearly every member of the House inside of a month after he first came to Washington." The paper then went on at length to extol his virtues and accomplishments.

The Scott (Kansas) *Republican*, reprinting from a Washington paper, gave Poley's reply to the whole matter. " 'I want to give you an interview,' said Congressman J. N. Tincher to the Capital Correspondent today. 'You know I seldom ever ask for publicity, but this is one time that I really want you to interview me. The newspaper boys with an energy that does them credit, and with a generosity that I don't deserve, have run me for about every office there is, including governor, U.S. senator and federal judge for Kansas, since I announced my forthcoming retirement from Congress. I just want to tell you and to tell Kansas folks that I am quitting Congress to get out of politics, not to get in. I am quitting to practice law, not to seek office. I am quitting to practice law in Medicine Lodge and make enough money so the Tincher family can live better in Kansas than they are living right now in Washington.' "[8] He added that there was nothing to the big oil story either, that if there had been he might have had the money to stay on in Congress.

Following all this, Tom Connally, Democrat of Texas, read a facetious newspaper article on the House floor, suggesting Poley Tincher for the Republican nomination for vice-president of the United States, on the same ticket with Speaker Nicholas Longworth for President. Poley's sarcastic reply "kept the House roaring with laughter." He declared that "he had no ambition to be vice-president and that he did not care to go to the Court of St. James. 'I could not wear the silk panties with any style,' he said, and added, 'I cannot even do the Charleston.' "

No doubt Mr. Connally was heartily sorry he had ever thought of poking fun at Poley, for the big congressman went on to refer to the Texas representative's Spanish-American War record, "a sore spot," and then stated that Connally was "much better fitted" than himself for the ambassadorship. "Gentlemen," he orated, "can you contemplate anything more grand than Tom Connally with silk pants coming down to his knees, and with little silver buckles on his slippers, at a court function in England?" He then quoted a mock conversation between Mr. Connally and the King of England, in which the Texan told the King that he (Connally) had served British interests well in Congress by opposing the protective tariff. Poley concluded by suggesting that, in his opinion, Connally would not even make a successful vice-president because "the function of a Vice-President is to sit still and keep his mouth shut."[9]

In February 1927, only days before his retirement from Congress, House debate on the McNary-Haugen farm bill reached the violent stage one morning when "in the lobby of the House two beefy Republicans from Kansas swung lustily" at each other. " 'You'll not talk that way to me,' bellowed Representative James G. Strong of Blue Rapids, Kansas. 'You're a liar,' replied J. N. Tincher of Medicine Lodge.

"Although Poley had about twenty-five pounds the advantage over his opponent, the heavyweight championship battle of the House drew to a scoreless tie when Speaker Longworth and Representative Hudspeth of Texas separated the pugilists before any fist had found a target."[10]

The Dodge City *Globe* applauded by remarking that although Big Seventh folks had been represented in Congress by a long line of fighters, who had walloped Wall Street, the Interests, Joe Cannon and Sweet Adeline, they would rather fight someone from New England than a Kansan. But, if necessary, they would take on a fellow Kansan in order to uphold the reputation of the Seventh.

On March 1, 1927, the Washington *Star* carried the following headline: HOUSE, AMID LAUGHTER, APPROVES TINCHER BILL FOR MEMORIAL IN HIS HOME TOWN. "Representative Poley Tincher of Kansas, the largest member in Congress and one of the most jovial, saw the successful passing of his bill to authorize an appropriation of $2,500 for erection of a memorial at Medicine Lodge to commemorate the 1867 Indian Peace Treaty. Said Representative Luce of Massachusetts, 'The gentleman from Kansas is retiring voluntarily from congress and he wants to take a memorial back home for both his constituents and himself to look at.' Amid laughter, the bill went through."

The Washington *Post* reported on March 5 that the House "adjourned in an outburst of song and play, with expressions of good will for all and enmity toward none. . . . There were swan songs by Senator-elect Vare of Pennsylvania and the jovial Tincher of Kansas, and rising and sincere tributes were paid to them."

The Washington *Star* likewise declared the close of the 69th Congress "was celebrated in the House by an impromptu concert, which was enjoyed by practically the entire membership and thousands of visitors who thronged the galleries and corridors." Tincher, leaving after eight years of service, "declared that the House leadership, both Republican and Democratic, is superior to that of any other legislative body in the world." Woodman of Virginia stood on his desk and while the Navy band, stationed on the House floor, played several numbers, led the entire multitude in singing.[11]

And so big Poley Tincher came home in triumph. Few men in Kansas had ever enjoyed as wide a personal acquaintance among national political leaders or had their speeches and activities so often reported in Washington and New York newspapers. But J. N. Tincher was by no means through with serving the state or the party he loved so well. Much in demand as a political speaker, he was a welcome and highly respected delegate to national conventions, where his fiery oratory was always cheered to the rafters. In 1928 he served as chairman of the big Republican convention in Kansas City, where, in a ringing speech, he nominated Senator Charles Curtis for the Presidency.

In his later years, due to his great weight, Tincher had trouble with his legs. He had, by this time, moved to Hutchinson, Kansas, and there, when he became unable to walk and took to a wheel chair, he had a ramp built onto his house so he could wheel himself to his car and ride to his office. Other than his home and his office, his favorite habitation was the Elks Club. His daughter, Coreine, often drove him to the club and turned him over to brother members, who wheeled him into the club rooms and relived with him the grand old days when good lawyers came up from the ranks the hard way, and most would rather try a case before a jury than eat. In those days, Poley declared, *cases went to trial*; few were settled by the court and almost none by private agreement.

On January 21, 1950, Hutchinson lawyers paid honor to J. N. Tincher at a huge banquet. Many well-known attorneys, including W. W. Harvey, chief justice of the Kansas Supreme Court, came to pay homage to their old contemporary who, for more than fifty years, was one of the outstanding trial lawyers of the midwest.

Less than two years later, on November 6, 1951, Poley Tincher died at the age of seventy-four. Most of the state's newspapers carried farewell tributes to him in their columns; among them this happy one: "This is to say farewell to Poley Tincher, one of the most successful citizens southwest Kansas ever produced and Hutchinson ever enjoyed. Poley was so full of human juices. He was a character in the most endearing sense of the word. He never flinched in standing by his friends and up to his enemies. In every way and at every moment he was able to find fun in life—able to find such great zest with the world and his place in it. That is what made J. Napoleon Tincher such a rare success."[12]

Among the letters written to the aged politician and saved by his sister, Mrs. Clara Downing of Medicine Lodge, two are of special interest. One, a Christmas letter written to Mr. and Mrs. Tincher in 1943, reads in part: "On this Christmas season, with its inspiration, I have many fond recollections of you two. I vividly recall often hearing Poley pronounce and argue his theories of government, with some of which I did not argue, but it is a pleasant recollection to recall his arguments, comments and illustrations, some of which may not have been appropriate for mixed and polite society, but they were always in point.

"I remember the night when I stayed at your home. When I went to my room, to my surprise, I found the reading light at the head of the bed turned on, a pitcher of water, a drinking glass, a nicely polished apple and a late magazine on the stand near the head of the bed. This thoughtfulness of Mrs. Tincher's showed me very clearly why she is so popular with all who know her. You, Poley, may not appreciate it, but I think a great deal of your popularity and success is come by, and should be attributed to, Mrs. Tincher." The letter was written by W. L. Cunningham, an attorney of Arkansas City, Kansas.

The other, from Congressman Charles A. Eaton of New Jersey, under a 1944 date, no doubt pleased Poley. Wrote Mr. Eaton, "It would be an immense comfort to me personally to have you wielding your keen edged intellectual blade on the floor of the House against the ogre of isolationism. . . . Unless we Republicans quit fighting among ourselves pretty soon, we might just as well lie down and let the New Deal finish the job of wiping off the map the old America which we have known so long."

Carry Nation, c1901. *Courtesy Kansas State Historical Society.*

TWELVE
Carry Nation
1899-1911

Carry Nation is, without doubt, the most controversial individual ever to reside in Medicine Lodge. Stories about her are endless and few of them are in accord, but on one point there is full agreement, that she was the town's most famous citizen of all time. As one writer put it: "Medicine Lodge has been the home of a number of well-known people, 'Sockless' Jerry Simpson, Chester I. Long, Tom McNeal, J. N. 'Poley' Tincher, but none of the others made headlines all over the world as Carry Nation did."[1]

Numerous writers and historians have dealt with Carry, many of them to her disadvantage. She has been ridiculed, pictured as masculine, coarse, rough, and unladylike, and berated for the causes she espoused. But among those who knew her best, her neighbors in Medicine Lodge, she was generally admired and respected. T. A. McNeal said of her: "She was a woman of pronounced faults and pronounced virtues, but her good qualities far outweighed her faults. She was generous to a fault and always ready to help the needy and afflicted. She was possessed of the courage of a crusader and the zeal of a bigot, with a frankness that was delightful when it was not embarrassing. In the singing her voice rose above all others in vibrant and triumphant peans of thanksgiving and praise, for with Carry Nation religion was no mere matter of form. Others might have doubts, she had none. Prayer might be with others largely lip service, but with her it was direct communication with the Most High."[2]

David Leahy wrote of her: "When she was in untroubled repose she not only was very agreeable and interesting, but sensible in her observations. . . . When under the spell of her whimsies I, like many others who knew she really had a kind and soft heart, liked the motherly old lady. We knew her to be charitable to the poor and needy beyond her means, and on the whole thought she did infinitely more good than harm during her stormy life."[3]

Zeal Johnson, the livery stableman's son, remembered her as a "great and grand woman . . . a gentle and kind soul."[4]

Carry Amelia Moore[5] was born in Kentucky in 1846, the daughter of well-to-do parents. An invalid during most of her childhood, she was not able to go to school and spent much of her girlhood reading the Bible. At the age of twenty-one she made an unfortunate marriage to a dashing young Civil War surgeon, Dr. Charles Gloyd. Drink ruined the young man and the marriage. After a brief but hard and bitter life together, Carry left him. Six months later he "filled a drunkard's grave," as Carry termed it.

With her sickly little daughter Charlene and the doctor's widowed mother, Carry set out to fend for them and herself. She managed to secure enough education to become a school teacher and followed that occupation for awhile. In 1877 she married again. Her new husband was David Nation, a minister of the Christian church and also a lawyer. Although the couple lived together for nearly a quarter of a century, it was a period of quarrels and strife, for they had little in common. No doubt the invalid daughter and the elderly mother of her first husband, both a part of Carry's household (the daughter until she grew up, the older woman until she died), did not help the marriage any.

David Nation became pastor of the First Christian Church in 1889; his wife, Carry, joined him in Medicine Lodge in April, 1890. As McNeal described their advent into the little town, "David *accompanied* his wife, Carry, for at no time did he attain to a higher rank than second lieutenant in that household." Carry, he added, "was always militant, always dominant, always in evidence. If she was not placed at the head of whatever procession she happened to be in, she organized another procession. I have often watched her and David on their way to church, Carry marching like a drum major some feet in advance, David bringing up the rear." Almost from the day of her arrival in town, Mrs. Nation was busy at gathering up food and clothing for the community poor and renting halls to start Sunday schools.

From the first, she was outspoken on her hatred for alcohol and tobacco. She had good reason to despise both. In those days the majority of adult males chewed tobacco, a filthy habit that kept sidewalks and the floors of most public buildings wet with the odorous "juice." Although she disliked the "weed" in any form, this phase of its use especially revolted her. She had spent most of her latter years in Missouri and Texas where saloons ran wide open, unfettered by legal restrictions. For this reason she had come gladly to Kansas where, since 1884, the manufacture and sale of intoxicating beverages had been illegal, except for medical, scientific, and industrial purposes. No doubt she had expected Medicine Lodge to be a city where whisky was despised, so one can imagine her dismay when she found as much drinking there as ever she had seen in the south; the town had seven shops where liquor was sold in open and accepted defiance of the law.

She first combated the evil of alcohol by making speeches against its sale at every opportunity and by helping in the local chapter of the Women's Christian Temperance Union. As jail evangelist for this organization, it was her duty to visit the inmates and render aid and assistance. Many told her how strong drink had been responsible for most of their troubles, and Carry became more and more incensed by the festering evil of the liquor trade. She began to rise frequently in church and prayer meeting to recite the names of the local whisky sellers and to demand why the city and county officials permitted them to operate in open violation of the state prohibition law.

On one occasion, however, as Zeal Johnson tells the story, she took advantage of one of the town's bootleg joints. In the country nearby she had discovered a widow with two children, fighting a losing battle to exist long enough to prove up on a homestead. The situation was beyond Carry's means to help in the usual way, so she marched to the saloon, entered, and asked the dive keeper if she could pray. The man at once removed his hat and bowed his head. Every man in the place did likewise, and Carry, kneeling beside a beer keg, offered up her prayer—for help and sustenance for the widow and her children who were without food, fuel, sufficient clothing, tools, money, or much of anything else needed to keep body and soul together. By the time she finished, the men in the dive were wiping tears on their bandannas and hauling out old wallets. The wolf would howl no longer at the widow's door, but Carry would visit many a saloon after that.

Because her speeches and recitations of saloon keepers' names had brought no results, Carry saw clearly that she would have to get on with the job herself. On a spring day in 1899 she hitched her old horse, Prince, to her buggy, loaded the rig with stones, and drove off to Kiowa where the saloons were not only permitted to operate but were encouraged to do so.

A monument stands today on the corner where she is said to have used her ammunition so effectively, but as late as 1935 some of Kiowa's residents insisted that the first saloon Carry smashed was the one across the street. Still another writer claims her target was the Lone Eagle, owned by Matt and Billy Lewis, and that clutching her apronful of stones she walked in singing "Where is My Wandering Boy Tonight?" and let go at the mirror with her rocks. Whichever "joint" it was, she did a good job. T. A. McNeal relates that she "threw overhand and wildly . . . but the bar extended from one end of the room almost to the other, and a rock heaved in that general direction was bound to hit something." The destruction was general but quite complete.

She was not arrested for that raid, although one story has it that she stood amidst the wreckage and dared the town marshal to do so. McNeal reports that when the marshal came running to see what the disturbance was all about, Carry gave him a good lecture, for she "had an extensive and virile vocabulary." And in the Medicine Lodge Stockade Museum one can see a partly full bottle of Edelweiss beer, rescued from the ruins that long ago day of the raid, by Sherm Holloway, who took it home and kept it until his death in 1957.

Carry drove home in triumph to Medicine Lodge, where the story of her attack had preceded her by telegraph, and a large crowd of her supporters waited to congratulate her. Encouraged by her first success, a few days later she made a ringing speech in front of the post office, charging Samuel Griffin, the county attorney, with taking bribes from the saloon keepers of Kiowa. Griffin countered with a slander suit for $5,000 damages, and won the case. Carry was fined one dollar, and the costs of the action, $113.65, were assessed against her.

One of Mrs. Nation's biographers, Ruby Basye, states that while Carry is best remembered with a hatchet in her hand she actually ran most of the Medicine Lodge liquor dealers out with prayer meetings. She held her meetings in front of the saloons and "while her words were directed to God, they were shrill enough to penetrate through the barred doors of the dens of iniquity."[6]

One Saturday afternoon that summer of 1899, Carry and Mrs. Wesley Cain, wife of the local Baptist minister, put on their best dresses and bonnets and headed for Mort Strong's saloon. They had with them a wheezy hand organ and they sang as they marched. By the time they reached the saloon they had gathered a crowd of some two hundred followers. The Basye account states that they went into the bar and began to pray, and that Mort grabbed Carry by the arm and hurried her roughly into the street while she flailed at him with her umbrella and shrieked at the top of her voice. Mort kept his hold on her, but accidentally bumped her against the town marshal, James Gano, who had been summoned and was standing by "in an agony of indecision." "Go easy, Mort," he begged, and the dive keeper then let Carry go.

Another account[7] relates that Gano met Mrs. Nation at the saloon door and said, "I wish I could take you off the streets."

"Yes," the crusader replied, "you want to take me, a woman whose heart is breaking to see the ruin of these men, the desolate homes, and the broken laws—and you a constable, oath-bound to close this man's unlawful business." She then pushed into the saloon and Strong immediately put her out. With tears streaming from her eyes, Carry continued to sing and hurl curses at the saloon keeper, the account goes on, and Mrs. Cain and the other woman joined in the song, which sounded over the town. Soon five hundred people had collected, some encouraging Mrs. Nation and her band, others shouting against them.

After several more unsuccessful attempts to enter the saloon, Carry headed for home, still singing. The women went with her, and through the rest of the afternoon they sang and prayed, while the crowd hung about outside, calling for more action.

By evening great excitement ran through the town, for the story of the morning affair had grown until rumor had it that Mort Strong had horsewhipped a woman. Feeling was so intense that about midnight the mayor and several councilmen went in a body to Strong's place—and were "surprised and indignant at finding beer and whisky on the premises." They sternly told Strong he must leave town at once or take the consequences. He left the next morning.

The Basye story relates the ending slightly differently. The women of the town, she writes, spent the evening knocking on the marshal's door and demanding that he do something about Mort Strong's manhandling of Carry Nation. Finally, in desperation, the marshal called the city council together, mostly for his own protection, and at midnight went with them to Mort's place. There they pounded on the locked door and demanded admission, and when they found a quiet poker game going on inside, they expressed great surprise and indignation and ordered the dive keeper to leave town or suffer the consequences.

In any case, Mrs. Nation won an important victory and encouraged by her success promptly sent the other six saloon keepers proper warnings. They knew she meant business and took precautions by being careful to open their barred doors only to trusted drinkers. But barred doors were no deterrent to the determined little crusader, who next set her sights on Henry Durst's saloon. Both accounts agree that she did not try to enter that liquor shop but, with a drunkard's wife beside her, knelt in the street in front of the barred door and began to pray. While his customers slipped out the back door and fled up the alley, Durst unbarred his front door and stepped out to have a look. Carry spied him, leaped to her feet, and caught him by his coat lapels. Then she shook him vigorously and threatened him with a prayer meeting twice a day until God smote him. It seemed too big a chance to take, so Durst departed in haste from Medicine Lodge.

The embattled ladies turned next to Hank O'Bryon's restaurant, for Hank also did a lively business in liquor in the back room. Carry accused him, threatened him, and prayed for him until he could stand no more and promised to lock the back room. He did, and thenceforth sold only food.

Three more "joints" closed their doors at the request of the badgered and harassed city and county officials, and that left only one, O. L. Day's drugstore. Carry knew that Day did not have a permit to sell liquor for medicinal purposes, and she knew that all the town's heaviest drinkers were now doing their loafing at his place. When she learned that a suspicious looking keg had been unloaded at Day's back door, she called a meeting of her temperance union. Shortly afterward the women marched on the store.

Mrs. Nation and another woman confronted Day and asked about the keg. He admitted possession, but explained that it was only California brandy, which he could dispense on prescription as soon as his permit arrived. But Carry swept by him to the back room and found the keg. At her triumphant call another woman rushed back to help her and they rolled the keg into the front room. In vain the druggist protested that it was only his harmless California brandy, while Carry insisted it was whisky, "the Devil's broth."

By the time Marshal Gano, perspiring and unhappy, arrived to help Day, the store was full of militant women, determined to possess the keg. "This is private property, Mother Nation," Gano said, trying to help Day hold onto the unwieldy barrel. "It's the broth of hell," Carry retorted, as she and her helpers fought for a better hold for themselves. The marshal then straightened up and caught Mrs. Nation by the arms and pulled her away. She cried and fought him. Then another woman leaped at the marshal from behind, grabbed him by the collar, and yanked him backward. Day then let loose of the barrel and stepped back, and Carry, jerking away from the marshal, helped roll the keg into the street, and, so one account says, smashed it with a sledge hammer borrowed from the blacksmith across the way.

One of the stories adds that Day sold his store as quick as he could and left town. At any rate, for the first time since Kansas was voted dry, Medicine Lodge was a place where one could not buy a drink.

With her town now good and dry, Carry Nation had to look for new fields to conquer, and Wichita seemed logical, for it was recognized by all anti-liquor organizations as the center of the entire illegal business in Kansas. If the saloons and warehouses there could be put out of order many counties in the state would be dry, for awhile anyway.

The boy, Zeal Johnson, hitched Carry's horse to her buggy for the saloon-smashing trip to Wichita. "I didn't know she was going to smash a saloon," he said, "but I was proud that I hitched up her horse on that occasion. She drove to Wichita, smashed a picture and other articles in the old Carey saloon, got herself arrested and put in jail, and came out a nationally known hero."

And from David Leahy, who was there, we have the detailed story of Mrs. Nation's activities on that historic visit. "It was on December 26, 1900, that she gathered up an apronful of rocks, brickbats and other missles, which, after a night of prayer, she hurled next morning in the famous temple of Bacchus adjoining the Carey Hotel."

Carry first attacked the famous picture of Cleopatra At Her Bath that hung back of the bar, sending two rocks through the painted beauty and leaving two horrible rents that "bibacious critics of art wept over for a week." She then hurled the rest of her stock of ammunition at the handsome arrays of Stoughton bottles, decanters, mirrors, and such like that decorated the temple.

"It was by mere accident," Leahy wrote, "that I got into the picture of Mrs. Nation's first dramatic performance in Wichita. I was the only available man at the *Eagle* office that morning when the report came in that a mad woman was breaking up things in Mahan Brothers saloon. I hastened to the place and got there as Mrs. Nation was being led away from the scene of devastation. I viewed the wreck, interviewed the barkeeper and wrote the story."[8]

Mr. Leahy then refutes a number of tales that were published concerning the crusader's famous Wichita raid, making much of the alleged ill-treatment she received in that city. It was stated, he said, that Carry vigorously boxed Park Massey's ears when he arrested her, and that she dragged Sheriff Simmons all over the floor of the railway station by the ears. (It would appear that the ill-treatment was the other way around.) But if she had done all that, Leahy went on, he was sure the authorities would have charged her with assaulting policemen, rather than for smashing illegal saloons. And the truth was, when Mrs. Nation was presented to Chief of Police Cubbon, he treated her with great courtesy and offered to liberate her immediately, so she could go home to Medicine Lodge for a happy New Year with her family, provided she would not put on any more shows in Wichita.

She refused scornfully. "No indeed," she said. "The moment I can get out of this hell-hole and gather up a few rocks I shall reduce every murder shop in this city to splinters."

Not knowing what else to do with her, the chief turned her over to Sam Amidon, the county attorney. Sam, a Democrat, promptly and properly passed her on to Republican Henry Schad, marshal of the city court. Now Henry, during the late war, had stood without flinching before the canon's mouth when it was spitting hot shot over the scenery, but after a few verbal projectiles from the mouth of Mrs. Nation he sought help and protection from Sheriff Simmons. The sheriff, a strict respector of womanhood, at first thought to make her his house guest, "but when she referred to him as Ahab and his amiable wife as Jezabel," it seemed best to turn her over to Dicky Dodds, his jail warden. Dicky was undersize and underweight and had a childlike disposition, just the type a motherly old lady would be glad to treat with maternal affection. Furthermore, he had no dissipations whatever. But Carry refused to recognize him as a member of the human family. Instead she ranked him with the crustacea and habitually referred to him as a shrimp.

Dicky was patient with her, but one evening when she was unusually clamorous for her freedom, he opened the back door wide and told her she could go. He even offered to call a hack to make her escape easier. But Carry, like the fellow who demanded his money at the bank, then turned it down when he saw he could have it, refused to leave. "And this," states Leahy, "was the sort of persecution she suffered in Wichita. No, Mrs. Nation was never persecuted in Wichita. Not a hair on her head was even disarranged during her raids."

In addition, it was intimated that Victor Murdock of the Wichita *Eagle* was the main persecutor of the whimsical old lady. Leahy found this ridiculous, stating he had known Murdock for forty-four years and that he was the poorest hand at persecution he had ever known. He and Murdock were together, he said, for most of the three weeks that Mrs. Nation was in Wichita, and he couldn't recall Murdock writing so much as a single unkind line about her.

As a matter of fact, Leahy went on, Victor was the first person upon whom Mrs. Nation made a friendly social call after she was released from jail. He remembered the call very well because he was with Murdock and they had their corncob pipes well smoked up when she came to the door. "After expressing the great sorrow she felt at seeing two young men taking a short cut to eternal damnation by the nicotine route, she settled herself cozily in the editorial chair and entertained us for an hour in the most amiable conversation. It was during that conversation that she revealed to Victor that her chief antipathy was against the use of tobacco, and that it was inherited. She called it a birthmark." In the course of that sociable visit, according to Leahy, Carry Nation conceived the idea of using a hatchet, rather than rocks, as the handiest weapon for saloon smashing.

In conclusion, he wrote, "Her whole life was full of inconsistencies. She was considered a religious fanatic, although she could never conform to the discipline of a church. She loved the sisters and abused them roundly. She held all preachers to be stumbling blocks to the advancement of Christ's kingdom upon earth. She was tolerant only with sinners, and was excommunicated for her friendship for unfortunate women. Her own conduct was above reproach. She probably hated a pipe smoker worse than a swindler."

After her pleasant visit with Leahy and Murdock, Carry went out and bought her first hatchet. On January 21, 1901, with three other women she attacked James Burne's saloon. From there they went to John Hareg's place, where they were arrested. Released a few days later, after the W.C.T.U. paid their bail of $1,000 each, Carry went home a famous woman.

People in other counties then began writing to her urging her to free their towns of saloons. She promptly obliged. Enterprise, Kansas, was first, then Topeka, where she was jailed again, and then on into other states. Known all across the nation by then, the progress of her crusade against the illegal liquor traffic was watched with interest and growing sympathy by a vast reading public.

After one of her raids, Carry Nation and a little woman by the name of Blanche Boise were jailed on a charge of disturbing the peace by breaking some windows and otherwise damaging some saloons. When this was published abroad the reaction was loud and clear. As T. A. McNeal wrote, there is a certain love of fair play in the mind of the average American, and it revolted at the transparent injustice of punishing a couple of women while saloon keepers were plying their unlawful business, unmolested by officers of the law.[9]

As for her generosity and willingness to help the needy and afflicted, the same writer stated: "She would have smashed a joint until it was an utter wreck, but if the next day she found the joint keeper in want or sickness she would have nursed him back to health and given of her substance to feed him and his family."

Mrs. Nation was crusading in Columbus, Ohio, when she heard that David Nation had brought suit for divorce. An item in the Medicine Lodge *Index* for February 20, 1901, notes that "Captain David Nation is kept rather busy these days answering press dispatches. Last Wednesday he got three from the New York *Journal*. The first stated a report was current that he had begun proceedings for a divorce because Mrs. Nation persisted in traveling over the country, and an answer was asked. Mr. Nation replied that it was a lie. The next one stated a report had been sent out from Wichita that he had told parties there that if his wife did not confine herself to Kansas he would sue for a divorce. Mr. Nation wired back to New York that anything sent out from Wichita is a lie. The third telegram asked him to write 200 words concerning Mrs. Nation's work, what she has accomplished and her future plans, which he did."

The same paper said: "The smart newspaper correspondents refer to Capt. David Nation as 'Mr. Carrie Nation.' " Also: "Mrs. Carry Nation is expected home today. The temperance women of the city have organized a hatchet brigade and will meet her at the depot."

Mr. Nation was granted a divorce that same year; he died two years later, in October 1903.

In September 1901, the Barber County court ordered Mrs. Nation's home in Medicine Lodge sold for the nonpayment of the costs in the Griffin slander suit of 1899. By then Carry was paying her way by selling little souvenir hatchets wherever she appeared, and by revenues from her speaking engagements, and so was able to save her home.

The remainder of her life was spent in fighting the liquor interests. She lectured on the stage and Chautauqua platform in most of the states of the union. She traveled in Mexico, Canada, England, and Scotland, always preaching prohibition. She published books and magazines, writing most of the material herself. But for years she came home to Medicine Lodge at every opportunity to visit her beloved friends.

And there were many in the little town who loved her very dearly. Elderly ladies who were young girls when Carry lived there speak of her today with sincere affection and respect. Mrs. Daws Grigsby is one of them. Mayme Cole Grigsby, daughter of P. B. Cole, rescuer of the Maddox girl at the time of the great flood, remembers Mrs. Nation well. "She was my Sunday School teacher when I was a girl, and I thought so much of her. She organized many Sunday schools in the community and did a great deal of good among the people." And she smiles as she remembers one sunny Sunday morning when she and George Moore, Mrs. Nation's nephew, started off to Sunday school themselves. There had been a big rain the night before and Antelope Creek was up. Swarms of fish were coming upstream with the high water, and when the children came to the creek they forgot all about

Sunday school and got busy catching fish. Mayme was catching them in her pretty little white apron, while George was scooping them out anyway he could. And then the young fishers looked up and saw "Aunt Carry" coming down the hill in her buggy. "Ah! we knew we'd catch it then, for missing Sunday school," Mrs. Grigsby laughs.

Later, when George Moore was a young man, he worked three years for Mr. Cole, saved his money, and went to Kansas City, where he put it all into a team and dray and went into business for himself. But one of his horses died right away, crippling his undertaking, until Aunt Carry heard about it; she quietly bought him another horse and put him on his feet again.

Of them all, Alice Martin MacGregor probably knew and loved Mrs. Nation best. The Martins came to Kansas in 1884, to a claim about eighteen miles north of Medicine Lodge. When Mr. Martin had a camp ready on the homestead, Mrs. Martin and her six-month-old baby came to Harper on the train. Her husband met her the next day, driving four horses hitched to the running gears of his wagon. Letting out the reach to make the wagon longer, he loaded it with enough lumber to build their first little house, then roped a rocking chair on top of the boards. Since the May day was blazing hot, he strapped an umbrella to the chairback, and Mrs. Martin and the baby rode home in style and comfort.

Alice's grandparents came to a farm nearby and built a good four-room "modern" house. Modern because, through an ingenious feature, it had running water inside. The well, put down in the middle of an inner room, had a windmill above it on the roof of the house, and water, pumped by the mill, ran through a tank in the room, keeping milk and butter fresh and cold, only a step from the kitchen door.

The Martins later moved into Medicine Lodge and Alice remembers the house well because it was just south of the Nation house, with a picket fence between. A frail, tiny child, she remembers how she loved to squeeze through the pickets to go to Aunt Carry's house. She fondly recalls how Mrs. Nation held her close and rocked and sang to her. "She had a beautiful voice until after she was horsewhipped one time for smashing a saloon," Mrs. MacGregor says. "After that it was too hoarse."

"Aunt Carry used to feed me hoe cakes, too, slathered with butter, to make me grow. And how I did love them. But I didn't like Mr.

Nation. He was always so cross and gruff with Aunt Carry, and whenever he came in I always ran home."

"She was so kind and good," Alice MacGregor goes on, "always helping people. She used to drive old Prince up in front of our gate and call out from the buggy, 'Oh, Sister Martin, bring the children and a knife and come out here. Somebody baked me a carmel cake and I want to give you some.' She had probably paid some poor woman a dollar to bake the cake."

Later, when Alice was older and Mrs. Nation was traveling abroad, her friend sent or brought her lovely things from faraway places. Mrs. MacGregor shows with pardonable pride the beautiful bracelet, set with cat eyes, cameos, and pearls, which Carry sent her from Mexico, and the solid silver spoon from Liverpool, England. She has the delicate brooch, with Mrs. Nation's picture in it, which the gallant crusader gave her mother long ago, and a splendid long string of glittering cut steel beads, and boxes of letters and cards from many states and countries. Alice MacGregor treasures them all, along with the memories they hold for her of a dear friend who was never too busy to remember her.

There are as many conflicting stories of Mrs. Nation's size and appearance as there are of her activities. Some have her tall and mannish looking. Most refer to her husky build; a few call her fat. These people who knew her say she was no more than five feet, eight inches tall, not large at all, but solidly built. She was an attractive woman, Mrs. MacGregor says, and she had lovely clothes. "She always looked nice."

As to the afflicted daughter so often mentioned, Charlene did not live in Medicine Lodge with her mother and few living there now remember her at all. However, she visited her mother one summer, Alice MacGregor recalls, and she was a grown young lady then. She cannot remember any scars on Charlene's face, or any other signs of affliction.[10] "She used to visit with my mother and there was nothing wrong with the way she talked." At any rate, she married well and had eight children.

As to Carry Nation's treatment by the citizens of Medicine Lodge, it was good, for the most part. But there were some, mostly rough men who disliked her interference with their "rights" to drink and smoke, who treated her rudely at times. A Bill Horn (said to have been a brother of the Wyoming killer, Tom Horn), who drove the stage from Hutchinson to Medicine Lodge in those days, is supposed to have kicked her off his stage once. One also frequently reads of Carry snatching cigars from the mouths of men she met on the street. "But do you know why she did that?" asks pretty Alice MacGregor. "It was because they walked up and blew smoke in her face." Most of the local churches gave only lip service to Carry's fight against the open saloons early in her Medicine Lodge career, and later, when the liquor forces and their prominent supporters attacked her with venom, some church groups—even some W.C.T.U. groups—weakened, regretting and ridiculing her actions, piously hoping she would desist and act in a more ladylike manner.

In 1903 Mrs. Nation sold her home in Medicine Lodge and used the money to make a down payment on a Kansas City home for the wives of drunkards. At that time she was making enough money from her lectures and souvenir enterprises to support herself, maintain the Kansas City establishment, and, as she finally grew old and tired, to buy herself a little farm near Eureka Springs, Arkansas. There, away from the heat of the summers, she retired to rest awhile.

Part of each year she lectured against liquor and for women sufferage, and continued to do many other good works. In the winter of 1910-11 she became ill in St. Louis, where she was lecturing, and returned to Kansas City to see her doctor. When he advised her to go to a hospital, she chose the Evergreen Hospital in Leavenworth, where she died six months later on June 9, 1911. Her death was ascribed to "nervous trouble due to unusual activities which caused a weakening of the heart." And *this* was said of one of the stoutest hearted women of her time. She is buried in Belton, Missouri.[11]

When her old home in Medicine Lodge was about to be torn down, the local W.C.T.U. ladies bought the house for $4,500, borrowed from Daws Grigsby, retired rancher. The women held their own meetings in the basement hall they fitted up in the house, and derived some revenues from renting the hall to other organizations. Donations from Carry Nation admirers and profits from the sale of souvenir items have brought in funds sufficient to maintain the house and to pay off the loan.

Mrs. Nation's own furniture had long since been moved away, leaving only the empty shell of her old home. But the foreward looking ladies, by diligent effort and with the backing of most of the community, were able to gather up enough furniture, almost identical to that used by the crusader, to refurnish the house. One piece of extremely good fortune came their way when Carry's own little organ came back to its old home, where it stands today in the very corner it occupied over sixty years ago. Its tones are still as sweet and strong as when Carry and her courageous followers stood about it singing their hymns of praise and war.

Across the room from the organ are glass cases containing her Bible and her hatchet, a few of the little souvenir hatchets left over from the hundreds of thousands she sold during her crusading days, and copies of her own magazines and newspapers, along with copies of British newspapers dealing with her stormy visits to that tight little isle.

On a shelf in the Stockade Museum, next door to the Nation home, stand a pair of dark brown bottles labeled "Malto-tone, special brew for medicine, Kansas City, Missouri." The bottles were discovered in August 1969, stashed away in a dark corner of the basement of the Hibbard drugstore of Medicine Lodge. Speculation among the townspeople is that they were likely hidden from Carry Nation, some seventy years ago, for the Hibbard drugstore is the same one, in the same building, once owned by O. L. Day.

When the local American Legion post was organized in 1919, a temporary charter was granted it under the name of the Carry Nation Post Number 1. However, the next year a permanent charter was granted under the prosaic title of Barber County Post Number 69.

Years later a fine new bridge was built to carry U.S. Highway 160 across the Medicine Lodge River at the west edge of town. It was proposed that the bridge be named the Carry Nation Bridge, but when the matter was put to a vote it failed to carry—an unfortunate disregard of an opportunity to perpetuate history.

However, the determined little lady has a firm niche in the Kansas State Historical Society museum in Topeka. There, in a glass showcase, a copy of her famous magazine, *The Hatchet*, featuring her slogan "To Cut Out The Evil," is prominently displayed. There are real hatchets in the case, too, some used by the dauntless Carry in her raids, others given to her as tokens of respect by organizations that believed in her work. There are also souvenir pins featuring her campaigns; and temperance badges; and a few whisky bottles, beer mugs, and wine glasses from saloons she broke up, but which she missed as she smashed her way through the furnishings. On the wall above the case hangs the last bar mirror she attacked, complete with the crack she put in it with her hatchet.

> Toll the bell softly and sing a Sweet song,
> Hushed be the voice of the world's Mighty throng.
> Step very lightly with slow gentle tread.
> The brave Home Defender, Carry Nation is dead.[12]

THIRTEEN

The Murder of Sheriff McCracken

1908

Carry Nation's raids on Kiowa's saloons produced one kind of excitement among the townspeople. A few years later, on a night late in March 1908, another and tragic kind of excitement swept through Kiowa. Under the banner headline ALL BARBER COUNTY MOURNS, the *Index* for March 25 reported: "Never in the history of Barber County were our people so horribly shocked as they were last Thursday night when the awful, heartrending news was flashed over the wires that Sheriff E. L. (Bud) McCracken was shot and mortally wounded at Kiowa by James Clark, better known as "Dad" Clark, while attempting to serve a warrant on him.

"Clark is a notorious bootlegger who has been hanging around Kiowa for a number of years. He worked, at times, at the cobbler trade as a side issue to cover his real business. The day before the shooting he was wanted as a witness in a petty larceny case and a subpoena was issued for him, but when Deputy Sheriff Downtain went after him he had left and secreted himself. Later in the day a warrant was issued, charging him with selling whisky. In the evening he returned to his house and barricaded the doors. Sheriff McCracken and City Marshal Bunton, of Kiowa, learned of his return and went to the house to arrest him."

From outside Clark's door, the officers told the old man who they were and what they wanted and asked him to come out. Clark did not answer them. Finally they broke down the door, talking loudly, for the bootlegger's benefit, of setting the house afire. This frightened Clark, who escaped through a window and ran into the outdoor privy. The sheriff followed, circling the little building several times and telling the old man he must come out.

By then it was nearly time for the train back to Medicine Lodge to come along, so the sheriff decided to waste no more time. The privy door was partly open and he could dimly see Clark standing inside. It looked to the officer like the old man had his hands up, so he reached for him. At the same instant Clark raised his revolver, stuck it against McCracken's chest, and fired. He then pushed the door shut and pressed himself into one corner. The sheriff lifted his own revolver and began firing into the tiny building. He fired four times, putting a bullet into each of three corners of the outhouse but missing the one where Clark stood. At the fourth shot Clark suddenly dashed out the door and ran off through the darkness.

Marshal Bunton, standing some thirty feet from the privy, then fired at Clark, striking him in the leg and knocking him down. His gun flew from his hand and he at once began to beg for mercy. Bunton got him on his feet again, McCracken joined them and the three started toward the depot. But after a few steps the sheriff said to Bunton, "I'm all in," and fell to the ground.

All three of Kiowa's doctors tended the wounded sheriff that night, none of them holding out any hope that he would live until morning. But he did, and the next day three more doctors, one each from Anthony, Medicine Lodge, and Wichita, hurried to Kiowa to do what they could to save the man. The sheriff himself, the *Index* reported, was cheerful and hopeful until near the end, which came at 12:10 on Saturday afternoon.

Following the shooting, feeling ran high, for the sheriff was a prominent and popular man. Knowing the temper of his fellow citizens, McCracken, even while he lay on his bed of intense pain, ordered his officers to keep the old man safe from harm. To insure against a premature end such as the Sheriff feared, Clark was hurriedly taken to the jail at Wellington, seventy miles east, a precaution that undoubtedly saved him from hanging.

The dead sheriff's body was taken from Kiowa to Medicine Lodge on Sunday morning, "accompanied by two hundred sorrowing and tearful Kiowa citizens." The funeral was held in the Christian church, "of which he was a faithful member," with all the ministers in the town taking part in the service. The city officials of Kiowa were honorary pall bearers and the funeral, according to the *Index*, was the largest yet held in Medicine Lodge. The church seated over five hundred people, the account adds, but only a small part of the assembled throng could find even standing room inside.

Reverend W. H. Moore, an intimate friend of the sheriff's, did not mince words in his funeral sermon, but "hit hard" at a great many people, including "some Christian persons who are passive on the question of law enforcement," in fixing the responsibility for the sad and tragic death. "We have no doubt," concluded the *Index*, "that his sermon has offended some people, but that he told cold facts is patent to every person who heard the discourse."

One of the saddest aspects of the whole affair was revealed in a paragraph at the end of the newspaper story. "During all this terrible tragedy Mrs. McCracken was confined to her bed, which makes the calamity thrice sad. She gave birth to a child two days before and hence was in no condition to withstand such a shock. But she has displayed most remarkable courage and no serious results are feared. She is a brave woman. . . ."

The sheriff, the *Index* noted, was fourty-four years old and the father of eight children besides the infant born at the time of his death. The paper concluded with a long and heartfelt eulogy for the murdered sheriff, and beneath it these words, in boldface type, "What a Price." Carry Nation would have agreed with all her heart.

A day or two before the shooting, Sheriff McCracken had gone to Kiowa to arrest Charles Chandler, John McGarrah, and Roy Brannon for the illegal sale of whisky. Chandler, taken before the judge, pled guilty, was fined, and sentenced to thirty days in jail. McGarrah was released on a $250 bond, but Chandler, Brannon, and a third man, Robert Arnold, were taken to Medicine Lodge and put into jail. The last two, on a complaint by James Clark, were then charged with stealing $15 from the old bootlegger. After reaching the jail, Brannon was released from the bootlegging charge, then immediately rearrested on the larceny charge. The trial on the latter charge was to be held in Medicine Lodge and the sheriff had gone to Kiowa to bring Clark back as a witness in his own case against the men he believed had stolen the money from him.

A good man had been killed, a fine woman was widowed, nine innocent children were left fatherless, and a ne'er-do-well old man, wounded and sick, had been spirited out of the hands of an avenging mob and lodged in a distant jail. But, as Mrs. Nation's determined assault had roused the country against illegal saloons a few years earlier, so the sheriff's untimely death stirred up the populace again. "Public sentiment," to quote the *Index*, "is aroused against bootlegging and general lawlessness."

The neighboring town of Hardtner likewise got in line behind the sentiments of its citizens: "No shot was ever fired that created more excitement and indignation among the people of this locality than the one fired at Bud McCracken at Kiowa. Everyone, regardless of politics, excepting those in sympathy with lawlessness, admits that Barber County never had a better sheriff. It is a great calamity to our people to have such a man, while fearlessly doing his duty, shot by one who was a known violator of the laws of the state.

"Will it not have the effect of awakening to a realization of their duty every law-abiding citizen in the county, will not the better class of our people now see that it is their duty as citizens to sacrifice even a little of their business that [they] are so fearful of hurting and do more toward assisting the officials in enforcing the law? But so long as we permit these lawless acts to go on before our eyes, and for fear of injuring our business keep quiet, just that long we are in a sense aiding and abetting such acts of violence."[1]

McCracken's last request was that W. I. Stranathan, his brother-in-law, should be appointed to "settle up his effects," which were considerable, including an unencumbered 1,500-acre ranch, cattle and horses, and $20,000 in life insurance with three different companies. A week later the *Index* reported that the Great Western officials of Kansas City had sent the widow a draft for $4,000 in full settlement of their policy on the sheriff's life.

This prompt payment apparently also settled some doubts in the community about the soundness of the insurance company, a new one which was offering better contracts than its older rivals in that part of Kansas. The rivals had spread and backed the "doubts," and the new company, hearing opportunity knocking loud and clear, had hastened to open the door. For, as the *Index* observed, "The prompt settlement of this claim has already put a quietus to those who have been 'knocking', and the cry that the company cannot meet its losses . . . will not be heard in this section of the country again soon, at least not while this transaction is fresh in the public mind."

The widow, writing to the Great Western on the day she received the draft, just ten days after her husband was shot, acknowledged receipt of the money and stated, "This is the first settlement made by any company and I wish to thank you for your promptness in this matter. Yours truly, Ella McCracken."

A rather odd and somewhat amusing event followed the murder. A young man, Will Clark, and his mother, Mrs. Jack Clark, were in Emporia at the time of the shooting in Kiowa. In Strong City, on their way home to Medicine Lodge, they read about the murder in the newspaper, and that the man who fired the fatal shot was a James Clark. Whereupon Mrs. Clark "became very nervous and feared at once that the man referred to might be her husband," since the description of the murderer resembled that of her spouse, Jack Clark, and she thought there might have been a typographical error in printing the name.

She at once persuaded her son to take her to Wellington so she could see for herself. When they arrived at the jail and asked to see the prisoner, Will was immediately searched on suspicion, then arrested for carrying a revolver. He was fined one dollar and costs, the latter amounting to more than thirteen dollars. A little later, when the sheriff of Sumner County learned the facts, "he regretted having arrested Mr. (Will) Clark, but the fine had been paid and there was no way of remitting it." Clark explained that he had once been "worked" (robbed) while traveling, and that was why he carried the gun. After his Wellington experience he no doubt felt he had been "worked" again.

As for the seventy-year-old murderer, "Dad" Clark, the "old inebriate" died in the Wellington jail the Monday following his incarceration there. The shot he had taken in his leg that night in Kiowa had broken one of the bones and gangrene followed. The leg was amputated but the old man died anyway, which was "most fortunate," according to the *Index*, for "it was doubtful if the populace could have restrained themselves when the old fiend would have been brought here [Medicine Lodge] for trial."

FOURTEEN

Cyclones, Railroads

1907-1935

A year preceding the killing of Sheriff McCracken, violence of a different kind visited Barber County. On Sunday, June 23, 1907, a thunder head arose in the sky to the west of Medicine Lodge. Though the wind that stirred the dust in the streets that afternoon was *from* the south, the cloud moved *south* against it, slowly growing bigger and blacker, while weather wise residents watched it uneasily.

"As the cloud gathered in size," reported L. M. Axline, editor of the *Cresset*,[1] "it took on a whirling motion and advanced to a point almost west of the city. All watching it realized that a terrible storm was at hand and the question was whether it would expend its force in the upper air or reach the ground, and if it came to earth where would it strike?

"As is usual with tornado and cyclone clouds, as soon as well formed it took an easterly course and traveled in that direction for ten or twelve miles. Damage was done from a point about seven miles west of town and through the north end of town to a point about four miles southeast."

Before the storm had fully developed into the twister that did so much damage, two funnel shaped clouds formed. "One of these seemed to be an outlet for the disturbance above it, for the vapor could be plainly seen pouring into it from the upper end and descending to the ground. The tail could be seen to sway back and forth, as a snake's tail when the head is held in the hand. The other end gathered from below and everything was carried upward."

The action of the cloud must have been horrifying to watch. Mr. Axline describes the whirling columns of vapor that constantly broke from the main cloud and were hurled to earth, doing tremendous damage wherever they struck. These "pieces of cloud" broke away, two or three at a time, and fell to earth, ripping and splintering everything they touched, but leaving clear spaces in between.

About half past six in the evening the two funnels joined together and "the storm broke in all its fury, enveloping the city and surrounding country in a whirling mass of vapor, rain and hail. Those that watched up to the last moment before the heavy downpour shut off the view witnessed a sight they must wish never to see repeated. The clouds reached to the earth and small masses of what seemed to be a vapor were continually shot from the ground into the clouds above, while the lightning and thunder were so continuous and awful that connected thought was impossible."

All who could took refuge in cellars, the rest waited in their homes for "the shock that all felt would surely come." The awfulness of the short period when the whirling winds were kneading the town is beyond description. And even though the tornadic winds soon lifted again into the upper heights, the storm was not yet done; for, after a momentary hush almost as frightening as the roar of the holocaust, rain, hail, and a fierce southeast wind rushed in to fill the vacuum left by the departing funnel.

But at last it was over and the late rays of the June sun revealed "a scene of destruction and waste. Nearly every building in the northwest part of town was in ruins or had vanished. The beautiful rows and groves of trees that had added so much to the beauty of our town were shorn of their leaves and branches, their naked arms outstretched to the sky, or else were torn out, root and branch, and piled with all manner of wreckage along the streets.

"Walnut Street was almost impassable, being filled with telephone poles and wire, trees of all sizes and varieties, dead horses and cattle, and chickens with their feathers stripped. That many people were not killed can only be accounted for by the lifting or suction power of the air, which in some places picked up the houses and left the occupants unharmed upon the floor, instead of a depressing force which sometimes crushes the houses and causes so much loss of life."

Altogether twenty-eight houses had been destroyed or carried away, and fifty or sixty barns totally wrecked. The west front of Jones grocery store was blown in and the stock badly damaged. Six miles west of town John Jesse's house was blown down and John's crippled leg was broken again in two places.

Delilah Spriggs, a woman still living in Medicine Lodge today, well remembers the storm. A young woman then, she was visiting the R. H. Faxons in the north part of town. With the young couple and their baby, she was in the kitchen of the six-room house. There was a terrible streak of lightning, she said, a terrific clap of thunder and then "a sudden awful wind." Windows and doors were crashing into the house in the other rooms and Mr. Faxon ran to the kitchen door to hold it shut. Delilah grabbed the baby, the young man yelled for help to hold the door, and the two women ran to throw their weight against it, too. Mrs. Faxon was praying, she said, and Mr. Faxon was cussing. "Hold your damnedest, it'll be hell in here if the door goes," he shouted. So they all held with all their might and the door stayed shut. When the storm was over and they dared leave the kitchen to look around, they found it to be the only whole room left in the house. The walls of all the other rooms were smashed in and the house was off its foundations.

Senator Long's home, just north of Faxon's, had not been seriously damaged but two Shetland ponies that had been grazing in the yard were gone. They were found the next day, two miles north: one hanging in the fork of a tree a good many feet above the ground, alive; the other grazing nearby.

The Alexander family, not far from the Faxons and just north of Highland Cemetery, fared much worse. As the house went to pieces around them, Charley Alexander put his arms around his wife and baby girl, "and amid the crashing timber, the roar and hiss of wind, hail and rain, the three were hurled into the midst of the storm." Somewhere outside the father managed to get hold of a tree. Putting the woman and baby next to the trunk, he shielded them as best he could, taking a fusilade of sticks, stones and debris of all kinds on his back, which was cut and bruised in a shocking manner.

The cemetery itself was thoroughly wrecked. "The scene was desolate in the extreme. Scarcely a stone or monument was left standing." It was later most difficult to determine the correct sites of many of the graves.

But to a man named J. Bradney was left one of the strangest of all experiences. Bradney was on the road about five miles west of town, driving one team to a hayrack, leading another, and hurrying to get home before the storm struck. Suddenly he was lifted from the wagon and whirled through the air, then dropped to the ground. A moment later he was airborne again, and this time he flew along for nearly half a mile, sometimes quite close to the ground. He was carried along so rapidly, he said, that he was unable to catch hold of anything that might have stopped his flight.

Another man, G. W. Marshall, working at the Currie farm that day, was standing in the barn door watching the gathering cloud when Jerry Gano and his wife dashed up in their buggy and drove into the barn. They intended to make a run for the Currie cyclone cellar, they said, and begged Marshall to go with them, but he declared he was not afraid and would stay in the barn. When the barn was carried away a few minutes later, he was bombarded by boards and timbers, then blown some twenty feet away and knocked down. He could hear and see objects of many kinds passing above him, so stayed where he was. The Gano team and buggy flew over him with a whizzing sound, he said, whirling in the wind and headed east. When it was over and the damage assessed, it was found that Marshall's collar bone was broken, the smashed remains of the buggy was scattered around a hundred yards from the barn, and the horses were located in a pasture half a mile farther on, crippled but on their feet.

That no human lives were lost was attributed in part to the fact that nearly everyone in the area had gone underground, into caves or cellars. The property damage, however, was estimated at $200,000. The tale concluded with the *Cresset's* comment: "People from the adjoining country came in Monday by the hundreds to view the effects of the cyclone in this city."

Violence, however, had not finished with the valley of the Medicine. Nature assaulted the lovely land again twenty years later in the spring of 1927. J. C. Hinshaw, in the April 21 edition of the *Index* commented on the extremely ominous weather experienced in Kansas that season, and noted that "Medicine Lodge and Barber County are very fortunate in escaping the brunt of the general storms over the country, although it looked for awhile Monday noon like it might be pretty bad right here in town." On May 7 the worst tornado ever to strike came down on the area. Three persons died and property damage ran to more than half a million dollars before it was over.

"After a close, sultry day," wrote Mr. Hinshaw, "the storm took form in the southwestern part of the county and between the hours of five and eight o'clock had torn its way across the county, missing Medicine Lodge by only a quarter to a half mile and making a complete circle around the town.

"With a roar that could be heard for miles, the storm gave warning of its approach and the threat of its fury, which was such that it could not have been equalled by tens of thousands of unleashed demons gone mad. No matter how one describes the aftermath of the storm or its effect, it must be remembered that it is still worse than any words can express. With fiendish design it swooped down on farm houses, tearing them to splinters, and scattering the timbers from the farm barns and outbuildings, granaries, sheds, corrals, fences, over miles of territory. Great trees were torn from the ground, broken off, twisted off, uprooted, the bark peeled from the trunks until today they stand like bleak, whitened old stumps that had died many years ago, mute reminders of prized trees in full leaf only a few days ago."

The three persons killed were Mr. and Mrs. Sayres and Mr. Coffman. Guy Sayres and his wife, at their home three miles southeast of town, died instantly. They were evidently preparing their evening meal; Mrs. Sayres was still grasping the handle of a skillet when her badly broken body was found some distance from where the house stood. Mr. Sayres was found farther away, across a small canyon in a grove of trees. Both bodies, stripped of clothing and plastered with mud, were bruised and mangled almost beyond recognition. Frank Coffman, who lived two miles north of town, was killed when the wall of his brick home toppled on him as he and his father left the house to make a run for a cave.

"Barber County in the path of the storm presents a scene of wreckage which could only have found its equal in the devastated warfields of France a few years ago. Well tilled fields are covered with splinters, boards, timbers and pieces of farm machinery, twisted, bent and broken. Fences are strewn across the roads and fields, wires are hanging from trees. . . .

"Bits of torn clothing may be found in trees. Huge masses of wire, rolled and matted together, were sent hurtling across pastures. Automobiles have been more completely wrecked than a salvage concern could have done, and the pieces scattered to the four corners of the compass.

"Horses, cattle, hogs, chickens and turkeys were found hundreds of yards and sometimes miles from the nearest farm home, with every bone broken, the larger animals with their heads driven into their bodies. So great was the strength of the wind that great holes were torn into the sod, some to the depth of a foot, and ten to twenty feet long or wide."

The path of the storm varied in width from a hundred yards to a mile or more, and its destruction was so complete that "a feeling of depression that could not be shaken off seemed to settle down over the town and country." Small knots of men gathered on the streets, telling of some new freakish thing done by the wind, then turning away as if lacking the will to clean up and begin over again. "It was a catastrophe," stated the *Index*, "that it will take years to overcome." And indeed it would, for whole groves of trees were torn and dead, and the fine big steel cantilever bridge over the Medicine River a mile south of town on the Kiowa road was thoroughly wrecked, its heavy spans and flooring twisted and splintered into useless junk.

On the G. E. Alexander ranch, thirteen miles southwest of town, a five-ton Holt catapillar tractor had been rolled over and over for a hundred feet, then abandoned on its side. A twisted iron bedstead and a few splintered boards were all that was left of the Thomas home a mile southeast of the village. And so it was on farm after farm, all along the storm king's path.

Presently, as always after such overwhelming disasters, stories of miraculous escapes began to make the rounds. There were the Joe Fussells, east of town. The storm blew away their house and outbuildings and overtook the family as they fled across a freshly listered field, seeking shelter in a canyon on the far side. All they could do then was flatten themselves in the shallow lister rows. The sixteen-year-old daughter, who carried the year-old baby in her arms, put the infant in the row beneath her, but both were picked up by the wind and carried a quarter of a mile away. Although they recovered from the harrowing experience, their condition when found was frightful. Stripped naked and fearfully bruised, their "backs were driven full of sand, gravel, grass and sandburrs, their heads coated with mud."

Mrs. Walter Friend, a newly married young woman, was getting ready to take a bath when her husband ran in, shouting, "Quick, let's get to the cellar. There's a cyclone coming!" Snatching a coat, she put it on as they ran. When they came up from the cellar after the storm had passed, their house and everything in it was gone, leaving the bride with nothing whatever but the old coat to wear.

Then, as if the Devil's wrath was not yet appeased, a fierce hail storm struck another section of the county a day or two later, mowing down newly greened wheat fields the tornado had missed, ruining crops in Valley, Sharon, and Medicine Lodge townships. Stones seven inches in circumference pounded the land and fell in such quantities that even the next day they could be shovelled up by the wagon loads. Birds and chickens were killed wholesale, cattle and horses were beaten, bruised, and bleeding, windows by the scores were broken, flooded creeks did heavy damage.

To round off the disasters of that spring, the insurance company that had written the bulk of the policies covering the damaged area went broke trying to meet its obligations in the path of the hail storm, leaving many of its policy holders with little or nothing to show for premiums paid.

But again, as always at such times, the neighbors rallied round and the unhurt, or least hurt, helped the others. Long lists of names appeared in the weekly *Cresset* through the rest of May and into June, the names of the folks who donated to the ever-growing "Relief Fund." The amounts given ranged from twenty-five cents on up to banker Chandler's $250 donation. All of it helped replace some of the clothes, buildings, furniture, cows, and horses lost in the big tornado. Even more, it helped instill new hope and courage in the beaten and hopeless.

From March 1908 until May 1927, a period of nearly twenty years, the records reveal no untoward violence or excitement in Medicine Lodge or Barber County. The First World War burst on the nation and passed into history. But the county prospered, paid off a portion of its burdensome debt, built needed bridges and roads, and acquired quite a few more miles of railroad track.

Jacob Achenbach, the man who carried in his hip pocket the funds to start Kiowa's bank, was responsible for the extra track mileage. Achenbach had done very well with his various business enterprises, so well that he was financially able to back the Kiowa, Hardtner and

Pacific Railway Company, organized in 1908 for the purpose of building ten miles of track from Kiowa, the end of the railroad, on to Hardtner, which had long bemoaned its lack of railway facilities.

Jacob called the first meeting of his company on July 9, 1908, and laid plans to build the road. All went well until it came to crossing his road over the main line of the Santa Fe. "They did not want us to cross their road," Jacob said. "But after putting our crossing in on the Denver, Enid and Gulf line one Sunday, we were ready to cross the Santa Fe line. Then their superintendent, Mr. Shafer, blockaded the crossing by having his private car stopped there. About forty or fifty cowboys gathered on Mule Creek and sent word to the superintendent that it would be best for him to move his car, as they intended to put in the crossing that day. If he refused to move it, they said, they would shoot it all to h——, well, they'd riddle it with bullets."[2]

Poly Tincher, then a Santa Fe attorney and in Kiowa at the time, was told of the trouble and advised to go tell Mr. Shafer it would be best for him to move his car before the riled cowboys got there as they would surely start something that would be hard to stop. Mr. Tincher drove out to the blockaded crossing and delivered the message, but Shafer laughed it off. The threatened raid, he said, was just a bluff. But when he saw the army of cowboys come over the hill, their horses on a dead run, he hurriedly changed his tune and ordered the engineer to get his car off the crossing and back to town, pronto.

The cowboys had all the necessary tools with them, and in less than three hours the crossing was laid.

Achenbach's bobtailed railroad triggered others. One, the Wichita Falls and Northwestern, built to Forgan in Beaver County, Oklahoma, a hundred miles west of Hardtner. And there the road ended, seven miles short of Beaver, the county seat. The people of Beaver then undertook to build the road on to their town but soon ran out of money. At that point they came to Achenbach for help. After due consideration, he "saw the possibility of developing the Oklahoma Panhandle . . . and decided to extend the road which split the Panhandle wide open." The road was completed in 1915.

At the time Achenbach began building his Beaver, Meade, and Englewood Railroad west of Forgan, no other railroad was under construction, or even contemplated, in that part of the country. The Missouri-Kansas-Texas had stopped at Forgan years ago and the Santa

Fe had ceased laying track at Elkhart, in the southwest corner of Kansas, a long while back. "When we reached Hooker [forty miles on west], the Rock Island sat up and took notice," Achenbach said, "and as we extended our road farther west the Santa Fe became interested, but for years our B.M.&E. was the only company building a mile of track in the state of Oklahoma."

But by the time Achenbach's road reached Keyes, Oklahoma, 105 miles from Forgan, the Chicago, Rock Island and the M.K.&T. were both trying to buy sixty-five miles of the road. In November 1930, after long deliberation, the Interstate Commerce Commission decided in favor of the M.K.&T., a company that in the beginning had refused to have anything to do with the road, claiming it would never earn sufficient revenue to buy grease for the engine.

In 1935, Jacob Achenbach, at the age of eight-nine, was still operating his first little railroad, the K.H.&P., and carrying on his cattle feeding business near his town of Hardtner.

J. N. "Poley" Tincher, the "Big Congressman from the Big Seventh."

Lucille Mulhall, waiting for steer roping competition at the 101 Ranch rodeo, June 11, 1905. *Courtesy National Cowboy Hall of Fame.*

1907 tornado results. Home of R. H. Faxon, secretary to Senator Chester Long. Later purchased by Sheriff Ben Harbaugh in 1922. *Courtesy Lloyd Weidner.*

First Barber County courthouse, paid for twice before it was finally built in 1886 at a cost of $40,000.

Carey Hotel bar, Wichita, Kansas, smashed by Carry Nation, December 27, 1900. *Courtesy Kansas State Historical Society.*

Carry Nation's Medicine Lodge home, c1960. *Courtesy Kansas State Historical Society.*

Whites and Indians who took part in the search for the actual 1867 peace treaty site. I-See-O is in feather headdress. The white man with no hat, in back row, is John C. Best, first president of the Peace Treaty Association. The man with hat, in back row, is General Winfield Scott, under whom I-See-O served as a scout at Fort Sill, Oklahoma. The Indian at far right is George Hunt, interpreter for I-See-O.

Wagon train scene from pageant.

1967 pageant scene. *Courtesy Kansas State Highway Commission.*

Stagecoach hold-up scene from pageant.

Indian attack on wagon train scene from pageant.

Isaiah Hewitt.

Vinton Clifford Sleeper.

Frank Pleasonton Hewitt and Ida Levara Sleeper, married in 1898. Parents of I. N. Hewitt.

The winning track team of Medicine Lodge High School, 1923. Back row, L to R: Brick Case, Clay McCoy, Coach Bryan, C. B. Fullerton, Ted Kenny. Front row, L to R: Trice Newsom, Jibo Hewitt, Glenn Nixon.

FIFTEEN

More Outlaws

1927

Before the community had recovered from the shattering effects of the tornado, it "experienced a series of thrills on Saturday afternoon, August 13 1927, when it became known that the Isabel State Bank had been robbed and that a posse was in pursuit of the robbers. The excitement did not abate until Sunday morning, when the two men were captured in a silo on the Chriss McGuire farm near Sharon."[1]

The robbers were Roy and Lawrence Turner, brothers, who had formerly lived in and near Medicine Lodge and were familiar with the town and its buildings, especially Roy who, before moving to Wichita two years back, had worked for the local branch of the Bell Telephone Company. On the Saturday of the robbery the pair had spent most of the day loafing in Isabel. About four in the afternoon, when the streets were nearly deserted, they had gone to the bank.

Finding only two men inside, Clyde Boots, assistant cashier, and a customer, Wilbur Irby, the unmasked robbers ordered them to lie down on the floor, then proceeded to ransack the money tills. With the cash and some bundles of travelers' checks, they ran out, got into a touring car, and headed south out of town. Boots jumped up, grabbed a gun, and fired several shots after the car. The Turners returned the fire and their bullets somewhat damaged the bank's south window. (All the rest of the afternoon anyone stopping at the post-office for the mail came on around the corner to take a look at the bullet holes in the window frame.) Helen and Roberta Tudor, busy at their switchboard in the nearby telephone office, heard the shots and spread the alarm. Within a few minutes dozens of men were giving chase.

Barely two miles south of town the bandits, with the usual bad luck of Barber County outlaws, crashed their vehicle into a car parked in the road beside a farmyard where a public auction was going on. Leaping from their car, the pair ran to another, parked on the far side of the machine they ran into, and sped on. But the new car was smaller and slower than their own and with the pursuing cars gaining on them they were forced to abandon the purloined car and hide in a corn field beside the road.

By then at least 300 men had joined in the chase. Armed with weapons of every kind, some dating back to the Civil War, the posse surrounded the cornfield and the capture of the robbers seemed certain. But fate, always capricious where bank robberies in that part of Kansas were concerned, now took another sudden turn. Before the army could close in on the hidden men, a severe wind storm struck the field, filling the air full of dust and flying debris; then came a heavy downpour of rain, and the pursuit had to be abandoned until the storm was over.

The tracks of the two men were then picked up, still leading south, and Sheriff Ben Harbaugh and a small force of picked men followed them all night. After awhile the tracks began to cross and recross, and even to double back on earlier trails; possibly because the robbers were lost, more likely due to a deliberate attempt to mislead the posse. At any rate the tracks were finally lost altogether. With dawn the sheriff and his deputies went into Sharon and recruited more help. Throwing his whole force in a circle around the spot where they lost the trail, it was soon picked up again, leading on into another cornfield.

But while the volunteers were covering that field, Sheriff Harbaugh walked over to a nearby group of farm buildings and peered into the silo. Sure enough, the pair was hiding there, and when the sheriff stuck his shotgun through the door and ordered them to put up their hands and come out, they did so without argument. It was a blue and sorry looking brace of desperadoes that faced the forty or more men in the posse. Worn-out by their long flight and sleepless night, their clothes and shoes mud-caked and filthy, they were quickly searched and relieved of $568 in stolen bills and change.

On the way back to Medicine Lodge the outlaws told how several times during the night members of the search party had been within a few feet of them, where they lay hidden in pools of rain water in the field. They freely and profanely declared that if they had had one more hour of darkness, or if it hadn't rained just when it did, or if they could have found another car, they would have made their getaway a sure thing.

Sheriff Harbaugh was generous in his praise for all the Barber County men who so quickly responded to the alarm. Without the aid of present-day radio and other high-speed communications media, they had, within a very short time after the holdup, blocked every road in the whole area; every person not known to the posse was stopped and made to give an account of himself. In addition to the men of Hardtner, Kiowa, Hazelton, Sharon, Medicine Lodge, Isabel, Lake City, and Sun City, the American Legion boys and every other man in the county had turned out to help as soon as the word got around.

By the time the Turners were lodged in the county jail they seemed to have recovered their good spirits and had, according to the *Index*, "assumed a jaunty air." Arrainged on Monday, they pled not guilty. On Tuesday they waived their hearing and were of necessity bound over to the district court and placed under a bond on $10,000 each. Since neither could give the bond, they were to be held in jail until the October term of court. As later events proved, their assurance of nearly three months in the old and inadequate jail was responsible for their quick rise of spirits. Any outlaw, faced with ten to twenty years in the pen, was a pantywaist for sure if he couldn't figure out a way to spring himself from a calaboose like this one.

At the hearing the pair wore neat grey suits and appeared not to have a care in the world. Their unrepentant attitude quite incensed the crowd that filled the courtroom, many of them people from Isabel who remembered how the two had fired from their fleeing car, "shooting with an evident intention to kill if possible." No doubt there was some discussion of another necktie party. However, the Turners were returned to the jail where, reported the *Index*, "special care is being taken to guard against any attempt to escape, especially as there are several other pretty desperate characters in the jail at this time."

Everybody concerned felt even better about the success of the big bandit roundup when it was learned that Roy Turner was already under a heavy bond for a recent diamond robbery in Wichita, where he had apparently taken $2,000 in jewels from one Louise Hughes. And still better when the Santa Fe agent from Attica identified the

Turners as the fellows who had robbed his station a few nights before the Isabel robbery. Then a pair of detectives came to town to see if they could get any trace of the American Express Travelers Checks that had disappeared with the cash at the time of the robbery. And then additional charges turned up, charges of other thefts and of bond jumping. The posse had patently done quite a scope of Kansas a good turn when they caught the notorious thieves.

Their satisfaction was short lived, for in spite of the "special care," whatever it may have been, on the night of August 29, just a little over two weeks after they were jailed, the Turners and a "wheat thief," Clyde Pennington, broke out of the jail, swiped a big blue Hudson coach belonging to George Teegarden, contractor for the new Medicine Lodge high school building, and left for parts unknown.

The escape was not discovered until morning, when Under-sheriff Mills went down to the basement jail to unlock the cells and release the men for breakfast. All the other prisoners, a collection of drunks and bootleggers under thirty- to ninety-day sentences, swore that they were sound asleep the whole time that the three men facing long prison terms were getting away.

The escape plan wasn't hard to figure out, and few seemed to blame the sheriff. Under the circumstances he had done about as well as anyone could. There were only three iron-barred cells in the old jail room, with a toilet in each cell. Major criminals, when there were any, were locked in the cells. All minor offenders were simply locked into the main room in a body. Since these men, too, must have access to one of the toilets, Harbaugh had met the problem by leaving Pennington's cell unlocked at night. The Turners were kept shackled in the main jail room during the day, but at night were unshackled and locked into separate cells.

The morning after the escape it was found that an iron bar on the inside of each of the locked cell doors had been twisted off by the Turners and handed out to Pennington who, probably with the help of one or more of the soundly sleeping inmates, forced the end of the bar into the loop of the padlock and broke the lock. With the same bar they had no doubt dug a hole through the west wall of the jail room and crawled out under the floor of the courthouse hallway above, then north to a trapdoor in the floor of the woman's toilet, and so to freedom.

It was believed that Roy Turner, during his former residence in the town, had learned the floor plan of the courthouse and jail, and doubtless also knew that the outside jail walls were of such a soft brick and lime construction that, as Sheriff Harbaugh said, "It was an easy matter to dig through them with most any sort of a tool." His big mistake, the sheriff sadly admitted, was in leaving Pennington free at night and the Turners unshackled.

All peace officers within 300 miles were alerted immediately: the robbers were described, and also the big Hudson coach, which Teegarden had considerately filled with gas the evening before, enabling the outlaws to drive a long way before the necessity for a stop.

The outlaws' run of good luck was almost too short to notice, for the *Index* of September 8 announced triumphantly that the three had been captured in Phoenix, Arizona, and charged with transporting a stolen car from one state to another. The Phoenix chief of police promptly wired Sheriff Harbaugh to ask if "he still desired the men, and Mr. Harbaugh wasted no time letting him know he certainly did." The men were to be returned to Medicine Lodge as soon as possible, where, by agreement of the county commissioners with the sheriff, they would be held under "day and night armed guard and no effort or expense will be spared to see that they are kept secure until the next term of the district court." The *Index* of September 15 noted that the three prisoners were "back in jail after a short vacation."

On the Sunday following his return to Medicine Lodge, Roy Turner took the officers to the spot where he and his brother had hidden the travelers checks under "a bunch of yucca just west of the first turn of the Isabel road north of where the old 'crooked bridge' used to be." With their recovery it seemed that all the stolen money had been found.

Back in their cells again, the three men talked freely of their escape. They had dug the hole through the wall several days before they used it, they said, and during the day kept it covered with a dish towel. The night of the jail break, Pennington had gone out first, to make sure the plan would work, but when he came back into the basement he could not get back through the hole into the jail. Although they hadn't intended to make their break for another day or two, the Turners now had to crawl out too, for the discovery of Pennington's absence would have given the whole show away. They had then looked around for the right kind of an escape car, something big and fast and powerful. Teegarden's big new Hudson was just the thing, and by sunup they were almost to Texas.

The trio was on the way to California when their luck gave out in Phoenix, where they missed the right road out of town and got lost. In trying to find their way again they drove into a side street filling station to ask directions. An alert policeman happened into the station before they got away. He concluded, right off, that the situation didn't add up as it should. For one thing the men were too poorly dressed to be the owners of such a fine car; for another, they were too far from home (they had replaced the Kansas license plate with one stolen from an Oklahoma car) to be traveling without any luggage. So, on general principles, he took them to the police station. When a letter from the Turners' sister, addressed in care of the Medicine Lodge jail, was found in Roy's pocket, the game was over.

The prisoners pled guilty at a special session of the district court and were quickly sentenced: the Turners to ten to twenty years at hard labor in the penitentiary at Lansing, Pennington to five years in the state penitentiary. Until they were taken away to begin their sentences the men, in addition to the twenty-four-hours-a-day armed guard posted over them, were kept in shackles and handcuffs in their locked cells. They also had an empty jail room before them, as all minor offenders were held in the unused women's ward for the duration. They were even transported to the penitentiaries with the shackles on their legs and their hands handcuffed behind them. As the *Index* observed, "Every precaution against their escape was taken." And once the thieves were safely lodged in prison, Barber County congratulated itself that its record was "practically clean, so far as bank robberies were concerned."

SIXTEEN

Peace Treaty Pageant

1927-1970

With the approach of the year 1917, Medicine Lodge citizens remembered that in October it would be a half century since the five tribes had met somewhere in their vicinity to sign the Peace Treaty of 1867. Nothing had ever been done to mark or commemorate either the site or the event, it was pointed out, so why not do something now? Committees were appointed and plans laid. A bill asking an appropriation was introduced into the Kansas legislature by Senator Price and another was prepared by Senator Charles Curtis for introduction before Congress in Washington. Before anything more could be done the United States went to war in Europe and all plans were dropped or laid by.

By the fall of 1925, with the war finished and the nation's economy beginning to boom again, some of the people who had promoted the commemoration idea eight years earlier decided it was time to take it up again. Once more committees were appointed and plans discussed. On March 11, 1926, a meeting of all committees and interested persons was called to order in Mrs. George Hibbard's home, and the Medicine Lodge Indian Peace Treaty Association was born.

The first project taken up was the definite location of the famous treaty conference, for legend put the site in many spots along the Medicine, all the way from Turkey Creek in Sun City township to a point southwest of Medicine Lodge. No one then living anywhere in the area had been on hand at the signing, nor for quite a few years afterward, but Mrs. Hibbard reported that she had located a Kiowa Indian who had been present at the famous meeting. The man was Sergeant I-See-O of Fort Sill, Oklahoma, who had written that he could find the place and would be willing to come to Medicine Lodge if his expenses were paid.

The new Association was penniless—until Frank Chapin remembered an old fund of $60, left over from some past Fourth of July celebration and lying unused in the Home State Bank. With this for a start, plans went forward to bring I-See-O to Medicine Lodge. On April 5, in company with his nephew George Hunt, the aged Indian chief came back to the valley between the rivers. An eighteen-year-old horse tender at the time of the peace treaty conference, he had later served in the U.S. Army. Now nearly eighty years of age, the old chief said he would know the place when he saw it again.

I-See-O brought with him old Kiowa tribal records or picture writings, showing the attendance of his tribe at the Council of 1867 and giving the name of the place as "Ay-Y'addle-d'ah," meaning "Timber Hill." The signing of the treaty, the old Indian said, "took place on the north bank of the Medicine River and southeast of another stream of considerable size that flowed into the Medicine from the north. The banks of the stream flowing into the Medicine were heavily wooded with elm and cottonwood and near the point where the two streams met the ground was flat and rather marshy, with some springs. On this level ground, in the angle formed by the confluence of the two streams, was a large grove of tall elms. Looking southwest from this grove over the Medicine River could be seen, about five miles away, an isolated hill with cedar trees on it. The treaty was signed in this grove of elm trees."[1]

Beginning on Turkey Creek, the committee and I-See-O visited all points on the river to which the description could apply. At each place west of Medicine Lodge the old chief shook his head and said the hills were too near, the stream coming in from the north was too small and the general contour of the land was not right. But just south of Medicine Lodge, where Elm Creek flows into the Medicine, I-See-O nodded his satisfaction. This was the place, he said, for here was a large piece of level ground, north of the Medicine and southeast of a stream that came in from the north. The ground was damp with spring seepage, one isolated peak of the Gyp Hills could be glimpsed over the south bank of the river, and before them were the stumps of a circle of huge old elm trees, felled long ago. The treaty had been signed in that very place, once shaded by the vanished grove, he declared.

The old chief then prepared and signed the following statement: "I the undersigned I-See-O do under oath make the following statements concerning the location of the signing of the Peace Treaty between the five tribes of plains Indians and the United States Government in October, 1867, on the Medicine River in Barber County, Kansas, known as the Medicine Lodge Treaty. That I was present at the said peace treaty as a member of the Kiowa tribe of Indians, and that for a period of about three weeks during the said October while the negotiations were going on, I became well acquainted with the surrounding country. That the Peace Council met just below the confluence of two streams of water, the one coming from the northerly direction, called the Medicine River. That the stream coming from the northerly direction was heavily wooded with elm trees, and that for some distance above its mouth it passed through a low, swampy, heavily wooded country. That this creek was about the size of the creek, now just east of the present city of Medicine Lodge, Kansas, known as Elm Creek.

"That the ground whereon the peace Council was held was heavily wooded with elm and some cottonwood. That from the location of the Peace council could be seen a solitary mountain or great hill some six or eight miles in a southwesterly direction, called by the Indians Ay-Y'addle-d'ah, meaning Timber Hill. That there were three locations of the Indians on the Medicine River during these treaty negotiations: the first being the site of the Peace Council, the second being a location some two or three miles above the spot where the Peace Council met, and the third being some few miles above the first and second locations. That after the Peace Treaty was signed the Indians, desiring better forage for their ponies moved about three miles up the Medicine River, and there received annuities and presents from the Government. That the Cheyenne tribe was camped on a third location still farther up the Medicine River, being afraid to bring their families down to the Peace Council, only the men coming down to attend the same. I recollect stories told by some of these Cheyennes that great droves of turkeys invaded the camp at the above location.

"After closely studying the ground from a point below Medicine Lodge City of today up the Medicine River to Sun City, and being uninfluenced by any motive other than a desire to locate the exact place of the signing of the Medicine Lodge Peace Treaty, I unhesitatingly state—that the Peace Council met just below the confluence of the two streams of water known as Elm Creek and Medicine Lodge River about one-half mile southwest of the present city of Medicine Lodge, Barber County, Kansas. [signed] I-See-O."[2]

The old Indian's statement helped clarify conflicting stories as to all of the areas which had been pointed out as the peace conference site. But now with the spot definitely located the Association could go ahead with its plans, for to Medicine Lodge alone belonged the honor of claiming and commemorating the Council headquarters. A corporation was formed immediately and a state charter applied for, after which the Chamber of Commerce and practically every other local club, organization, and association got in line to render aid and assistance. All that summer and fall the people labored, for the project to which they had put their collective shoulder was truly enormous.

Senator Curtis and Congressman J. N. (Poly) Tincher offered to do all they could to get a suitable appropriation from the government for the erection of a monument and the staging of a suitable memorial celebration. John Best,[3] first president of the Medicine Lodge Indian Peace Treaty Association, appointed committees right and left, the dates for the big celebration, October 12-14, 1927, were set, and blueprints for the commemorative monument were drawn and approved. Riley MacGregor looked into the possibility of securing government troops for the pageant, which Professor F. L. Gilson of Emporia was commissioned to write and direct. The town band had to be revived and readied, numerous proposed pageant sites had to be investigated and a selection made. When Oklahoma promised to send a large group of Indians, a committee had to be appointed to find out how to feed and house the tribespeople at the pageant site.

By spring 1927, work on the big undertaking was in high gear. A final choice of the available sites had been made, the selection falling on a huge natural amphitheater about a mile east of town where the beholder gazes across an inspiring vista of plains extending for miles to the southwest. Funds to underwrite the huge production were raised by subscription, by the sale of memberships in the Association, and finally by borrowing the last $2,500 from local businessmen—to be paid back if and when the show netted enough to do so.

Wagons, buggies, ox carts, stage coaches, horses, and gear of all kinds had been rounded up. Teachers were drilling scores of very young school children for their parts as elves and prairie flowers. Hundreds more of the town and country folks were practising for the various episodes, following a plan still used today, that of putting each scene together separately, honing it to perfection and timing its length to the second, then putting them all together *for the first time* at the first showing of the big pageant. From the beginning the plan has worked perfectly and scene has followed scene like clockwork.

The great show exceeded the fondest hopes and expectations of Barber County residents. Attendance was estimated at 27,000, and when all expenses and debts were paid the Association wound up $2,400 to the good. With all that money and experience, to say nothing of the fun they'd had, it wasn't surprising that the community decided to repeat the pageant every five years.

The only disappointment had been in the failure of the monument appropriation to come through in time to erect the memorial statue for the first pageant. Not until February 1929 could President Best call a meeting to advise the Association that $2,500 had been appropriated for the monument provided it was used prior to July 1. A location was promptly approved, a Wichita architect employed, and soon the impressive memorial—depicting a white soldier and an Indian warrior clasping hands in friendship—was erected on the southwest corner of the school grounds on Main Street.

In 1930, Elbert S. Rule, a pioneer resident of Barber County, purchased 160 acres of the land where the pageant was held and presented the tract to the Medicine Lodge Indian Peace Treaty Association, thus assuring the pageant a home in perpetuity. The following year the Kansas legislature appropriated $10,000 for the purchase of an additional 320 acres adjoining the original 160. The entire 480-acre tract provides the Association abundant space in which to operate.

Shortly after the second successful performance of the Peace Treaty pageant in 1932, President Best was transferred to Buffalo, New York, with the National Gypsum Company, and Riley MacGregor was elected to head the Association in his place. The third pageant took place on schedule in 1937, but the next five-year span was shortened by a year in order to hold the fourth pageant in conjunction with the state-wide Coronado celebrations of 1941, commemorating the 400th anniversary of the Spanish explorers' visit to the land that is now Kansas.

In the forty-three years that have passed since the first pageant performance, eight more have been held in the beautiful Memorial Peace Park amphitheater.[4] However, the two-hour panoramic dramatization of the tremendous acts of history that were played out in this section of the plains between 1541 and 1867 has changed but little since the 1927 re-enactment.

Here still, in the great saucer-like depression overlooked by the magnificent red hills and bluffs, the Spirit of the Prairie, a lovely young woman, does her graceful symbolic dance, calling to life the flowers and elves of the lovely land. In sequence follow scenes depicting in vivid color and immense grandeur the Ages of Discovery, of Exploration, and of Settlement, and finally the Signing of the Great Peace Treaty. Here the Spanish friars, Coronado and his men, the French and the English parade across the vast hill-rimmed stage. Here Lewis and Clark and Captain Pike play their brief parts on Time's dais. Here is portrayed that violent period when Kansas first became the crossroads of the nation, with hunters, trappers, traders, and travelers passing on horseback, in ox carts, stage coaches, and covered wagons. Here, too, cowboys hurrah their way into the history of the plains, then give way to the settlement period; and always there are the Indians in colorful panoply, first friendly, then bitterly hostile. And finally there come the generals in full dress uniform, the statesmen in their tall hats, the soldiers and reporters, and the members of the five great Indian tribes with their proud chiefs, all vividly bringing to life one of the most magnificent dramas ever played out on the American scene.

The tops and slopes of the hills surrounding the valley offer perfect seating for the 20,000 or more spectators who attend each of the three afternoon performances. But it is next to impossible to do justice, with mere words, to the spectacle they see there. Without a doubt it surpasses many an impressive Hollywood extravaganza.

In the 1967 centennial pageant, as in the first, more than 2,000 Medicine Lodge and Barber County folks took part, along with some 500 Indians, most of them descendants of the chiefs of the five tribes who signed the treaty one hundred years ago; the names of Little Raven, Tall Bear, Yellow Bear, Stumbling Bear, Little Coyote, White Horse, and Curley are prominent among them. For the horse lovers of America this is a splendid show; hundreds of horses are used in the scenes with Coronado, the cowboys, the Indian attack on the covered wagons, and the cavalry charging to the rescue.

Some forty officers and directors co-ordinate the big show and delegate duties to more than one hundred committee chairmen who oversee the myriad ramifications and details of the whole affair. Many, perhaps most, of these people also play the parts of important characters in the pageant itself. Jibo Hewitt, a director, plays Kit Carson in the early settlers scene and Colonel F. S. Tappan in the treaty scene. Another director who has taken part in all but three of the pageants is Mrs. Mayme Grigsby. This delightful lady, collector par excellence of antique furniture, glass, and china worth a fortune, has helped with the wagon train scene six times, one year as sole supervisor of this graphic section. She has also ridden sidesaddle in every pageant parade except the first one. Wearing her authentic and elegant turn-of-the-century riding habit, she is an imposing figure on her prancing Palamino, Paula. About a year before the pageant of 1967, Mrs. Grigsby fractured her hip. Her many friends sadly figured this would put her out of the parade, on horseback anyway. But it didn't. Jaunty as ever, she and Paula went the whole mile-long route. At the age of ninety, she plans to ride again in 1970. It is people such as these who stage this delightful and meaningful panorama of history every five years or so.[5]

Now known nation-wide, "The World's Largest Production on the World's Largest Stage" attracts visitors from every state. Medicine Lodge, of course, with only the Grand Hotel, two motels, and its several hundred hospitable homes, cannot begin to house and feed the hordes of guests that descend upon it come pageant time. But this is a small matter, for the surrounding towns, Pratt, Harper, Kiowa, Anthony, even Wichita, are all within convenient driving distance. Visitors can take in the big show in the afternoon; visit the colorful Indian village spread over the nearby swales, the Stockade, Carry Nation's home, and other places of historic interest in Medicine Lodge; stay for the big Indian dance in the evening; and then trundle off over excellent hardtop highways to their night's lodgings.

Kansas' governors have always attended the pageant, as have her senators and congressmen; her present senator, Bob Dole, is a faithful supporter. All are proud of the place Medicine Lodge has made for itself—and Kansas—in the world of history and entertainment.

The pageant directors' greatest disappointment in this respect was back in 1927, when Chief I-See-O didn't live long enough to return to Medicine Lodge to be the honored guest at the first big show. No other person who had been present at the original peace treaty conference was ever found, but Tom McKinney of Albuquerque, New Mexico, one of the twin sons born in 1887 to Wayne McKinney and the widow of Wiley Payne, intends to be on hand in 1970.

At the conclusion of the 1967 pageant it was agreed by Association president Bill MacGregor and the directors to hold the next pageant three years later, rather than the usual five. Among the reasons for stepping it up two years was the fact that 1970 marks the centennial of the arrival of the first domestic cattle into the valley of the Medicine. Although the first large herd came in 1872, a few small bunches were wintered there in 1870, near where Forest City later stood. Furthermore, George H. Fritz, great-nephew of Emil Fritz whose fortune was the indirect cause of the famous Lincoln County war in New Mexico, was slated to be the incoming president of the Kansas Livestock Association in 1970.

Emil, who went to New Mexico after the Civil War, became ill and went home to Stutgart, Germany, where he died a short while later. His brother and sister, Charles and Emilie, of Lincoln County, were heirs to a $10,000 insurance policy on his life. They tried to collect from the New York company, which was in difficulties and refused to pay. The heirs then hired Alexander McSween, of Lincoln, New Mexico, to go to New York and get the money. Some two years later, when the cash had been paid to McSween and deposited in his bank account, they sued to collect their inheritance. Since Emil had been a partner of L. G. Murphy & Company in Lincoln County, there were various connections of his estate with the murky doings of the whole violent business that developed there between Murphy, McSween, and others, including Billy the Kid and Hendry Brown.

George H. Fritz is the son of Mr. and Mrs. George L. Fritz, who came to Barber County in 1879 and went into the cattle business southwest of Medicine Lodge. Managing editor and fieldman for the Kansas Livestock Association magazine, *The Kansas Stockman*, in the 1950's, he was later manager of the famous CK ranch of Brookville, Kansas. After the death of his parents, he went home to manage the family ranch. In 1960 he was elected president of the Kansas

Hereford Association and in 1970 president of the powerful Kansas Livestock Association.

At the tenth performance of the Medicine Lodge Peace Treaty Pageant, George H. Fritz will be honored for his lifelong connection with and service to the largest industry in the state—the raising and feeding of cattle, a business that began on these plains and water-courses one hundred years ago.

Over the years there had frequently been talk of constructing another stockade in Medicine Lodge, made in the likeness of the one built in 1874. In July 1959, I. N. "Jibo" Hewitt, the community's foremost booster, announced through his *Index* column of many years standing, "Jibes by Jibo," that a strong movement was under way to get financing approved for establishing a Barber County museum and stockade. This was especially timely in view of the fact that the state's one-hundredth birthday was coming up in 1961, and many Kansas towns and communities were already building museums, historical centers and exhibitions.

After a great deal of discussion by many people and organizations, the proposition was finally presented, in February 1960, to the Medicine Lodge Chamber of Commerce, which gave its approval and appointed a committee. Spurred on by the shortness of the time at their disposal, if they were to have a building before the centennial year was past, the committee quickly proposed a corporation to raise funds and erect a log stockade. Their plan being approved, directors were chosen and officers elected. An architect was found to draw the plans and a location was decided upon, next door to Carry Nation's old home, two blocks west of Main Street and fronting on U.S. Highway 160. A highway garage already stood on the site, which was owned by Jibo Hewitt. The cost of a log stockade, 500 feet by 100 feet, plus remodeling the garage into a museum building, would be $40,000. Forging right ahead, the corporation in 1960 put on sale $20,000 in debenture bonds and $20,000 in common stock. By the following January there was money enough on hand to order the logs, $6,000 worth, and begin construction. The first logs arrived from Colorado in April and the stockade rapidly took shape.

As the sturdy log walls and corner turrets neared completion, a fine old two-story, four-room log house, built by Robert Smith fourteen miles south of Medicine Lodge in 1877, was moved into town intact and set up inside the stockade walls. By the time the work was completed and the museum furnished and opened to the public, October 1, 1961, with three months of the centennial year yet to run, a total of 230 persons were on record as owning the Medicine Lodge Stockade by way of shares of stock in the handsome, sturdy structure, the only one of its kind in Kansas. Since the $40,000 raised through the sale of stocks and bonds was not enough to underwrite purchase of the land too, Hewitt, to expedite the whole matter and get the building under way, had turned the land and garage over to the corporation, to be paid for monthly from entrance fees collected at the door.

Wide, barred gates in the front stockade wall swing open to admit visitors. In the museum inside a great deal of the history of Medicine Lodge and Barber County is handsomely displayed. Beyond the museum, in the spacious enclosure protected by the high walls, the Smith house, furnished throughout as it was nearly a century ago, is open to all comers. From the old dishes and cooking pots in the kitchen to the yellowed book laid down on the "center table" to the few articles of clothing hanging on hooks in the bedrooms, one has the feeling that the family just stepped out of the house no more than a few minutes ago.

Out in the "yard" stand the iron lattice-work cells from the old jail, the ones from which the Turners escaped back in the twenties. Nearby is a "gypsum house." Built of native gypsum like that quarried and burned in the handmade kilns of a past century, it illustrates a type of structure that was "solid as a rock" and once quite common in that section of Kansas.

One can stand inside those stout stockade walls and see, in the mind's eye, how it must have been back in the days when the first stockade was new, when men, women, and children from miles around, together with their livestock, carried on the business of daily living there: cooking, washing, milking the cows, cleaning their guns, loading ammunition. And one can almost hear the merry tunes of a mouth harp or an old fiddle to which barefoot men and women, forgetting their fears and cares, danced out the measures of "circle to the left and swing the girl that you love best."

From the visitors who pour through the stockade come strange tales too. It was one of these who recognized her ancestor in the picture of the outlaws who held up the bank in 1884. "Why, we have one of those pictures," she said, "and that's my grandfather," indicating the young man looking over the shoulders of Smith and Wheeler. She went on to tell the story of how he financed his wedding trip to Niagara Falls, and added that they still had the letter from the New York *Times*.

Another visitor, a lady from California, told Mrs. A. I. Gigstad, one of the alert curators of the museum,[6] that her grandparents had homesteaded on the Medicine in the days when Indians still roamed the valley. Her own mother, the lady said, had been a little girl then, and when a fast growing tumor developed on her throat one summer, her father, much concerned, made plans to take her to Chicago to a specialist as soon as he sold his cattle. In the meantime a band of Indians visited the Medicine and the medicine man came to the house to beg for coffee, sugar, and other delicacies. When he saw the growth on the child's neck he asked to examine it. The old Indian felt of it and said, "I can cure. Either she grows to be a tall squaw or she has not many moons left." The father concluded the medicine man couldn't hurt the child, and he might help her, so told him to go ahead. The Indian said he'd need a bag of striped peppermint candy, and while the father made the trip to the store after the candy the Indian went out and gathered herbs from along the river. The father came home with the candy, and while he prepared and mixed his herbs the old medicine man sucked on stick after stick of the candy. When his potion was ready he applied it to the growth, which soon went away, permanently cured.

Another visitor told of an old recipe given her family by these same Medicine River Indians. Many years later a friend developed a pernicious form of skin cancer. She went everywhere, consulting every known specialist, and was told by all that nothing could be done for her, so she came home to die. Then her home town doctor, who had seen the old Indian recipes, came and asked for them. As a last resort he went out and found the right plants, mixed the ingredients, and applied them; the first to burn off the cancer, the second "which smelled to high heaven" to heal the burn. She was cured and lived many more years.

Another highly specialized annual production of the busy Medicine Lodgers is the great annual Easter Sunrise Service, held at the Memorial Peace Park. Here, before a huge cross erected on the north rim of the basin, the story of Easter is told in tableau, narration, and song. Sponsored by the Barber County Scottish Rite Masons, the first service was held in 1952. That year the tableau was presented on the floor of the basin, pageant style.

Luke Chapin, prominent young Medicine Lodge attorney, was president of the twenty-man committee; Jibo Hewitt was secretary. At the conclusion of that first performance the group decided to stage the next service on the north rim of the basin, rather than on its floor. This proved far more successful.

There, with the sun rising over the red hills, the people gathered by the thousands, some to sing and act in the matchless story, the rest to watch, and probably to pray. Scenes portrayed are: The Last Supper, The Garden of Gethsemane, The Betrayal, The Trial, The Crucifixion, The Burial, The Empty Tomb, and The Ascension. The glorious songs of the final scenes rolled out across the hills as the sun's first rays shone on the cross and the empty tomb, renewing the good news broadcast to mankind two thousand years ago, "Christ the Lord is Risen Today."

Attendance, very good for the first few years when people came from miles around, began to slip in the sixties, partly due to other towns and communities developing and holding their own sunrise services and drawing off those from a distance, and partly because nowadays people seem more and more reluctant to get out of bed so early.

So why not, reasoned the directors, have the service on the night before Easter. Since the park was well lighted by powerful lights, darkness would be no problem. As a consequence, the impressive service is now held at night, with the final scenes running well past midnight and into Easter morning. Attendance has gone up into the thousands again, as visitors seem to enjoy the novelty of the nighttime presentation; and anyway, the drama, with its huge choir of nearly 200, is well worth seeing at any time. This show, too, proves that the lively people of Barber County are cheerfully willing to go to almost any length, both in effort and expense, to provide dramatic and worthwhile entertainment.

Jibo Hewitt in his role as Kit Carson in the Peace Treaty Pageant.

SEVENTEEN

I. N. "Jibo" Hewitt

1884-1970

Since I. N. "Jibo" Hewitt, Medicine Lodge's most ardent and faithful promoter, has spent most of his life in the town, his story is, perforce, also the story of Medicine Lodge, for Jibo's forebears arrived in the valley of the Medicine in 1884, when the village was but little more than a decade old. On the paternal side he was represented by his grandparents, Mr. and Mrs. Isaiah Hewitt of Ohio, where his great grandfather had once been captured by Indians and held captive for a time. On the maternal side his grandparents were Mr. and Mrs. V. C. Sleeper of New Hampshire.

The Hewitts settled on a ridge northeast of Medicine Lodge and Jibo's father, Frank, was the boy of twelve who touched the dead bodies of Hendry Brown and Ben Wheeler the morning after the shooting and hanging of April 30, 1884. The Sleepers, who had lived for awhile in Wellington, about seventy miles east of Medicine Lodge at the forks of the rivers, built a two-room frame house on a little slope above a bend in Sand Creek, northeast of town. Mr. Sleeper, one of the men who built a raft and assisted in the rescue of victims in the big flood of 1885, continued to live in Wellington most of the time and tend his meat market there. At stated intervals he made the long drive to the homestead, taking supplies to his wife and children. Both families were caught up in the big Indian scare of the summer of 1885.

This came about when rumors of unrest among the Cheyennes down in Oklahoma began to run rife in south central Kansas, from Wichita to Caldwell and on west beyond Barber County. All the weekly newspapers of the region carried the scare stories and Governor John A.

Martin became so concerned that he asked the War Department to call out the army to patrol the border. The Wichita *Eagle*, on June 27, reported that five companies of the Fifth Cavalry had just passed through that city by special train, headed for Oklahoma. The Santa Fe agent at Kingman on July 8 announced the Indian scare had reached "gigantic proportions and hundreds of families had flooded into town from points as far west as forty miles."

The Anthony *Enterprise* countered with the statement that there were no hostile Indians in Kansas. The Attica *Advocate* of July 9 likewise discounted the reports of hostile Indians and laid the tales to an attempt on the part of cattlemen to "magnify the situation into a huge Indian war" to drive out the settlers west of Barber County. Because the Cheyennes and Arapahoes, with their squaws and papooses, had been in Medicine Lodge, Lake City, and Sun City, trading around and dickering as usual and because some timid settlers were always frightened at the sight of Indians, scare stories spread.

In mid-July, the Attica *Advocate* reported a large force of U.S. soldiers concentrating in the Indian territory south of Kansas, more than enough to cope with any force the Indians could possibly put into the field. No hostile action on the part of any Indians was reported, the story went on, but the uneasiness of the governor and the people had resulted in some 1,250 men being called into the area—fifteen companies of infantry and ten of cavalry.

At one time this large force of troops were encamped near the small village of Crisfield, about fifteen miles southeast of Medicine Lodge where, on July 24, the troops were reviewed by Colonel Henry A. Morrow, Twenty-First Infantry. About 250 teams and thirteen coaches of people (some 2,000 persons in all) from Harper and Attica journeyed to the village on an extremely hot and dusty day to watch the great military show.[1] However, when no Indian trouble developed, the troops were later dispersed. A few remained in Kansas in permanent camp at Fort Riley; most were sent on to Arizona.

It was while this Indian scare was at its height that five Cheyennes came to the Sleeper house on Sand Creek. The parents and their son Nick were away and only the two teenage girls, Ida and May, were at home. Of course the girls were terribly frightened when the Indians came to the door, but there was nothing they could do when the red men came on in and began picking up whatever took their fancy. One

Indian, who wore a full feathered headdress and may have been a chief, became interested in the small organ the family had brought to the homestead with them. He picked and poked at it, looked into its working parts, and finally made motions toward the girls and then toward the organ. Not knowing what else to do, Ida went to the instrument and began to play. The Indians listened intently while she pumped out several tunes, then suddenly left the house and rode away on their ponies. They hadn't touched the girls and they took nothing with them except a quarter of beef that was hanging in the smoke house.

The Sleepers, like most of the homesteaders, lived in crowded quarters while getting a start on the land. Beside the organ and the bed, there was room in the little house for only the most necessary pieces of furniture: stove, table, cupboard, a chair or two. So at night the two girls and their young brother climbed a ladder to the loft, where they slept on corn shuck mattresses laid on the floor.

The family got its start in cattle in a novel way. A winding canyon road passed the bend in the creek below the house where some springs welling up at that point made it a favorite camping place for travelers passing by. The Sleeper girls and their brother often fished in the bend, and one day while tending their lines the three found a pack rat's nest. In going through the accumulation of junk the rat had horded, they found some chewed up bits of paper money. Gathering the pieces together, they took them home to show their father when next he visited the homestead. Mr. Sleeper sent the fragments to Washington D. C., and presently a letter came back with a twenty dollar bill enclosed. The money was invested in a fine heifer calf, the Sleeper "foundation herd," which in time put them into the cattle business.

Frank Hewitt and Ida Sleeper were married in 1898. After a few years on a ranch and a few more in the village of Nashville, up in Kingman County, they moved to Medicine Lodge in 1913. One of their six children was Ivan N. Hewitt, nicknamed "Jibo" while yet a small lad. Jibo early showed the ambition and initiative that have prodded him down through the years.

As a boy growing up in the little town he got into all the mischief most boys do, yet found time to hustle all manner of money-making jobs for himself: shining shoes, selling papers, trapping in winter, printer's devil for the *Cresset*. There were eleven cafes in the village while Jibo was in high school and he washed dishes in all of them. During these pursuits he saw practically all of the day-to-day goings-on in the town he came to love so well.

He well remembers the ice business of Medicine Lodge, owned by H. Tisdale of Lawrence, and managed by the county sheriff, Jim Gano. As the season of deep cold approached, Gano turned a good head of water into the "middle lake" of the chain of three fed by the old Elm Creek ditch. If it was a "good winter" the temperature would fall low enough and stay low long enough to freeze a deep, uniform thickness of ice on the lake. The ice harvest, when the crews went out on the lake to saw the cold stuff into blocks, was always a busy, exciting time. From the lake the blocks slid down a chute into the big icehouse, half above ground, half below, where they were packed in straw to await the next summer's hot weather. The same boys who, in mittens, stocking caps, and overshoes, watched the ice "put up" in winter followed the ice wagon, barefooted, in summer, snatching ice splinters from the wagon as the iceman made his daily rounds.

Another interesting feature of village life in the first quarter of the present century had to do with the omnibuses or hacks that met the passenger trains to pick up passengers and baggage for transportation to the hotel. Jibo, delivering his papers on Main Street, enjoyed the noise and confusion of meeting the trains. Competition between the drivers of the various buses was keen and each had his own "dodge" for securing a major portion of the business.

H. Tisdale also owned one of the omnibuses and Sheriff Gano was its manager. His head driver was Bill Horn, an old time stage coach driver. Gano also ran a dray wagon, for hauling heavy freight, but had only one team for both the dray and the bus. Parking the bus on Main Street, he went about his freight delivery business until he heard the whistle of the incoming passenger train. Then, in a lightning switch, he and Bill Horn transferred the team from the wagon to the bus and dashed down the hill to the depot, where Bill "sold his outfit against the others."

Numerous salemen rode the trains from town to town in those days, getting off at each station with their bulky sample cases. In Medicine Lodge the route most of them traveled was from the depot to the sample rooms in the Grand Hotel, and each driver, standing by his bus, tried to out shout the others with, "Here is your ride uptown.

Four long blocks, all uphill. We can carry your baggage, too," and grab the biggest share of the lucrative trade.

In the hustle and confusion anything might happen. It was while meeting a train on a very windy night late in December, 1901, that Gano's bus came near setting the town afire. For some reason the team took fright at the engine, steaming and whistling up to the depot, and "put out for home." As the horses dashed across the tracks the lamp upset, setting fire to the rig. With the blazing bus in tow, they raced up Kansas Avenue, stopped for a moment at the bus barn, then whirled and dashed on to the Central livery barn. There the mobile firebrand was stopped and the fire doused before it set the barn, and quite likely the rest of the town, on fire. The *Index* of January 1, 1902, reported that Gano was in the depot waiting room when the runaway started, but did not say where the driver was. Except for the running gears, the bus was a total loss.

Jibo was in the eighth grade when he first discovered he could run —by beating a freshman who was considered, by himself and others, to be pretty fast. When he started his freshman year in high school, he was washing dishes in a restaurant two or three blocks from the school. At the first BONG of the morning bell, Jibo could fling the soapsuds off his hands, light out for the schoolhouse, and be there in time not to be counted tardy. "It was good practice for a runner," he said.

Then a friend noticed his fast footwork and offered to give him a few pointers. The friend was Clifford Moore, a Negro boy two or three years older than Jibo. Clifford, a high school athlete, met him in an alley down by the depot every evening and there taught him how to make fast starts, how to have his feet already in the air when the gun went off. It worked, and the lad soon began to make a track record for himself.[2]

Jibo, who grew up on a steady diet of Horatio Alger books, was ever on the lookout for ways to get rich. And so, in the spring of his junior year in high school, he had some ideas for renovating the old opera house, unused for many years. The first floor of the building was then in use by the Ford dealer as a show room and office, but the huge upstairs room, once the scene of many a fashionable affair, was a desolate place, its windows broken, inhabited by bats and spiders, filled with dust and debris.

Hunting up the Ford dealer owner, the lad asked him if he'd like to have the upstairs room cleaned and repaired. The owner said he'd like it fine and Jibo told him he'd do it all for nothing if he could have the use of it, rent free, for the next year. The bargain was struck right there, and Jibo marshaled his forces and went to work.

He first advertised his plan for holding dances, wrestling matches, and other entertainment in the opera house, and then promoted a contest for a catchy new name for the place—the prize to the winning *couple*, free admission to all the dances. While the couples were racking their brains for names, Jibo recruited a work force from among his friends by promising them a free dance ticket or two and they tackled the junk, bats, spiders, dust, and broken windows. He secured most of his paint, window glass, and lumber for his stage by offering the local dealers free passes to the wrestling matches.

His schedule was slowed somewhat when the hardware store owner offered him a job for the summer. Jibo took it, and spent his days clerking in the store or putting corn binders together in the yard at the back, but evenings were free for cleaning up the old hall. By fall his entertainment emporium was spic and span and the prize for its high-sounding new name, "Tokio Garden," had been awarded, by his three high school coed judges, to Houston Case and Eva Bragg.

Jibo ordered enough Japanese lanterns and other oriental decorations to turn the fifty-foot-long room into a fairyland of subdued light and color and had the ancient grand piano, relic of the old hall's halcyon days and still in the place when he took over, dusted and tuned. Hiring the best orchestra he could find, he opened his 1923 "season" with a Halloween masquerade dance. The Garden was filled that night and the dance such a triumphant success that his future as an entertainment promoter was assured.

That September a carnival starring Jack Roller, a 240-pound heavyweight wrestler, had come to Medicine Lodge. Before the show went on its way, Jibo had signed Roller to stay on in town for the winter and appear in regular matches on the stage in his Garden. "We had three good heavyweight wrestlers in our district," Jibo said, "Orville Brown, a local boy; John Pesek, of Hastings, Nebraska, an ex-world champion; and Dick Daviscourt, a well-known wrestler from Wichita."

Jibo put on a good match about once a month, but he'll never forget the night of a much advertised match between Pesek and Roller.

The Garden filled so rapidly that soon the only space left was on the stage where the bout was to take place. So he sold ringside standing room there, too. "Only I didn't know when to stop," he said. The match was about to start when suddenly the overloaded stage went down with a crash.

The standees fell only some three feet—to the solid floor below, but some of them, sure they were about to plunge all the way to the street floor twenty feet beneath, were yelling bloody murder and desperately trying to find something to catch hold of. Jibo saw the stage go down, saw the mad scramble of the men among the splintering lumber—and froze where he stood. When Roller yelled in his ear, "Jibo, get yourself home, and stay there for thirty minutes," he came to and did as advised. When he ventured back to the hall a half hour later the wreckage had been cleared away, the match was on, and everybody was good-natured again.

His winter calendar of wrestling matches was highly successful, not only for Jibo but for the wrestlers. Especially for Brown, who went on to become a world champion.

In his spare time that winter young Hewitt carried on his usual outside activities: washing dishes, shining shoes at Newkirk's barber shop, cleaning three offices (including their ever-present spitoons) and the Episcopal church. By graduation day the young hustler, besides making passing grades and lettering for the third year in basketball, football, and track, had cleared over $1,000 on his various enterprises. That fall he turned the Tokio Garden back to the Ford dealer and went off to Kansas University at Lawrence.

During his sessions at the shoeshine stand Jibo had gotten well acquainted with J. N. Tincher. When he came home from school the next summer the congressman asked him to go back to Washington with him. It was late in the fall before young Hewitt got started for the capital. He drove a big truck to Chicago for his brother, covering the first leg of his journey without cost to himself; he stayed on in the windy city for awhile, earning expense money for his assault on the nation's capital by continuing to drive the truck. A stranger in the big city, he and the truck once got lost in Lincoln Park in a snow storm. He hadn't meant to get into the park in the first place, but once in he couldn't seem to find his way out. A policeman finally hailed him to a stop to tell him he was not supposed to be there. Jibo assured him he knew it, and was doing his best to get out. The officer then showed him the nearest way out.

Hanging onto what little cash he had, Jibo hitchhiked the rest of the way to Washington and reported to Poley Tincher. Through the congressman's assistance he got a job in the Department of the Treasury, then under Andrew Mellon, and also enrolled in George Washington University. In the treasury building he worked in the "issue and redemption" department where his main job was destroying old paper money. Because he was broke upon his arrival in the capital, Jibo borrowed a twenty dollar bill from Mr. Tincher to tide him over until his first pay check, and the big congressman ever after liked to tell how the Kansas boy had to borrow "eatin' " money though he was "burning" millions every week.

Jibo vividly remembers the Ku Klux Klan parade he witnessed while working in the treasury building. For five hours the robed Klansmen paraded past the building. "Every little bit," he said, "I would go out on the front steps and watch awhile, then go back to work."

Toward spring Jibo, dissatisfied with his treasury job because of its inadequate salary, resigned and hired out to a real estate company. For awhile he almost starved to death at his new job, but before the summer was over he was making good commissions. He did well the following winter, both in school and at his work. In the spring of 1926 he accompanied his university track mates over to Pennsylvania State University and won a gold medal in the relays there. At the close of the school year he went to Jersey City and hired out to an elevator company. He liked the work and might have stayed on in the east except that his father got sick and the family wanted him to come home.

He arrived in time to take part in the first Medicine Lodge Indian Peace Treaty pageant, where he helped take the wagon train through. In 1929 he opened a bakery and confectionary in his home town, and on the side served as scout master for the local Boy Scout troop. Things were beginning to get tough all over by the time he sold his bakery in 1930 and launched out on a new kind of sales business.

Loading his car with all manner of "notions," small items needed daily by almost everybody: aspirins, razor blades, needles, paring knives, anything he could profitably sell for a nickel or a dime, he set out to visit crossroads stores, drugstores, barbershops, all the little places the regular salesmen passed by. He sold directly from the stock in his car and he sold for cash or its equivalent. "I'd take most anything in payment," Jibo said, "a meal, a room for the night, gas for my car."

When many others were out of work and most of the nation was lamenting the hard times of the depression years, Jibo was selling steadily and building a good business, the Hewitt Sales Company. Before long he had twenty salesmen on the road, selling variety store merchandise in Nebraska, Oklahoma, and Texas, as well as Kansas. By 1932 he was doing so well he could afford to buy a home and marry the girl of his choice, pretty Bess Harbaugh, daughter of Ben Harbaugh, the settler who breakfasted Ben Wheeler and his friend on the morning they held up the Medicine Valley Bank and who later served as Barber County sheriff.

A loyal Democrat, in 1933 Hewitt organized the Young Democrats of Barber County and was elected president of the group. The following year he was elected chairman of the Barber County Democratic Central Committee and headed the first March of Dimes drive in the county. His political activities soon attracted the attention of the state organization and in 1936 he was elevated to the office of state secretary-treasurer of the group. Appointed State Parole Officer by the governor of Kansas in 1937, he handled 500 parolees of all ages and all degrees of law breaking during the next two years. A year later he moved up to the vice-presidency of the Young Democrats of Kansas. That same year, 1938, the office of treasurer of the state of Kansas was vacated and the young Hewitt was appointed by Governor Huxman to fill it, making him the first Democrat ever to hold that position in the state. On the side he held the state vice-presidency of the Junior Chamber of Commerce and helped organize the Wichita Jaycees.

Succeeding to the presidency of the Young Democrats of Kansas in 1940, he helped Louis Levand, one of the owners of the Wichita *Beacon*, organize and carry out a very successful state-wide March of Dimes drive. That August he held a big rally of the Young Democrats in Medicine Lodge, and for his main speaker secured Lyndon B. Johnson of Texas and Washington D. C. That afternoon, after the program, he took Johnson home with him for a brief rest and visit before he left town. Jibo still lives in the same house and still owns the chair the future president of the United States sat in that day.

All of his life Hewitt has liked to tinker and invent things. One of his inventions was a very successful tool for use in aligning the front wheels on automobiles. "It sure worked, too," one of his Medicine Lodge neighbors said, when telling about it. It must have, for it was soon in use in garages in all the forty-eight states and in Canada and Mexico. Jibo advertised the tool in national magazines and set up a company to handle orders from wholesalers. In 1954 he sold the business to a St. Louis firm.

With his facility for keeping ahead of the times, Jibo early saw the potential of his town as a tourist stop. Located at the Kansas "Crossroads of the Nation," where U.S. Highway 160, east and west, crosses U.S. 281, north and south, it was a logical overnight stop for some of the countless thousands of travelers who would be using these transcontinental roadways as soon as they were black topped all the way to the nation's borders. Anticipating the future travelers' needs for food and lodging, he built, in 1945, Medicine Lodge's first motel and cafe unit, fronting on U.S. 160. Like the log hotel of 1873, the demand had outgrown the supply before he had even finished his basic unit of four cabins and he hurried to build fifteen more.

The longer a visitor could be held in the area the more profitable it would be for the community, and as a native of the beautiful Gyp Hills Jibo knew his country had much to offer sightseers. It was simply a matter of making the one known to the other. Therefore, shortly after the staging of the 1952 Indian Peace Treaty pageant, he put out his famous orange-tinted mailing folder, courtesy of his "Gyp Hills Motel, Cafe and Trailer Park." A well-drawn map shows all that section of Kansas from Coldwater to Sharon, from Hardtner and Kiowa to Greensburg and Pratt, but with hard-sell emphasis on Medicine Lodge and the Gyp Hills.

The story of the famed 1884 bank robbery is told in vivid detail and illustrated with pictures of the bank (long ago torn down), the prisoners (all dead a few hours after the picture was taken), the armed posse (all long dead, too), "Jackass Canyon" (very little changed by the eighty-six years that have passed over the red hills since the robbers trapped themselves there), and the hanging tree (a beautiful old elm in the city park, with a stout, horizontal limb that could have served, but didn't). Attention is called to the Carry Nation home, to

David Nation's grave in Medicine Lodge cemetery, to Flower Pot Mountain, and, of course, to the next big Peace Treaty pageant.

But twenty years ago the Plains country highways were a far cry from what they are today. Poorly marked by highway signs and with long unpaved stretches, Highways 160 and 281 were good examples of bad highways. Especially 281, the great north-south artery from Canada to Mexico. Well aware of the necessity of overcoming these disadvantages if tourists were to be coaxed to travel the cross-country highways to and through his town, Jibo began agitating for road improvement and for landscaping and beautifying the Plains highways where needed.

A firm believer in beginning at home, he first tackled the hard-topped stretch of roller coaster road that connected Medicine Lodge with Coldwater, forty miles west. With the help of his local Lion's Club, the Boy Scouts, and anyone else he could persuade to get into the act, he set out young native cedar trees along the fence lines that border the highway. The first trees put out, now nineteen years old, are tall, shapely firs, while jack rabbits can still jump over the latest plantings; and every year there are more of them. As Alvin Dunder observed, no one seems to have a "bark count" on the planting but many hundreds of trees are today a living memorial to Jibo Hewitt and his chief collaborators, Clarence Benefiel and Bill Austin, retired hardware merchant and rancher, now both in their eighties.[3] Long after they are gone, Cedar Tree Lane will delight motorists zooming across the hills of southern Kansas.

As a result of his enthusiasm for highway improvement, Hewitt was soon involved state-wide, and then nation-wide. Elected national president of the Highway 160 Association in 1951, by 1954 he headed up the Kansas Highway 281 Association, and was vice-president of the national association for the same road. At the state meeting of the association that year, the national president reviewed the twenty-five year history of the highway's struggle and presented its needs. Envisioned as the great north-south life line of the nation, carrying its traffic from Canada to Mexico, it had grown all too slowly during the quarter century. Kansas was the first of the six states it crossed to pave every one of its own 250 miles. Nebraska had completed only part of its share. North Dakota was second to Kansas in finished miles; South Dakota, Oklahoma, and Texas hadn't paid too much attention to the project. Consequently, a good many of the 1,806 miles between the borders were still only dirt or gravel grades. And if Kansas was ever to have maximum returns from its own paved portion of the transcontinental highway it would have to prod the other states into finishing the considerable gaps in theirs.

As national president of the association in 1956, Hewitt did just that, by attacking the weakest link in the chain, South Dakota. Throughout the past eight years, national presidents had tried to organize a South Dakota state association and all had failed. Even when the national association met at Aberdeen, South Dakota, in 1952, its members hadn't been able to stir enough enthusiasm among the South Dakotans to persuade them to organize and get behind road improvement in their state. The opposite had been true in North Dakota when, at the national convention in Jamestown the following year, that state had organized, affiliated with the national association, and then gone ahead in a whirlwind of road building that completed 281 almost to Canada by the end of 1957.

So now the new president made a frontal attack on the problem. He ordered telephone directories from every town along 281 across the state of South Dakota and wrote a personal letter to every businessman in each of the towns,[4] urging him to help line his town up and get it on a paved highway instead of a dirt road. It was easy to enthuse every merchant, cafe, and gas station operator about the advantages of being located on a paved cross-country highway that could soon be carrying hundreds of thousands of travelers in front of the business establishments. In no time at all Jibo not only had South Dakota organized and boosting, but he had enthused Plankinton into inviting the national association to meet there in 1958.

"That was the best convention we ever had," Jibo said. Plankinton's 600 residents went all out to house and entertain the sixty delegates present. At the meeting North Dakota reported its share of the highway blacktopped all the way to the Canadian border. Nebraska had only two little eight-mile stretches yet to do. Reports from Oklahoma and Texas were good, and South Dakota was fast closing its longer gaps. At long last the dream of an all-paved U.S. 281 from border to border was almost a reality.

By the time Jibo retired in 1961, at the end of his fifth year as president, he had driven from Mexico to Canada on the great "palms to pines" all-paved highway and could point with pride to the handsome signs that proclaimed it the "American Legion Memorial Highway." He had worked hard and with unflagging enthusiasm. He had attended annual meetings all the way from Texas to North Dakota, most of the time as president, and he had a right to be proud of the end result.

While the roads leading to it were being improved, Jibo had been busy advertising his state and his town by other means. As a member of the local Lions Club, in 1951 he began attending the order's international conventions. Well supplied with his Gyp Hills circulars, he traveled down to Mexico City, and by convention's end quite a few people from all over the world knew quite a lot about Medicine Lodge, Kansas, "Crossroads of America," home of the famed Peace Treaty pageant, and even that it offered "good fishing—when wet."

In 1954, as president of both the Medicine Lodge Lion's Club and the Chamber of Commerce, he was deep in plans for celebrating the upcoming state centennial in 1961. At the national Lion's Club convention in San Francisco in 1957 he was ready with centennial promotional material, and again in Chicago the next year, where delegations from all over the world marched down Michigan Avenue in colorful panoply. Jibo wore his Kit Carson get-up, appearing just as he does in the big Peace Treaty pageant, and his Kansas delegation placed seventeenth in the big parade of more than one hundred entries. His all-out push came during the New York City convention of 1959 where, as a member of the Kansas Centennial Commission and chairman of the Lions State Centennial Committee, Jibo did his best to see that the United States *and* the world got invited to Kansas for the big celebration. As a long-time member of the Masons and Elks, a life member of the Kansas State Historical Society, a vice-president of the National Little Britches Rodeo Association,[5] an International Lions Club Counselor, and a member of the Tourist Committee of the State Chamber of Commerce, he hustled all that year of 1960, more than doing his share in making the Kansas centennial a jubilee long to be remembered.

Jibo's community has not been lax in showing its appreciation. In 1961 the Junior Chamber of Commerce presented him a high trophy, its annual Senior Citizen's Award; and in 1969 Medicine Lodge elected him mayor, an office he holds with humble pride and administers with friendly efficiency.

That the genial mayor, now past three score years of age, keeps a benevolent eye on the goings-on in his town is evident from occasional items appearing in the classified section of the *Index*; this one, for instance: "NOTICE. Our policemen are friendly, nice human beings, so kiddies say 'Hello, Chief,' 'Hello, John,' 'Hello, Guy,' or 'Hello, Carl,' when you see them on the street; ask them a question and see how friendly and helpful they can be. And do be careful riding those bicycles at night, without lights. Signed, I. N. 'Jibo' Hewitt, Mayor." Or maybe it is his picture in the paper, with "four pretty girls looking on," the night he threw the switch that turned on the Medicine Lodge Christmas lights.

In January, 1970, he went to Denver for a Little Britches Rodeo meeting, and in March, as in previous years, he helped with the big Easter pageant in the Memorial Peace Park. In April he teamed up with Govan Mills, dinner chairman, to head a reunion honoring a favorite former teacher. With the special loyalty of small western towns to those who have made outstanding contributions to the growth and culture of their people, Medicine Lodgers have, for thirty-four years, annually honored Miss Ruth Payne, teacher of mathematics and Spanish in their high school from 1918 to 1922. Her former students come from neighboring states and from many towns to pay her homage. In 1969 the Ruth Payne Club established a $200 book memorial to Miss Payne and purchased thirty-two books and six volumes of state history for the local library. This year seventy-six former students attended the dinner and program and another $100 for the book fund was donated when "the hat was passed around." Members of the club represent many professions, all ardent admirers of "our Miss Payne."

October will find Jibo with shoulder-length wavy grey locks again, his neatly trimmed mustache full-grown, and his trusty long gun cleaned and oiled, all in readiness for his role as Kit Carson in the great Peace Treaty pageant.[6]

EIGHTEEN

Medicine Lodge Today

1970

Today Medicine Lodge is a fascinating little city of about 3,000 souls. Its paved up-town streets are amazingly wide and clean, its business buildings modern and attractive. Its churches, schools, public library, hospital, and courthouse are capacious, handsome structures. There are many beautiful homes, both old and new, and neat little cottages along its shady streets. The city park is a lovely place, well furnished with a swimming pool, playground equipment, and scores of fine old trees, many of them flowering varieties.

On the southern edge of town one may still follow narrow winding lanes through a thick stand of brush and trees entwined with ancient wild grape vines. Here the scene must be much as it was before the awful flood of 1885 swept down upon the campers of that long ago spring evening.

As one travels away from the block-wide up-town thoroughfares, the town's streets begin to jog and turn, sometimes they just end, and those on the outskirts meet the open farmland suddenly. In the end, one concludes that in spite of the up-and-coming bustling efficiency of its main business section, Medicine Lodge is really just a pleasant country town with a restful rural serenity.

Its one industry, other than agriculture, is the big gyp mill. Now a multimillion dollar concern, the mill's history is as unique and interesting as that of the community it helps to support. As the *Index* wrote of it in 1952, "Started in 1889, the gypsum mill . . . has grown through the years—and hell and high water—to become one of the outstanding industries in Kansas today." The first mill stood on the west side of the Medicine River, until a spring flood washed out the dam that supplied its water power. The next plant, built on the city side of the river, was destroyed by the 1907 tornado. The new, and better, mill that replaced it burned down in 1916. Undaunted, the owners spent $600,000 to rebuild.

These men, the owners, were interesting in their own right. In 1887 Thomas Best, an Englishman, was planning a pleasure trip through the United States. When he learned, through the London office of the Santa Fe Railroad, that there were promising gypsum deposits near Medicine Lodge, Kansas, he routed his journey to that dot on the map. Thomas took some samples of the white mineral back with him to England, where his father owned several gyp mines. His brother William found the samples good enough to encourage the brothers in establishing a gypsum mill in the little Kansas town on the Medicine in 1889. They named their outfit Best Brothers Keene's Cement Company, Ltd. The "Keene's" was a gypsum cement process developed in Britain, which the Bests were to use in the new location. An extremely hard white plaster, it is still used as a background for setting cornice tile and for ornamental moldings.

The gypsum was then mined in the hills five miles southwest of town and hauled to the mill over crooked trails and across frail, shaky bridges in ox carts. Only about a dozen men worked at the plant before 1900, the year Tom Best made a deal with a big St. Louis contractor to supply Medicine Lodge gypsum for the cement he was using in St. Louis' fine new downtown buildings. Sales boomed from then on and the plant grew rapidly.

In 1907, when the Santa Fe was extending its line twenty-eight miles west of Medicine Lodge, heavy dynamiting was required to level the ground. The blasts dislodged boulders of exceptionally fine white gypsum. Learning of this, the Bests at once prospected the area and bought several thousand acres of the land.

By this time the ice and bus business in Medicine Lodge was fading rapidly away and Sheriff Gano was available. The Best brothers hired him and made him manager of their new quarries. Since 1930, however, the company has mined rather than quarried its gypsum, and of course the ox carts were long ago abandoned in favor of the railroad as a means of transportation.

John Best, son of William, succeeded to the presidency of the company in 1926, and when the entire operation was sold to the National

Gypsum Company, a giant eastern corporation, John Best went with it, a company vice-president with offices in Buffalo, New York.

Today the ultra modern mill represents the outlay of well over $5,000,000 and is actually five factories in one. Its wallboard plant is 838 feet long and 240 feet wide, the largest building in the western half of Kansas. A year's output would make a wall eight feet high from New York to San Francisco and back again to Kansas. The gypsum deposits, now mined near Sun City and used in the plant, are the purest in the world and reserves are estimated at more than thirty million tons,[1] enough to last through hundreds of years of present full-scale operation.

The plant's product has scores of uses, all the way from dental casting plaster and fine paper to the sturdiest of home and factory building materials. Many of the finest federal buildings in our nation's capital include Medicine Lodge gypsum in their construction and your own bathroom and kitchen is probably plastered with it.

Under the able management of Lester Gilmore, another Medicine Lodge boy who followed the Horatio Alger pattern and worked his way up from the bottom at the mill, the plant today employs 160 persons, with a payroll of approximately $1,000,000 per year. Additional Santa Fe trackage from the mainline to the plant was added years ago and today the freight tonnage shipped from the town is greater than that of any other point on the entire Panhandle division.

It was the burgeoning gyp mill with its growing work force, attracting new families to town, that spurred the building of the town's $265,000 hospital, its $250,000 elementary school, and its $60,000 swimming pool.

Today Jibo Hewitt looks back on his life in the town and finds it good. His roots and his memories go deep—back to his boyhood when he fished the Medicine River with his best friend, his father, back to the many "Decoration Days" when he helped his grandmother Hewitt put bouquets, made from the abundance of her big flower garden, on the graves of sixty Civil War veterans, including David Nation, in old Highland Cemetery. But, true to the creed of his Horatio Alger heroes, the Mayor of Medicine Lodge would rather look ahead to victories yet to be won by him and his neighbors, for a people who have triumphed over a past such as theirs need not fear the future.

APPENDIX

Treaty of Confederation, Kiowa and Comanche Tribes Concluded at Medicine Lodge Creek, October 21, 1867

Articles of a treaty and agreements made and entered into at the council camp, on Medicine Lodge creek, seventy miles south of Fort Larned, in the state of Kansas, on the twenty-first day of October, one thousand eight hundred and sixty-seven, by and between the United States of America, represented by its commissioners duly appointed thereto, to-wit: Nathaniel G. Taylor, William S. Harney, C. C. Augur and J. B. Henderson, of the one part, and the confederate tribes of Kiowa and Comanche Indians, represented by their chiefs and headmen, duly authorized and empowered to act for the body of the people of the said tribes (the names of said chiefs and headmen being here-to subscribed), of the other part, witness:

Article I. From this day forward all war between the parties to this agreement shall forever cease.

The government of the United States desires peace, and its honor is here pledged to keep it. The Indians desire peace and they now pledge their honor to maintain it. If bad men among the whites, or among other people subject to the authority of the United States, shall commit any wrong upon the persons or property of the Indians, the United States will upon proof made to the agent and forwarded to the commissioner of Indian affairs at Washington City, proceed at once to cause the offenders to be arrested and punished according to the laws of the United States, and also to reimburse the injured person for the loss sustained.

If bad men among the Indians shall commit a wrong or depredation upon the person or property of anyone, white, black or Indians, subject to the authority of the United States and at peace therewith, tribes here named solemnly agree that they will, on proof made by him, deliver up the wrongdoer to the United States to be tried and punished according to its laws, and in case they willfully refuse so to do, the person injured shall be reimbursed for his loss from the annuities or other moneys due or to become due to them under this or other treaties made with the United States. And the President, on advising with the commissioner of Indian affairs, shall prescribe such rules and regulations for ascertaining damages under the provisions of this article as, in his judgement, may be proper; but no such damages shall be adjusted and paid until thoroughly examined and passed upon by the commissioner of Indian affairs and the secretary of the interior; and no one sustaining loss, while violating or because of his violating, the provisions of this treaty or the laws of the United States, shall be reimbursed therefor.

Article II. The United States agrees that [the][1] following district or country, to-wit: commencing at a point where the Washita river crosses the 98th meridian, west from Greenwich, thence up the Washita river, in the middle of the main channel thereof, to a point thirty miles by river, west of Fort Cobb as now established; thence due west to the north fork of the Red river, provided said line of Red river east of the one hundredth meridian line, and thence down to said north fork, and in the middle of the main channel thereof, from the point where it may be intersected by the lines above described, to the main Red river; thence down said river in the middle of the main channel thereof to its intersection with the ninety-eighth meridian of longitude west from Greenwich; thence north, on said meridian line, to the place of beginning, shall be and the same is hereby set apart for the absolute and undisturbed use and occupation of the tribes herein named, and such other friendly tribes or individual Indians as, from time to time, they may be willing [with the consent of the United States] to admit among them; and the United States now solemnly agrees that no person except those herein authorized so to do and except such officers, agents and employees of the government as may be authorized to enter upon said Indian reservation in discharge of duties enjoined by law, shall ever be permitted to pass over, settle upon, or reside in the territory described in this article, or in such territory as may be added to this reservation for the use of said Indians.

Article III. If it should appear from actual survey or other satisfactory examination of said tract of land that it contains less than one hundred and sixty acres of tillable land for each person who at the time may be authorized to reside on it under the provisions of this treaty, and a very considerable number of such persons shall be disposed to commence cultivating the soil as farmers, the United States agrees to set such additional quantity of tillable land adjoining to said reservation, or as near the same as it can be obtained, as may be required to provide the necessary amount.

Article IV. The United States agrees at its own proper expense to construct at some place near the center of said reservation, where timber and water may be convenient, the following buildings, to-wit: A warehouse or storeroom for the use of the agent, in storing goods belonging to the Indians, to cost not exceeding fifteen hundred dollars; an agency building for the residence of the agent, to cost not exceeding three thousand dollars; a residence for the physician, to cost not exceeding three thousand dollars; and five other buildings, for a carpenter, farmer, blacksmith, miller and engineer, each to cost not exceeding two thousand dollars; also a school house or mission building, so soon as a sufficient number of children can be induced by the agent to attend school, which shall not cost exceeding five thousand dollars.

The United States further agrees to cause to be erected on said reservation, near the other buildings, herein authorized, a good steam circular saw mill, with a grist mill and shingle machine attached, the same to cost not exceeding eight thousand dollars.

Article V. The United States agrees that the agent for the said Indians in the future shall make his home at the agency building, that he shall reside among them, keep an office open at all times for the purpose of prompt and diligent inquiry into such matters of complaint by and against the Indians as may be presented for investigation under the provision of their treaty stipulations, as also for the faithful discharge of other duties enjoined on him by law. In all cases of depreciation on person or property he shall cause the evidence to be taken in writing and forwarded, together with his findings to the commissioner of Indian affairs, whose decision, subject to revision of the secretary of the interior, shall be binding on the parties to this treaty.

Article VI. If any individual belonging to said tribes of Indians or legally incorporated with them, being the head of a family shall desire to commence farming he shall have the privilege to select in the presence and with the agent then in charge, a tract of land within said reservation, not exceeding three hundred and twenty acres in extent, which tract, when so selected, certified and recorded in the "landbook" as herein directed, shall cease to be held in common, but the same may be occupied and held in the exclusive possession of the person selecting it, and of his family so long as he or they may continue to cultivate it. Any person over eighteen years of age, not being the head of a family, may in like manner select and cause to be certified by him or her for purposes of cultivation, a quantity of land not exceeding eight acres in extent, and thereupon be entitled to the exclusive possession of the same as above directed. For each tract of land so selected a certificate containing a description thereof and the name of the person selecting it, with a certificate indorsed thereon that the same has been recorded, shall be delivered to the party entitled to it, by the agent, after the same shall have been recorded by him in a book to be kept in his office, subject to inspection, which said book shall be known as the "Kiowa and Comanche land book." The President may, at any time, order a survey of the reservation and, when so surveyed, Congress shall provide for protecting the rights of settlers in their improvements, and may fix the character of the title held by each. The United States may pass such laws, on the subject of alienation and descent of property on all subjects connected with the government of the said Indians on said reservations, and the internal police thereof, as may be thought proper.

Article VII. In order to insure the civilization of the tribes entering into this treaty the necessity of education is admitted especially by such of them as are or may be settled on said agricultural reservations: and they therefore pledge themselves to compel their children, male and female, between the ages of six and sixteen years, to attend school; and it is hereby made the duty of the agent for said Indians to see that this stipulation is strictly complied with; and the United States agrees that for every thirty children between said ages who can be induced or compelled to attend schools a house shall be provided and a teacher competent to teach the elementary branches of an English education shall be furnished, who will reside among said Indians and faithfully discharge his or her duties as teacher. The provisions of this article to continue for not less than twenty years.

Article VIII. When the head of a family or lodge shall have selected lands and received his certificate as above directed, and the agent shall be satisfied that he intends in good faith to commence cultivating the soil for a living, he shall be entitled to receive seeds and agricultural implements for the first year not exceeding in value one hundred dollars, and for each succeeding year he shall continue to farm for a period of three years or more, he shall be entitled to receive seeds and implements as aforesaid not exceeding in value twenty-five dollars. And it is further stipulated that such persons as commence farming shall receive instructions from the farmer herein provided for, and whenever more than one hundred persons shall enter upon the cultivation of the soil a second blacksmith shall be provided, together with such iron, steel and other material as may be needed.

Article IX. At any time after ten years from the making of this treaty the United States shall have the privilege of withdrawing the physician, farmer, blacksmith, carpenter, engineer and miller herein provided for; but in the case of such withdrawal an additional sum thereafter of ten thousand dollars per annum shall be devoted to the education of said Indians. and the commissioner of Indian affairs shall, upon careful inquiry into the condition of said Indians, make such rules and regulations for the expenditure of said sum as will best promote the educational and moral improvement of said tribes.

Article X. In lieu of all sums of money or other annuities provided to be paid to the Indians herein named under the treaty of October eighteenth, one thousand eight hundred and sixty-five, made at the mouth of the "Little Arkansas," and under all treaties made previous thereto, the United States agrees to deliver at the agency house on the reservation herein named, on the fifteenth day of October of each year, for thirty years, the following articles, to-wit:

For each male person over fourteen years of age, a suit of good substantial woolen clothing, consisting of coat, pantaloons, flannel shirt, hat and a pair of homemade socks. For each female person over twelve years of age, a flannel shirt, or the goods necessary to make it, a pair of woolen hose and twelve yards of calico and twelve yards of "domestic."[2]

For the boys and girls under the ages named, such flannel and cotton goods as may be needed to make each a suit as aforesaid, together with a pair of woolen hose for each; and in order that the commissioner of Indian affairs may be able to estimate properly for the articles herein named, it shall be the duty of the agent each year to forward him a full and exact census of the Indians on which the estimates from year to year can be based; and in addition to the clothing herein named, the sum of twenty-five thousand dollars shall be annually appropriated for a period of thirty years, to be used by the secretary of the interior in the purchase of said articles, upon the recommendation of the commissioner of Indian affairs, as from time to time the condition and necessities of the Indians may indicate to be proper; and if at any time within the thirty years it shall appear that the amount of money needed for clothing under this article can be appropriated to better uses for the tribes herein named, Congress may by law change the appropriation to other purposes, but in no event shall the amount of this appropriation be withdrawn or discontinued for the period named; and the President shall, annually, detail an officer of the army to be present and attest the delivery of the goods herein named to the Indians, and he shall inspect and report on the quantity and quality of the goods and the manner of their delivery.

Article XI. In consideration of the advantages and benefits conferred by this treaty and the many pledges of friendship by the United States, the tribes who are parties to this agreement hereby stipulate that they will relinquish all right to occupy permanently the territory outside their reservation as herein defined, but they yet reserve the right to hunt on any lands south of the Arkansas [River] so long as the buffalo may range thereon in such numbers as to justify the chase [and no white settlements shall be permitted on any part of the lands contained in the old reservation as defined by the treaty made between the United States and the Cheyennes, Arapahoe and Apache tribes of Indians at the mouth of the Little Arkansas, under date of October fourteenth, one thousand eight hundred and sixty-five, within three years from this date], and they [the said tribes] further expressly agree:—

First. That they will withdraw all opposition to the construction of the railroad now being built on the Smokey Hill river, whether it be built to Colorado or New Mexico.

Second. That they will permit the peaceable construction of any railroad not passing over their reservations as herein defined.

Third. That they will not attack any persons at home, nor traveling, nor molest or disturb any wagon trains, coaches, mules or cattle belonging to the people of the United States, or to persons friendly therewith.

Fourth. They will never capture or carry off from the settlements white women or children.

Fifth. They will never kill or scalp white men nor attempt to do them harm.

Sixth. They withdraw all pretense of opposition to the construction of the railroad now being built along the Platte river and westward to the Pacific ocean; and they will not, in the future, object to the construction of railroads, wagon roads, mail stations or other works of utility or necessity which may be ordered or permitted by the laws of the United States. But should such road or other works be constructed on the lands of their reservation, the government will pay the tribes whatever amount of damage may be assessed by three disinterested commissioners, to be appointed by the President for that purpose, one of said commissioners to be a chief or headman of the tribes.

Seventh. They agree to withdraw all opposition to the military posts now established in the western territories.

Article XII. No treaty for the cession of any portion or part of the reservation herein described, which may be held in common, shall be of any validity or force as against said Indians, unless executed and signed by at least three fourths of all adult male Indians occupying the same, and no cession by the tribe shall be understood or construed in such manner as to deprive, without his consent, any individual member of the tribe of his rights to any tract of land selected by him as provided in Article III (IV) of this treaty.

Article XIII. The Indian agent, in employing a farmer, blacksmith, miller and other employees herein provided for, qualifications being equal, shall give preference to Indians.

Article XIV. The United States hereby agrees to furnish annually to the Indians the physician, teachers, carpenter, miller, engineer, farmer and blacksmiths, as herein contemplated, and that such appropriations shall be made from time to time, on the estimates of the secretary of the interior, as will be sufficient to employ such persons.

Article XV. It is agreed that the sum of seven hundred and fifty dollars be appropriated for the purpose of building a dwelling house on the reservation for "Tosh-e-wa" (or the Silver Brooch), the Comanche chief, who has already commenced farming on said reservation, and the sum of five hundred dollars annually for three years from date, shall be expended in presents to the ten persons of said tribes who, in the judgement of the agent, may grow the most valuable crops for the period named.

Article XVI. The tribes herein named agree, when the agency house and other buildings shall be constructed on the reservation named, they will make no permanent settlement elsewhere, but they shall have the right to hunt on the lands south of the Arkansas river, formerly called theirs, in the same manner, subject to the modification named in this treaty, as agreed on by the treaty of the Little Arkansas, concluded the eighteenth day of October, one thousand eight hundred and sixty-five.

In testimony of which we have hereunto set our hands and seals on the day and year aforesaid.

(Seal) N. G. Taylor
President of Indian Commission
(Seal) Wm. S. Harney
Brevet Major General
(Seal) C. C. Augur
Brevet Major General
(Seal) Alfred H. Terry
Brigadier and
Brevet Major General
(Seal) John B. Sanborn
(Seal) Samuel F. Tappan
(Seal) J. B. Henderson

Attest:

Ashton S. H. White
Secretary
Jas. A. Hardie
Inspector General, U.S. Army
Henry Stanley
Correspondent
A. A. Taylor
Assistant Secretary
J. H. Leavenworth
United States Indian Agent

Satank or Sitting Bear
(His X mark) (Seal)
Sa-tan-ta or White Bear
(His X mark) (Seal)

Wa-toh-konk or Black Eagle
(His X mark) (Seal)
Ton-a-en-ko or Kicking Eagle
(His X mark) (Seal)
Fish-e-more or Stinking Saddle
(His X mark) (Seal)
Ma-ye-tin or Woman's Heart
(His X mark) (Seal)
Sa-tim-gear or Stumbling Bear
(His X mark) (Seal)
Sit-par-ga or One Bear
(His X mark) (Seal)
Corbeau or The Crow
(His X mark) (Seal)
Sa-ta-more or Bear Lying Down
(His X mark) (Seal)
Parry-wah-say-men or Ten Bears
(His X mark) (Seal)
Tep-pe-navon or Painted Lips
(His X mark) (Seal)
To-sa-in or Silver Brooch
(His X mark) (Seal)
Cear-chi-neka or Standing Feather
(His X mark) (Seal)
Ho-we-ar or Gap in the Woods
(His X mark) (Seal)
Tir-ha-yah-guahip or Horse's Back
(His X mark) (Seal)
Es-a-nanaca or Wolf's Name
(His X mark) (Seal)
Ah-te-es-ta or Little Horn
(His X mark) (Seal)
Pooh-yah-te-yeh-be or Iron Mountain
(His X mark) (Seal)
Sad-dy-yo or Dog Fat
(His X mark) (Seal)

Note: On the same date, representatives of the Apache tribe also signed a similar treaty, and on October 28 the Cheyennes and Arapahoes signed a treaty with the same government representatives. *N.S.Y.*

NOTES

Chapter One

1. The "Legend of Flower Pot Mountain" (the Bard sometimes calls it simply Flower Mountain) and many of Orange Scott Cummins' poems are to be found in his book, *Musings of the Pilgrim Bard*, published in 1903 by the Eagle Press of Winchester, Oklahoma. The version of the "Legend" used in this present volume has been shortened from Cummins' original story, which, after the manner of his day, was very flowery and wordy. However, this version printed here has not been reworded; rather, the original has been condensed almost half, by omitting many lines and whole paragraphs.
2. This hill, locally known as Flower Pot Mountain, is a high, peculiar formation rising abruptly from the valley of a small creek about nine miles west of the town of Medicine Lodge. It is almost round, with sides so steep that it can be climbed only with difficulty. Its summit is about an acre in extent and its rim, once densely fringed with cedars, today bears only a lone tree leaning eastward on the eastern side of the strange hill.
3. The site of present-day Medicine Lodge.

Chapter Two

1. T. A. McNeal, *When Kansas Was Young*, 1.
2. Douglas C. Jones, *The Treaty of Medicine Lodge: The Story of the Great Treaty Council as Told by Eyewitnesses*, 19. Jones' valuable book is a narrative taken from the accounts of journalists present at the treaty negotiations.
3. Custer, still under arrest for being absent from his command

without proper authority, was not with his troops at the time. Major Joel H. Elliot, commander of the troops on the Medicine Lodge, would be killed by Indians on the Washita the following year, when Custer was again in command. Jones, *Treaty*, 30-40.

4. Ibid., 72.
5. Carson, who was to die only a year later of an old injury, was very helpful in getting the tribes to come in for the treaty conference.
6. Jones, *Treaty*, 74.
7. A. E. Sheldon, *History and Stories of Nebraska*, 79; LeRoy R. Hafen and Francis Marion Young, *Fort Laramie and the Pageant of the West*, 183.
8. Jones, *Treaty*, 91-92.
9. Ibid., 160. No doubt the supply was also running low in the other camp tents, leading to the story, still told in Medicine Lodge, that the treaty making came to an end when the whisky ran out.

Chapter Three

1. Reuban Lake needn't have worried about coyotes attacking him as long as he was still alive. Coyotes will not bother anything that has a strong man scent about it. In the early days, if hunters brought down a large animal and had no way to transport it home, they merely threw a coat or some piece of clothing on the carcass, then went for a horse or wagon, knowing the meat would not be bothered by the timid scavengers while they were away. Though the story told of some bolder coyotes coming over to bite and pull on the hide and of others putting their noses near Lake's face, this was likely an embellishment, either by Lake himself for appreciative audiences or by the later teller of the tale. The story is found in the *Barber County Index*, April 2, 1970, told by George Miller of Sawyer, Kansas; it was a prize winner in a Native Sons and Daughters of Kansas contest.
2. McNeal, *Kansas*, 6.
3. The 1873 records show that 127 persons were the most to vote in the first county election.
4. McNeal, *Kansas*, 7.
5. *Barber County Index*, Special Peace Treaty Edition, October 1967, "County Had Rough and Rugged Years in the Beginning." This thirty-six page special edition was put together in 1967 and published in time for the commemoration of the centennial of the 1867 peace treaty, October 12-15, 1967 (the centennial pageant lasted four days instead of the customary three). A most attractive edition, it is filled with splendid pictures of scenes from former Peace Treaty pageants and of old-time people and places in the town. Here, too, is related much of the early history of Medicine Lodge,

most of it taken from the pages of the town's first newspapers.

6. McNeal, *Kansas*, 7.
7. *Barber County Index*, Special Peace Treaty Edition, October 1967, "Barber County Was Once Big Headache To State." This story further relates: "It was such an embarrassing mess that the legislature appointed special committees to travel to the county to investigate the situation." Committee members, arriving in 1874 at the time of an Indian scare, found that most of the county's residents had moved into a stockade in Medicine Lodge. "The close proximity of the members of the two factions, the 'pro-commissioners and the anti-commissioners,' jammed together in a complete stage of full-blooded argument, caused more trouble than the Indians," states the writer. This article adds that Commissioners Samuel H. Ulmer, Lewis H. Bowlus, and James G. Kirkpatrick were indicted for their crimes, along with Milton D. Houk, county clerk. One went to the penitentiary and the others became fugitives.

Chapter Four

1. Alfred T. Andreas, *History of Kansas*, 1521.
2. Thoburn, *History of Oklahoma*.
3. During the months of freezing weather, oysters could be brought into the settlements by stage or freight, and later by train. They were a delicacy much favored by the pioneers.
4. McNeal, *Kansas*, 31.
5. Ibid., 23.
6. *The Barber County Mail*, October 17, 1878.
7. McNeal, *Kansas*, 21. A second newspaper weekly, the *Barber County Index*, made its first appearance in Medicine Lodge on June 10, 1880. The two papers flourished side by side for many years.

Chapter Five

1. Kiowa *News-Review*, Golden Anniversary Edition, April 8, 1935, "The Early Years on the Prairies Were Hard." This special edition was a thirty-two page issue comprised of the town's history and early day pictures and advertisements.
2. It is an interesting part of pioneer prairie history that at least one Jewish person settled in each new prairie town. Most of them were well liked by the other townspeople and were readily assimilated into the social setup of the community. Even in the Bard's verse, there was probably no anti-Semitism intended; had the hide merchant been of any other nationality the poem joke would have been played on him just the same. Although most towns had only

one Jewish family in residence, they frequently visited or entertained the Jewish families from other towns. In this way they kept alive their own customs and traditions and also saw to it that their young people met and married other young people of their own religion.

3. From a Dodge City newspaper clipping, yellowed with age; no date.
4. In the summer of 1886 the Comanche Pool shipped 4,000 calves from Kiowa to Kansas City for veal, an operation that proved the day of the cattle range was passing. Until then, the biggest cost in cattle production was the calf, after which the expense of making it into a prime beef had been no more than growing a chicken in a barnyard.
5. Harry E. Chrisman, *Lost Trails of the Cimarron*, 97-98.
6. As told to him by Mrs. Alfreda Achenbach, also of Hardtner, Kansas.
7. A standing, and standard, reward of ten dollars was paid for every wolf scalp brought to the county treasurer.
8. Kiowa *News-Review*, Golden Anniversary Edition, April 8, 1935, "Local Men Captured 'Two Toes,' Killer Wolf of the Range."

Chapter Six

1. Nyle H. Miller et al., *Kansas in Newspapers*, iii.
2. Ibid.
3. Kiowa *News-Review*, Golden Anniversary Edition, April 8, 1935.
4. By the early twentieth century, the Kiowa *Herald* had disappeared, but in 1910 Kiowa had two other weeklies, the *Journal* and the *News-Review*. That such small towns could, and often did, support two or more newspapers simultaneously was due in most cases to political rivalry; usually one paper was of Democratic persuasion and the other Republican, with each battling vigorously for its own faction while seeking ever more lurid and derogatory words with which to belittle and besmirch its opponents. Most readers in the area, enjoying the wordy wars, subscribed to both papers so as not to miss anything.

   Also, by 1910, most of the county's smaller villages boasted at least one weekly newspaper, usually two- or four-page editions. Isabel had a *Herald*, as did Hazelton, for example. The Hardtner *Press*, founded a few years later, lasted for a couple of decades. But today all these papers are gone, as is the Kiowa *Journal* and the Medicine Lodge *Cresset*. Nevertheless, the villages—Sun City, Hazelton, Sharon, Lake City—supply weekly news columns to the *Barber County Index*, thus keeping everybody apprised as to what everybody else is doing.

5. Kiowa *News-Review*, Golden Anniversary Edition, April 8, 1935.
6. Kiowa *Herald*, July 30, 1885.
7. Kiowa *News-Review*, Golden Anniversary Edition, April 8, 1935.

Chapter Seven

1. From the ballad, "Vengeance at Medicine Lodge," by Richard Wheeler. The Reading (Pennsylvania) *Gazette and Democrat* of August 2, 1873 carried an article, "A Duel to the Death," which begins as follows:

> A correspondent of the [New York] *World*, writing from Medicine Lodge, Indian Territory [sic], thus describes a recent duel between Hugh Anderson, of Texas, and Arthur McCluskey, of Kansas.
>
> Medicine Lodge is in the very heart of the Indian nation, about a hundred miles south of the Kansas frontier, and on account of its peculiar natural advantages as a hunting rendezvous is annually the resort of a large number of both whites and Indians. Directly on the main [line] of travel pursued by the buffalo in his migrations from south to north and vice versa, from being originally a simple trading station with the Indians it has risen to the dignity of a settlement, though the houses, with the exception of two rather good-sized buildings used for storage purposes, are but five in number and of most unimposing dimensions.
>
> In the centre of the "settlement" stands a huge log cabin occupied by Job Harding, a Kentuckian of enormous strength and stature, who, in addition to his pursuits as a hunter and trapper, adds to his income by keeping a small stock of goods, which he exchanges with the Indians for pelts and hides, and sells to such parties as happen to run short of supplies. . . .

The *Gazette and Democrat* article then goes on to describe at length and in detail the savage duel as witnessed by the *World* correspondent. As a boy, Richard Wheeler ran across a copy of this old newspaper and it fired his imagination about the romantic town of Medicine Lodge; this led to his writing, many years later, the ballad of the long-ago fight at the frontier town. In a letter to I. N. Hewitt of February 19, 1970, Mr. Wheeler comments on the relationship between his ballad and the newspaper article: "The facts are as I have presented them in the poem. You will note, however, that I changed the name 'Hugh Anderson' to 'Anderson Hughes'. I *had* to do this. The real name could not be fit into the rhyme and meter of the poem. But, outside of this, I have presented the story authentically. The facts in the article were so remarkable that they needed no 'special touches' by me!"

The ballad has been privately published in a sixteen-page booklet by Richard Wheeler, *Vengeance at Medicine Lodge: The Amazing Story of the Old West's Bloodiest Duel.*

2. Calcium flares were used by early-day photographers for the brilliant flash of light needed for indoor pictures.
3. McNeal, *Kansas*, 24.
4. Ibid., 19.
5. Medicine Lodge *Cresset*, May 29, 1879.
6. McNeal, *Kansas*, 19.
7. Many stories are told today about the "hanging tree." One is that the tree died within three months after the three outlaws swung from its limb; another, that the big tree was entirely chipped away by folks who wanted bits of it for souvenirs. And still another, no doubt the true one, that the man who owned the land where it stood cut it down, along with others, to clear the place for some buildings he wanted to put up. There are as many locations pointed out, "the real site of the hanging tree," as there are stories. Although the tree was outside the limits of Medicine Lodge in 1884, the town has long since built beyond the spot. According to Dillman Ash, whose grandfather was at the hanging and later showed his grandson the location, the site where the big elm once stood is in the northeast part of town, on the block bounded by West Kansas, Walnut, First, and Cedar Streets.
8. McNeal, *Kansas*, 41.

Chapter Eight

1. McNeal, *Kansas*, 49.
2. Robert R. Dykstra, *The Cattle Towns*, 144.
3. The Kid stated that he took the horses in lieu of wages he had earned but never received from Chisum.
4. James Hines, *Man's Adventure* magazine.
5. These were all descriptions of Brown used by writers in sensation-seeking papers and magazines in the years following the holdup and murders.
6. *Barber County Index*, Special Peace Treaty Edition, October 1967, "Medicine Lodge Bank Robbers."
7. McNeal, *Kansas*, 40.
8. Caldwell *Messenger*, Centennial Edition, May 8, 1961, Section F, 3.
9. Ibid.
10. Residents of Medicine Lodge say that the scenic box canyon was not called Jackass Canyon until the beginning of the tourist era, "but those tourists really go for it," they claim, smiling.

11. John W. Nyce, a pioneer banker of Caldwell.
12. Hardtner *Press*, February 8, 1934.
13. *Cresset*, May 8, 1884.
14. Mrs. Payne was among the heavy losers in the big cattle die-up of 1885. She later married Wayne McKinney, a cattleman and one of the posse members who helped catch the outlaws. Four more children were born to her and Mr. McKinney, including twin boys in 1887, named Ed and Tom, for men prominent in Medicine Lodge at that time: Ed Sample, a well-known lawyer, and Tom Doran, another cattleman of the posse.
15. Caldwell *Messenger*, Centennial Edition, May 8, 1961, Section F, 3.
16. *Guns*, February 1961, 55. Rickards is a British author then living in London, now in Canada, who is known for his authentic accounts of the American West.
17. At first glance the Pfost gun appeared to be one which had belonged to Wheeler, but closer examination produced some complications. The serial number of this gun is 336251, and this series was made in 1917, long after Wheeler's death. Therefore, the gun itself was not Wheeler's. However, the handgrips could have been, and undoubtedly were; grips were often changed from gun to gun. Is it possible that the *grips* now owned by Pfost in Medicine Lodge and the *gun* now owned by Leah in Todmorden were originally together as the gun which Rickards says Wheeler purchased in Caldwell during 1883? Very likely not. Wheeler's grips are dated 1882, whereas the gun was not purchased until 1883 and was stamped by Wheeler with that date; furthermore, the gun now in England carries the serial number 98218, a series manufactured in 1883. Therefore, we must conclude that there must have been three guns involved in this pattern: an 1882 (or earlier) gun, an 1883 gun, and a 1917 gun; the first two belonged to Wheeler, the third did not. How the grips were switched around must remain a speculation. Just another mystery in the strange robbery attempt on the Medicine Lodge bank in 1884.

Chapter Nine

1. *Barber County Index*, Special Peace Treaty Edition, October 1967, "A Mighty Water Spout."
2. Ibid.
3. A room in one of the town buildings, as the county still had no courthouse at this time.
4. No exact total either of lives lost or property damaged was ever agreed upon by the people of the community.
5. The last verse of a long poem, "The Flood," written by the Pilgrim Bard and published in the *Index*, May 7, 1885.

Chapter Ten

1. Wichita *Eagle*, July 15, 1934.
2. Ed Lemmon, *Boss Cowman.*
3. Donald Day (ed), *The Autobiography of Will Rogers*, 13.
4. Will Rogers spent a good many years at the Mulhall home in Oklahoma during his teen years. He later started his showman's career at a roping and riding contest supervised by Zach Mulhall in St. Louis in 1899.
5. Wichita *Eagle*, July 15, 1934.
6. Ibid.
7. The old black night stick Simpson used to keep order while marshal of Medicine Lodge is now displayed in the Stockade Museum in that town.
8. McNeal, *Kansas*, 52.
9. Ibid., 53.
10. The Zeal Johnson stories are from a yellowed newspaper clipping without a date and without the name of the paper, though it may be of Wichita or Hutchinson origin. The article is headlined "Knew Sockless Jerry" and carries the by-line Kent Eubank.

Chapter Eleven

1. Two Hutchinson *News-Herald* articles, January 22, 1950, and November 7, 1951, contain reminiscences by Poley Tincher. Much of the material in this chapter is taken from these two articles and from a letter written to Nellie Yost by Tincher's sister, Mrs. Clara Downing of Medicine Lodge.
2. Kiowa *News-Review*, October 24, 1924.
3. Ibid., October 21, 1924.
4. *Barber County Index*, October 23, 1924.
5. *Pretty Prairie Times*, October 30, 1924.
6. St. John *News*, February 24, 1926.
7. Wichita *Beacon*, February 24, 1926.
8. Scott *Republican*, March 18, 1926.
9. New York *Herald-Tribune*, April 7, 1926.
10. *Time*, February 21, 1927.
11. Washington *Star*, March 4, 1927.
12. From a worn old clipping without date or newspaper name.

Chapter Twelve

1. *Barber County Index*, Special Peace Treaty Edition, October 1967, "Carry A. Nation Declared War Against Social Evils."
2. McNeal, *Kansas*, 56.
3. *Barber County Index*, March 26, 1936.

4. From the clipping described in Chapter 10, note 10; article headlined "Carry Nation Acts Related by Pioneer."
5. Carry's mother was a Campbell and Carry sometimes used the name Carry Campbell.
6. *Barber County Index*, Special Peace Treaty Edition, October 1967, "Carry Nation's Hatchet Carried Her To Fame."
7. *Barber County Index*, Special Peace Treaty Edition, October 1967, "Carry A. Nation Declared War Against Social Evils."
8. *Barber County Index*, March 26, 1936.
9. McNeal, *Kansas*, 56.
10. It has often been told that she had a malformed mouth that interfered with her speech and that operations to correct the malformation left her badly scarred.
11. The family lived for some years near Belton, Missouri, and Carry's mother, Mrs. Mary Moore, was buried there in what became the Moore family burial plot. Since Carry and David Nation were divorced at the time of her death, she was buried in her family plot.
12. From the leaflet, "A Short Biography of Carry A. Nation," published by the W.C.T.U. of Medicine Lodge.

Chapter Thirteen

1. *Barber County Index*, March 25, 1908, "Hardtner News Items."

Chapter Fourteen

1. *Barber County Index*, Special Peace Treaty Edition, October 1967, "1927 Tornado Took Three Lives Here."
2. Kiowa *News-Review*, Golden Anniversary Edition, April 8, 1935, "Sketches From The Life History Of An Early Barber Settler."

Chapter Fifteen

1. *Barber County Index*, August 18, 1927.

Chapter Sixteen

1. *Barber County Index*, Special Peace Treaty Edition, October 1967, "Aged Indian Locates Site of Treaty Signing."
2. The document was sworn to before Notary Public J. Fuller Groom and witnessed by Mrs. George Hibbard, John Best, Samuel Griffin, Joseph Hinshaw, Frank Chapin, Sallie Woodward, J. Fuller Groom, Rachel Ann Nixon, George Hunt, and Lillian Hunt (George's wife). Dated April 7, 1926.

3. John Best was owner and manager of the Best Brothers Keene's Cement Co. Ltd., Medicine Lodge's chief industry at that time.
4. Pageant years: 1927, 1932, 1937, 1941 (Coronado anniversary), 1947, 1952, 1957, 1961 (Kansas centennial), 1967 (Peace Treaty centennial), 1970.
5. Attendance at the first nine pageants has averaged 14,000 per day during each three-day period. The 1970 pageant is again under the direction of Max Muller, artist and director from Lindsburg, Kansas, who has been associated with the production for the past nine years. Mr. Muller estimates that he has directed more than 6,000 community actors during his years with the Peace Treaty Pageant production. "We fill this vast stage with a cast of 2,000 actors and a host of horses and vehicles," he says, "and our covered wagons are visible for a mile in the distance as they wind along the trail leading into the arena."

   Over the years, when they could be found and when there was money to pay for them, the Association has purchased vehicles and gear until there is now a collection of working equipment worth $25,000. The Association owns eighty-five pieces of rolling stock: covered wagons, buggies, stage coaches, ox carts, and more. An authentic re-creation of Custer's Seventh Cavalry has been put together; its equipment includes a genuine army ambulance, forty-five McClellan saddles, and numerous army guns. All this collection, so essential to any authentic re-enactment, is housed in a long building near the amphitheater where it is kept in top condition ready for use when the proper year rolls around. Work on costumes continues almost constantly and additional ones are added to the collection annually, so that nearly all of the pageant's 2,000 actors are authentically clothed. The Indians, of course, furnish their own historic habiliments.
6. Mrs. A. I. Grigstead serves as a regular daily volunteer attendant at the Stockade. When, occasionally, she needs a little time off, other ladies from a small pool of volunteers fill in for her. The Stockade has averaged 7,500 visitors each year since it was opened.

Chapter Seventeen

1. Wichita *Eagle*, November 16, 1969, 1C.
2. The Moore family was one of three Negro families that lived in Medicine Lodge when Jibo was a boy. In the decade or two immediately following the Civil War many Negroes, seeking a place for themselves in the new scheme of things, migrated to the frontiers of the nation. The father, LeRoy Moore, worked in the gyp mill for years and his sons, Charlie and Clifford, grew up in the town, where Charlie, the elder brother, was an outstanding student

and athlete in the schools. By the time Clifford was helping Jibo make a track star of himself, Charlie was in Southwestern College at Winfield, Kansas, where he became its greatest athlete and one of its most brilliant students of all time. He went on to become a college teacher and Medicine Lodge today claims him as its most celebrated former student. Clifford, once a shoeshine boy in the same parlor where Jibo shined Poley Tincher's shoes in days gone by, now owns the establishment.

3. Hutchinson *News*, May 22, 1969, High Plains Column.
4. This was not as difficult as it may sound, for in the 220 miles across the state on U.S. 281 there were not many more than a dozen towns, most of them very small.
5. An association sponsoring rodeos for boys and girls eight to eighteen years of age. More than half a hundred such rodeos are now held each year, one of them in Medicine Lodge, and Jibo attends as many as he can.
6. When asked, years ago, to play the part of Kit Carson in the big pageant, Jibo read everything he could find on the history of the famous scout, and then made a trip to Taos, New Mexico, to get the feel of Carson's home and personality. He likewise studied every scrap of history he could uncover concerning Colonel Tappan, the dressy top-hatted army officer. Consequently, when he plays either character, he actually feels that he *is* Kit or the Colonel, whichever man whose hat he is wearing at the time.

Chapter Eighteen

1. Dean Richmond, *Design for Growth*, 36.

Appendix

1. The original treaty was written in black ink. A few words and phrases were added in black pencil; these are indicated by brackets in this printing of the treaty.
2. "Domestic" was a cotton cloth sold by the yard in most frontier stores of the period.

INDEX

Aberdeen, (South Dakota), 203
Achenbach, Jacob, 72, 97, 99, 135, 170, 171, 172
Adams, Jake, 89
Adams, Mrs. Margaret, 31
Adney, Miss, 60
Aetna, (Kansas), 64, 72
Albuquerque, (New Mexico), 186
Alexander, Charley, 166
Alexander, G. E., 169
Alger, Horatio, 196, 208
Alva, (Oklahoma), 62
Amidon, Sam, 150
Anderson, Hugh, 75, 77
Anthony, (Kansas), 68, 160, 185
Anthony *Enterprise,* 193
Arkansas City, (Kansas), 134
Arnold, Robert, 161
Atchison, Topeka and Santa Fe Railroad, 67
Attica, (Kansas), 68, 70, 175, 193
Attica *Advocate,* 193
Aubley, Bill, 99
Auger, General Christopher, 26, 29
Austin, Bill, 202
Axline, L. M., 164

Bad Back, Chief, 31
Baldwin, Levy, 78, 79
Ballinger, 50, 55, 57, 119
Barber County, (Kansas), founded, 41-44; Indians, cattle, 45-52, 56, 59, 62, 63; towns, 72-74, 75, 77, 79, 81; bank robbery, 83-97; flood, 110-116, 117, 119-20; churches, 121; famous people, 123-141, 153, 162, 164, 170, 175, 178; pageant, 179-186, 187-88, 190, 193, 200
Barber County *Democrat,* 126
Barber County *Index,* 56, 83, 110-11, 152, 159, 16-63, 167-68, 174-75, 177-78, 187, 196, 205, 206
Barber County *Mail,* 50, 53-4
Barber County Scottish Rite Masons, 190
Baricklow, G. W., 113
Barkley, Alben, 135
Beaver, (Oklahoma), 171
Beaver County, (Oklahoma), 171
Beaver, Meade and Englewood Railway Company, 135, 171-72
Bell, Mal, 60
Belton, (Missouri), 156
Bemis, C. C., 40, 42
Benefield, Clarence, 202
Bent, George, 34
Bent, Julia, 31
Bent, William, 31
Best Brothers Keene's Cement Company, Ltd., 207
Best, John, 182-3, 207-08
Best, Thomas, 207
Best, William, 207
Billie the Kid, 85, 90-92, 186
Black Kettle, Chief, 23, 27, 29, 30, 34

Blackwood, Lenora, 4
Blackstock, Ira, 135
Blair, William, 56
Blazer's Mill, 90
Bloom, Joe, 99
Blue Rapids, (Kansas), 139
Boise, Blanche, 152
Bond, Dr. C. C., 74
Boots, Clyde, 173
Bothwell, William S., 59, 60
Bowlus, L. H., 41, 43
Bradley, Lee, 88
Bradney, J., 166
Bragg, Eva, 197
Brannon, Roy, 161
Brewer, Dick, 90
Brookville, (Kansas), 186
Brown, George, 24
Brown, Marshal George S., 89
Brown, Hendry Newton, 85-8, 90-5, 98-103, 196, 191
Brown, J. H., 78-80
Brown, Orville, 197-98
Bryan, William Jennings, 130
Budd, H. J., 24
Buffalo Chips, Chief, 34
Bulkley, Solomon, 24
Bull Bear, Chief, 34
Bunton, 159-60
Bunton, Clark, 115
Bunton, Pearl, 64
Burnes, James, 152
Burton, Ben E., 92
Burton, Mrs. Ben, 102
Bushy Head, Chief, 55-6
Byron, (Oklahoma), 104

Cain, W. A., 121
Cain, Mrs. Wesley, 122, 147
Caldwell, (Kansas), 46, 73, 85, 87, 89, 90, 94, 100, 101, 103, 124, 191
Caldwell *Commercial*, 91, 93
Caldwell *Messenger*, 94
Campbell, 134
Campbell, W. E., 67
Cannon, Joe, 139
Capper, Senator Arthur, 136
Carey, (a Wichita hotel), 149
Carl, William, 49
Carr, B. O., 90, 91
Carson, Kit, 27, 185, 205
Carter, Thomas, 121
Case, Houston, 197
Castine, Effie, 82
Castine, George, 81-2
Castine, John, 81-2
Cattell, 69
Champion, Mr. 81
Champion, Mrs., 80
Chandler, (banker), 132, 170
Chandler, Charles, 161
Chapin, Frank, 180
Chapin, Luke, 190
Chautauqua County, 113
Cherokee Strip, 55
Cherokee Strip Livestock Association, 83
Chicago, Rock Island Railway Company, 172
Chickasha, (Oklahoma), 134
Chisum, John, 91
Chivington, Colonel J. M., 23, 27
CK Ranch, 186
Clark, (Lewis and Clark), 184
Clark County, 52, 56, 62, 113
Clark, Jack, 163
Clark, Mrs. Jack, 163
Clark, James, (Dad), 159-61, 163
Clark, Roll, 88
Clark, Will, 163
Cleveland, President Grover, 59, 125-26
Cochran, M. J., 52-3
Coffman, Frank, 168
Colcord, Colonel W. L., 56
Coldwater, (Kansas), 61, 64, 200, 202
Cole, P. B., 114, 116, 153-54
Cole, Sam, 114
Colson, Mayor A. M., 94
Columbus, (Ohio), 152
Comanche County, (Kansas), 51, 56, 61, 118
Comanche Cattle Pool, 56-7, 61, 83, 105
Conine, Julia, 115
Connally, Tom, 138
Cook, Mrs. Lois, 116
Cook, W. W., 106

Coolidge, President, 136
Coronado, 2, 183-85
Corson, 130
Cowley County, (Kansas), 62, 113
Crawford, Governor Samuel, 25
Cresset, 54, 57, 59, 78-9, 83, 87-8, 100, 101, 164, 167, 170, 194
Crisfield, 193
Crow, Chief, 31
Cubbon, 150
Cummins, Orange Scott, (Pilgrim Bard of Medicine Lodge), 1, 2, 36, 44, 50, 52, 58-9, 123
Cunningham, W. L., 141
Curley, 184
Curly Hair, Chief, 34
Currie, 167
Curtis, Senator Charles, 136, 140, 179, 182
Custer, 72

Denver, Enid and Gulf Line Railway, 171
Dodds, Dicky, 151
Dodge City, (Kansas), 46, 52, 73
Dodge City *Globe,* 136, 139
Dog Fat, Chief, 31
Dolan, 90, 91
Dole, Senator Bob, 185
Doles, Amp, 77
Doles, Dunc, 77
Doran, Tom, 56, 88, 115
Downing, Mrs. Clara, 141
Downtain, 159
Doyle, J. B., 49, 56
Dull Knife, 51-2
Dunder, Alvin, 202
Durbin, 50
Durst, Henry, 148
Dutton, Mr., 60
Dyer, Nina Cummins, 52

Eads, Tom, 126
Eagle Chief Cattle Pool, 55-7, 61
Earp, Miss, 60
Eaton, Charles A., 141
Eldred, Charles H., 101, 111
Elkhart, (Kansas), 172
Elliot, Major Joel, 26
Elm Mills, (Kansas), 74, 81-2, 119
Elmwood, (Kansas), 44
Emporia, (Kansas), 152
Enterprise, (Kansas), 152
Evans, 49, 56
Evansville, (Kansas), 56
Eureka Springs, (Arkansas), 156
Ewell, Oliver, 49, 50, 55, 125

Faxon, R. H., 166
Fayel, William, 25, 29
Flat, George, 89
Flato, W. F., 56
Fleming, John, 88
Flower Pot Mountain, 2, 8, 14, 19, 21, 202
Flynn, D. T., 66-7
Forest City, (Kansas), 47, 50, 72, 186
Forgan, (Oklahoma), 171-72
Fort Harker, 24-6
Fort Laramie, (Wyoming), 23
Fort Larned, 25, 116
Fort Lyon, 23
Fort Riley, 193
Fort Sill, (Oklahoma), 179
Fort Sully, (South Dakota), 23
Fosset, 90
Frame, Clarence, 74
Frame, Louis, 74
Friedly, Rev. George, 84-5, 88, 95-6
Friend, Mrs. Walter, 169
Fritz, Charles, 186
Fritz, Emil, 186
Fritz, Emilie, 186
Fritz, George, 186-87
Fritz, Mr. and Mrs. George L., 186
Fullerton, Chester, 104
Fussell, Joe, 169

Gano, James, 147, 149, 195, 196, 207
Gano, Jerry, 167
Garden City, (Kansas), 59
Garton, John, 80, 81
Geneseo Cattle Company, 55
George Washington University, 199

Geppert, George, 83-5, 100-03, 106, 119
Gibbs, Jerry, 112
Gigstad, Mrs. A. I., 189
Gilmore, Lester, 208
Gilson, Professor F. L., 182
Gloyd, Charlene, 144, 155
Gloyd, Dr. Charles, 144
Green, Reverend David, 4
Greensburg, (Kansas), 201
Gregory, A., 68-9
Grey Beard, Chief, 29
Grey Head, Chief, 34
Griffin, Samuel, 37-8, 146, 153
Griggsby, Daws, 156
Griggsby, Mrs. Daws (Mayme), 153-54, 185
Groom, J. Fuller, 202
Gyp Hills, 62, 180, 201, 204

Hadwager, Gus, 62
Hall, S. F., 24, 29
Hallowell, J. R., 128
Harbaugh, Ben, 99, 174, 176-77, 200
Harbaugh, Bess, 200
Harding, 75-6
Hardwick, 69
Hardwick House, 69, 70
Hardtner, (Kansas), 62, 72, 97, 121, 135, 162, 171-72, 175, 201
Hardtner, Dr., 72
Hareg, John, 152
Harney, General William S., 24, 26-7, 29, 30, 34
Harper, (Kansas), 56, 67-8, 70-1, 97, 115, 154, 185, 193
Harper County, (Kansas), 56, 62
Harrison, President, 126
Harvey, W. W., 140
Hastings, (Nebraska), 197
Haugen, 138
Hays, Miss, 60
Hazelton, (Kansas), 69, 71, 175
Heap of Birds, Chief, 34
Hegwer, August, 40, 66-7, 73
Heizer, Chester C., 93, 103
Henderson, Senator John B., 23-4, 29
Herrington, 88
Heskert, Cash, 132
Hewitt, Frank, 99, 191, 194
Hewitt, Isaiah, 99, 191
Hewitt, Ivan N., (Jibo), 185, 187, 190-91, 194, 205, 208
Hibbard, 157
Hibbard, Mrs. George, 179
Higgins, John, 111
Hillman, John W., 78-9, 80
Hillman, Mrs. Sadie, 78-9
Hinshaw, J. C., 167-68
Holloway, Sherm, 146
Hooker, (Oklahoma), 172
Horn, Bill, 155, 195
Horn, Tom, 156
Horney, George, 108-09
Horse Back, Chief, 31
Howland, John, 24, 29
Hubbell, Mayor, 90
Hudspeth, Representative, 139
Hughes, Louise, 175
Hugo, (Colorado), 62
Hulbert, 103
Hulpieu, Joe, 61
Hulpieu, John, 60
Hulpieu, Norton, 59
Hulpieu, Sarah, 60
Hunt, Frank, 89
Hunt, George, 180
Hunter, 49, 56
Hutchinson, (Kansas), 50-1, 81, 140, 156
Hutchinson, W. E., 40
Huxley, Thomas Henry, 130
Huxman, Governor, 200

Iliff, E. W., 54
Independence, (Kansas), 5
Indianola, (Nebraska), 92
Ingersoll, Robert, 130
Irby, Wilbur, 173
Iron Mountain, Chief, 31
Iron Shirt, Chief, 31
Isabel, (Kansas), 72, 137, 173, 175-77
I-See-O, Sergeant, 179-82, 186

Jackass Canyon, 95, 201
Jackson, 70
Jackson County, (Kansas), 128

James, C. W., 56
Jamestown, (North Dakota), 203
Jesse, John, 166
Johnson, President Andrew, 24, 26
Johnson, L. B., 200
Johnson, Zeal, 130, 144-45, 149
Jones, (grocer), 165
Jones, Andrew Jackson, 126
Justis, M. S., 49, 50, 55-7, 68, 125

Kansas City *Star,* 136-37
Kansas City *Times,* 125, 136
Kansas Hereford Association, 186-87
Kansas Livestock Association, 186-87
Kansas University, 198
Kein, Isaac, 46
Kelly, Will, 49
Kennedy, Elijah, 46
Key, Ben, 125
Keys, (Oklahoma), 172
Kicking Bird, Chief, 31
King, Henry, 66
Kingman, (Kansas), 137, 193
Kingman County, 194
Kingman *Leader-Courier,* 137
Kiowa, (Kansas), 66-8, 70, 72-3, 115-16, 123, 125-26, 134, 146, 159, 160-63, 169-71, 185, 201
Kiowa County, 56
Kiowa, Hardtner and Pacific Railway Company, 170-72
Kiowa *Herald,* 67, 70, 124
Kiowa *News-Review,* 135
Kirk, Major E. B., 56
Kirkpatrick, J. C., 41, 43

Lake City, (Kansas), 38, 42, 44, 50, 72, 175, 193
Lake, Reuban, 38-9
Lane, M. J., 68
Lane, Nat, 57, 119
Larash, E.Z., 113
Last Chance, (Kansas), 51-2
Lawrence, (Kansas), 78-9, 195, 198
Leah, Harry, 104
Leahy, David Demosthenes, 123-27, 129, 131, 143, 149-52
Lean Bear, Chief, 34
Leavenworth, Colonel Jesse, 25
Leavenworth, (Kansas), 24, 156
Lebrecht, Simon, 58-9, 129
Leedy, Governor, 80
Lemmon, Ed, 123
Lemon, Barbeque, 49
Leonard, Lewis, 133
Levagood, Maude, 94
Levand, Lewis, 200
Lewis, (Lewis and Clark), 184
Lewis, Matt and Billie, 146
Lincoln, (New Mexico), 186
Lincoln County, (New Mexico), 90, 91, 186
Little Bear, Chief, 31, 34
Little Big Mouth, Chief, 34
Little Coyote, Chief, 184
Little Horn, Chief, 31
Little Man, Chief, 34
Little Raven, Chief, 25, 29, 34, 184
Little Robe, Chief, 33-4
Livingston, Dr., 25
Lockwood, 37
Lockwood, Frank E., 108
Lodi, (Kansas), 50
Long, Chester I., 122, 125-27, 129, 131-33, 143, 166
Longworth, Nicholas, 138-39
Lottin, B. C., 50
Luce, Representative, 139
Lytle, Vernon, 88

MacGregor, Alice Martin, 120, 154-56
MacGregor, Bill, 186
MacGregor, Riley, 182-83
Maddox, Samuel, 113, 116, 153
Mahan Brothers, 150
Maize, Chief, 56
Male, George, 66-7
Marshal, G. W., 167
Martin, Howard, 88
Martin, John, 46
Martin, Governor John A., 192-93
Martin, Mr. and Mrs., 154
Massey, Park, 150
Maxon, 50
McAlister, Frank, 114

McCarty, J. A., 56
McCluskey, Arthur, 75-7
McCluskey, Chester, 75
McCracken, E. L., (Bud), 134, 159, 162, 164
McCracken, Ella, 161, 163
McCusker, Phillip, 30, 33
McGarrah, John, 161
McGrath, Charley, 60, 61
McGuire, Chris, 173
McKay, Judge, 133
McKinley, President, 72, 123
McKinney, Alec, 88
McKinney, Tom, 186
McKinney, Wayne, 88, 186
McNall, Webb, 80
McNary, 138
McNeal, J. W., 54
McNeal, T. A., 41-3, 57, 59, 79, 87, 93, 100, 102-03, 128-29, 143-44, 146, 152
McSween, Alexander, 91, 186
McWilliams, Miss, 52
Meade, (Kansas), 62
Meade County, 62
Meagher, Mike, 89, 90
Medicine Lodge, (Kansas), 40-2, 44; Indians, 46-8, 50, 52-3, 58, 64, 70, 72; first killings, 75, 77; more killings, 78, 82, 86; three men hanged, 86, 91, 93-5, 99, 100-04; Grand Hotel, 105, 109, 113-15; growth, 117-22; famous people, 123-41; Carry Nation, 143-58, 160-61, 163; cyclones, 164-70, 173-77; pageant, 179-90; Jibo, 191-208
Medicine Lodge House, 38
Medicine Lodge Indian Peace Treaty Pageant and Association, 179, 182-83, 199
Medicine Lodge Stockade Museum, 146, 157, 185, 188
Medicine Lodge Sugar Works and Refining Company, 118
Medicine Valley Bank, 82, 101, 104, 117, 119, 200
Melick, Erve, 60
Mellon, Andrew, 199
Memorial Peace Park, 184, 189
Merchants and Drovers Bank, 82
Middleton, Jack, 64
Milam County, (Texas), 92
Miller, Ben S., 101
Mills, 55
Mills, (under-sheriff), 176
Mills, Govan, 205
Milton, (poet), 54
Mingona, (Kansas), 72
Missouri, Kansas and Texas Railway Company, 171-72
Mobeetie, (Texas), 71
Moore, Carry Amelia, (Carry Nation), 144
Moore, Clifford, 196
Moore, George, 153-54
Moore, Reverend W. H., 161
Moreland, Jim, 89
Morrow, Colonel Henry A., 193
Mosley, E. H., 37, 40, 46
Mosley, Lt. John, 46-7
Mule Creek, (Kansas), 50-2, 73, 123, 171
Mulhall, Lucille, 123-24
Mulhall, Zach, 123, 125
Murdock, Victor, 151-52
Murphy, 90-1
Murphy, L. G. and Company, 186
Murphy, Thomas, 25-6
Murray, Tom, 52

Nashville, (Kansas), 194
Nation, Carry, 122-23, 135, 143-159, 161-62, 185, 187, 201
Nation, David, 135, 144, 152-53, 155, 202, 208
National Gypsum Company, 207-08
Nebraska, Kansas and Southwestern Railway Company, 42
Nelson, C. D., 56
New Kiowa, (Kansas), 67-9, 70-2, 115
New Kiowa *Herald*, 68-9, 71
Newkirk, 198
New Orleans, (Louisiana), 4
Noble, Albert L., 133-34
Norris, Mrs. Bessie, 116
Nyce, Mr., 98

O'Bryon, Hank, 148
O'Connor, Barney, 47, 88, 95-6, 103
Old Drab, (trapper, guide), 5-7
Oldham County, (Texas), 90
One Bear, Chief, 31
Osborne, Governor Thomas, 46
O'Shea, Marshal, 70

Paddock, George Washington, 78
Painted Lips, Chief, 31
Pardee, Gene, 52
Pardee, Horace, 50
Paris, (Texas), 86
Parson, 81
Payne, E. W., (Wylie), 52, 56, 82-4, 99-102, 106, 186
Payne, Miss Ruth, 205
Peck, George R., 127
Pennington, Clyde, 176-77
Penn State University, 199
Peoples, Willis, 62
Pesek, John, 197
Peters, Henry, 104
Pfost, Orville, 104
Phillips, Ben, 108
Phoenix, (Arizona), 177-78
Phoenix, Dick, 49, 56
Pike, Zebulon, 2, 184
Pixley, (Kansas) 72,
Plankinton, (South Dakota), 203
Poisal, John, 31
Poor Bear, Chief, 31
Pratt, (Kansas), 185, 201
Price, Senator, 179
Priest, Nate, 88

Rackdale, (Texas), 92
Ramsel, Plummer, 60
Rawlins, J. M., 56
Raymond, Joel, 16
Raymond, Nora, 17, 19, 20
Renolds, George, 49
Reynolds, Milton, 24
Rigg, C. F., 87, 98, 103, 111
Rigg, Dr. C. T., 40
Rhian, 41
Rice County, (Kansas), 81
Richards, 75
Rickards, Colin, 103
Ricker, Captain, 46-7
Roberts, Buckshot, 90
Robertson, Ben, 92-3
Rogers, 44
Rogers, Will, 123, 125
Rolla, (Missouri), 92
Roller, Jack, 197-98
Roman Nose, Chief, 34
Roosevelt, Theodore, 123
Rose, W. F., 119
Ross, Senator E. G., 25
Rothbun, Ed, 90
Rule, Elbert S., 183
Rumsey, Albert, 73
Rumsey, A. W., 66-7

St. Joseph, (Missouri), 50
St. Louis, (Missouri), 4, 24, 156, 201, 207-08
Sample, Ed, 102
Sanborn, John B., 24
Sandy Jim, (gambler), 93
Santa Fe, (New Mexico), 5
Santa Fe Railway Company, 127, 171-72, 175, 193, 207
Satank, Chief, 31, 34
Satanta, Chief, 25-6, 31-2
Sayres, Mr. and Mrs. Guy, 168
Schad, Henry, 150
Schluppe, 50, 55, 57, 119
Scott (Kansas) *Republican*, Secat, Porter, 113
Seegar, John D., 62
Sells, Superintendent, 48
Shafer, Mr., 171
Sharon, (Kansas), 70, 72, 121, 170, 174, 200
Shaw, Anna, 122
Sheldon, D. E., 40, 41, 44
Shepler, Frank, 112
Shepler, Mrs. Frank, 116
Shepler, Judge, 49
Sherlock, 55
Sherman, Lt. General William T., 24, 26
Sheets, 52
Shreeves, Orval, 103
Silver Brooch, Chief, 31
Simmons, 81, 150
Simpson, Jerry, 125-33, 143

Singer, 87
Sleeper, Ida, 193-94
Sleeper, May, 193
Sleeper, Nick, 193
Sleeper, V. C., 191, 193-94
Sleeper, Mrs. V. C., 191
Slim Face, Chief, 34
Smith, 88
Smith, Boardman, 111
Smith, Charles, 113
Smith, Eli, 38
Smith, John, (interpreter), 34
Smith, Robert, 187-88
Smith, William, 85-8, 99, 101-02, 189
Spotted Elk, Chief, 34
Spotted Horse, 93
Spotted Wolf, Chief, 34
Spriggs, Delilah, 166
Springer, 132
Standiford, W. A., 44, 49, 106, 111, 112
Standing Feather, Chief, 31
Stanley, Henry M., 25-9, 33-4
Steadman, Mrs., 80
Stephenson, Mr., 60
Stewart, Cornelius, 81-2
Stewart, David, 82
Storm, Chief, 34
Stranathan, W. I., 162
Strong City, (Kansas), 163
Strong, Mortimer, 147-48
Strong, Schuyler, 74
Stumbling Bear, Chief, 31, 184
Sumner County, (Kansas), 62, 163
Sun City, (Kansas), 42, 44, 46-7, 50, 72, 175, 181, 193, 208
Sutton, M., 40

Tack, Jack, 135
Talbot, Jim, 89, 90
Tall Bear, Chief, 34, 184
Tall Bull, Chief, 29
Talliaferro, Charley, 84-5, 88, 96
Tappan, Samuel F., 24, 29, 185
Tascosa, (Texas), 90-1
Taylor, James, 24
Taylor, N. G., 24, 26, 29, 30
Taylor, O. L., 119
Teegarden, George, 176-78
Ten Bears, Chief, 29, 31
Terry, General Alfred H., 24, 29
Thomas, 169
Thompson, Henry C., 120
Tincher, Andrew and Coriene, 133
Tincher, J. N., (Poley), 131, 133-41, 143, 171, 182, 198-99
Tisdale, H., 119, 195
Titus, Miss, 60
Titus, Ellis, 60
Titus, Jim, 133
Topeka, (Kansas), 152, 157
Trinidad, (Colorado), 119
Tudor, Helen and Roberta, 173
Tunstall, 90
Turner, Roy and Lawrence, 173, 175-78, 188
Tuttle, Solomon, 49
Two Toes, (wolf), 62-4

Ulmer, S. H., 41, 43
Updegraff, Alf, 115
Updegraff, Derrick, 38, 40, 105

Valley County, (Kansas), 170
Van Hook, Jim, 115
Van Slyke, D., 106, 111
Vare, Senator, 139
Vernon, (Texas), 86

Ward, Bunk, 111
Walters, 79, 80
Washington *Post,* 139
Washington *Star,* 139
Webster, Daniel, 22
Wellington, (Kansas), 108, 160, 163, 191
Wesley, John, 85-8, 98, 101-02
Wheeler, Alice, 92
Wheeler, Ben F., 85-8, 91-3, 98-104, 189, 191, 200
Wheeler, Richard, 77
Whirlwind, Chief, 34
White Antelope, Chief, 23
White Horn, Chief, 31
White Horse, Chief, 34, 184
White Rabbit, Chief, 34
White Spirit of the Whirlwind, 8, 10, 11, 12, 15-19, 21

Wichita, (Kansas), 47, 51, 62, 90, 125, 130-31, 149-50, 153, 160, 173, 175, 183, 185, 191, 197
Wichita *Beacon,* 90, 200
Wichita *Eagle,* 125, 150-51, 193
Wichita Falls and Northwestern Railway, 171
Wiley, Joe, 97
Wilson, John, 56
Wilson, John, (constable), 89, 90
Wilson, Tommy, 125
Wise, Squire, 81
Witzleben, Mr., 98
Wolf Sleeve, Chief, 31
Wolf's Name, Chief, 31
Woman's Heart, Chief, 31
Wood, George, 89
Woodman, 140
Woodruff, G. M., 120
Woods, George, 89
Woods, Meg, 89, 92
Woodward, R. M., (Dick), 38, 47, 50-1
Wright, Moses, 121
Wyat, 50
Wynkoop, E. W., 25

Yellow Bear, Chief, 34, 184
Young Colt, Chief, 34
Youmans, 44, 49, 106, 111
York, 125